Edexcel IGCSE
ICT

Student Book

Roger Crawford

D1149287

3 4114 00527 5036

A PEARSON COMPANY

Published by Pearson Education Limited, a company incorporated in England and Wales, having its registered office at Edinburgh Gate, Harlow, Essex, CM20 2JE. Registered company number: 872828.

www.pearsonschoolsandfecolleges.co.uk

Edexcel is a registered trademark of Edexcel Limited

Text © Pearson Education Ltd 2010

First published 2010

14 13 12 11 10
10 9 8 7 6 5 4 3 2 1

ISBN 978 0 435044 11 4

Original design by Richard Ponsford and Creative Monkey
Packaged and typeset by Naranco Design & Editorial / Alberto Gombáu [Proyecto Gráfico]
Original illustrations © Pearson Education Ltd 2010
Illustrated by Techset Photodisc
Cover design by Creative Monkey
Cover photo © Pearson Education Ltd: Photodisc
Proofread by Matthew Strawbridge
Index by Indexing Specialists (UK) Ltd
Printed in Spain by Grafos S.A.

Acknowledgements
The author and publisher would like to thank the following individuals and organisations for permission to reproduce photographs:

(Key: b-bottom; c-centre; l-left; r-right; t-top)

Alamy Images: Alex Segre 261, Anthony Hatley 7b, Art Directors & TRIP 29, David D. Green-technology 5b, Eddie Gerald 31t, Editorial Image, LLC 9, fStop 13t, GAUTIER Stephane / SAGAPHOTO.COM 264, Mar Photogtaphics 258, Mark Bassett 272, oliver leedham 17, Paul Thompson 284, picturesbyrob 8b, Qrt 12, Stephen Barnes / Technology 286, Synthetic Alan King 4b; **Corbis:** David Sailors 262; **Getty Images:** Alistair Berg 250, Lester Lefkowitz 265b; **iStockphoto:** Don Nichols 263, geopaul 11, joel dietle 6r, krzysztof Krzyscin 31b, Marcus Lindstrom 10, Michal Rozanski 7t, Rene Mansi 7bc; **Pearson Education Ltd:** Comstock Images 15, Gareth Boden 17tl, Ian Wedgewood 1, 270, Naki Kouyioumtzis 6l, Photodisc 17tr, 28t, Photodisc. Brofsky Studio Inc 260, Photodisc. C Squared Studios 4t, Photodisc. Kim Steele 265t, Photodisc. Life File. Michael Evans 275, Photodisc. Martial Colomb 196; **Photolibrary.com:** Comstock 254, 276, Photoalto 41b; **Science Photo Library Ltd:** Will & Deni McIntyre 282

The author and publisher would also like to thank the following for permission to reproduce copyright material:

p.185 & 186 Reproduced with permission of Yahoo! Inc. ©2010 Yahoo! Inc. YAHOO! and the YAHOO! logo are registered trademarks of Yahoo! Inc.; p.200 Image of the BBC Radio homepage reproduced with the written permission of the British Broadcasting Corporation. © BBC 2009.

Every effort has been made to contact copyright holders of material reproduced in this book. Any omissions will be rectified in subsequent printings if notice is given to the publishers.

Websites
The websites used in this book were correct and up to date at the time of publication. It is essential for tutors to preview each website before using it in class so as to ensure that the URL is still accurate, relevant and appropriate. We suggest that tutors bookmark useful websites and consider enabling students to access them through the school/college intranet.

Disclaimer
This material has been published on behalf of Edexcel and offers high-quality support for the delivery of Edexcel qualifications.

This does not mean that the material is essential to achieve any Edexcel qualification, nor does it mean that it is the only suitable material available to support any Edexcel qualification. Edexcel material will not be used verbatim in setting any Edexcel examination or assessment. Any resource lists produced by Edexcel shall include this and other appropriate resources.

Copies of official specifications for all Edexcel qualifications may be found on the Edexcel website: www.edexcel.com.

Contents

About this book

This book has several features to help you with IGCSE ICT.

Exercises

There are exercises throughout each chapter, which help you to test your understanding of the material as you work through the book. Some require short answers, others need a paragraph or for you to complete an activity using a computer.

Margin Boxes

The boxes in the margin give you extra help or information. They might explain something in a little more detail or guide you to linked topics in other parts of the book. The margin boxes include Did you know?, Hint!, Activity and Quick question boxes.

End of Chapter Checklists

These checklists summarise the material in the chapter. They could also help you make revision notes because they form a list of things that you need to revise.

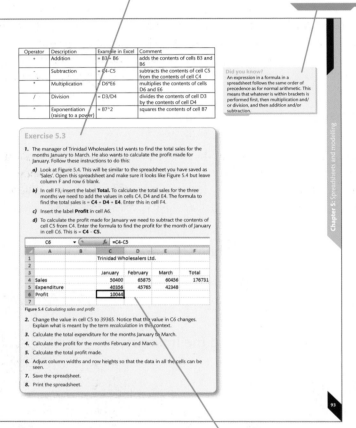

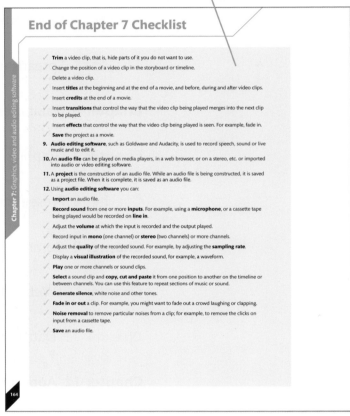

Figures

Throughout the book there are screenshots, photos and illustrations to clearly show what is being discussed in the text, for example where on the screen to click or how a system works.

Additional Materials and Answers

Additional material to use along with the Student Book is available at www.pearsonglobalschools.com/EdexcelIGCSEICT. For answers to the Exercises, teachers and parents can email icsorders@pearson.com.

Chapter 1: Hardware

ICT

In this chapter you will learn about the types of hardware used for input, output, processing and storage.

From the moment you wake, ICT affects you every day. In many cities, ICT systems control the power supply. Computers also print your electricity and telephone bills and many others. The milk you use at breakfast comes in a package marked with a bar code. The pattern of bars represents the identification number for the contents of the package. The checkout at the supermarket serves as an electronic point-of-sale machine, reading the pattern and recognising the number. The computer then knows which item has been purchased, and what its price should be. So the computer affects your breakfast! And computers are used to design and test many parts of the car, bus or bicycle that you use. The effects of ICT systems can be seen everywhere.

Input, output, processing and storage

A common feature of every computer is that its user always has some information to be processed. The user may type in the **data** (unprocessed information), then press a key or perform some other action so the processing can take place. When the job is complete, the answer is produced. So we have three stages: input, processing and output.

Figure 1.1 *Computers are now part of our everyday lives*

What is a computer?

A **computer** is an electronic machine that can follow a set of instructions to input, process, store and output data.

Let's look at each part of that sentence.

- **ELECTRONIC** – Computers are electronic devices. They use tiny electric currents, flowing through circuits, to do their operations.

- **MACHINE** – This is a device to do work easily.

- **INSTRUCTIONS** – The computer must have a sequence of instructions, given in a **program.** The computer will follow this sequence, so the program is essential in getting the computer to do its job.

- **INPUT** – is when data is typed in or otherwise entered into the computer.

- **PROCESS** – The computer processes data, just as you could process your ingredients to get a tasty cooked meal. Think of the computer program as a recipe with instructions to follow. Raw food goes in as input and, after processing, out comes the well-baked dish!

- **STORE** – A computer not only processes data, but can store or save it too.

- **OUTPUT** – This is when the computer displays text or graphics on the screen, prints, plays sounds or otherwise communicates to the user.

- **DATA** – This is the raw information to be processed – just like the raw food.

A computer is a *programmable* machine. Basically it can do whatever it is programmed to do. And notice carefully that it is just a machine. It automatically follows the set of codes or instructions given in a program.

What is the difference between data and information? **Data** means raw, unprocessed information. It could be numbers, or words and letters. **Information** is data that people understand. In order to understand *data,* you may have to interpret it.

For example:

> The number 10092004 is data.

This can be interpreted as:

- A date 10/09/2004

- A sum of money $100,920.04

The interpreted data is information. That is, the date or the sum of money is information.

We need to be careful how we interpret data as it can mean quite different things when it is information.

Typically, a computer inputs data, processes it following program instructions, and outputs information. This is often a cyclical process with the user inputting data, viewing the output, and responding to the output by inputting more data. While the data is being processed, data can be retrieved from backing storage or saved on it. This is interactive processing and it provides the user with an immediate response. This can be like an active two-way conversation between the user and the computer.

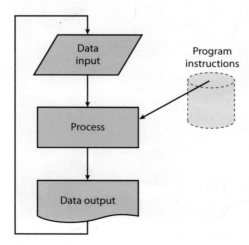

Figure 1.2 *Flow of data*

What is hardware?

Computer hardware is the equipment that makes up the physical ICT system. That is, the **keyboard,** the **monitor** screen, the **system unit** and everything inside it, and other devices connected to it, such as a **printer.** Usually, the monitor, keyboard and other devices are connected to the system unit.

- The **keyboard** has keys for alphabetic characters and numbers. There are extra keys for special functions.
- The **monitor** screen lets you see what you are doing.
- The **mouse** is your pointing device. As you move the mouse, a pointer on the monitor screen moves in the same direction as the mouse. You use the mouse to point, and click the mouse buttons to select.
- The **system unit** is the box where all the processing takes place. All the other devices are installed in it or connected to it.
- The **microprocessor** or **Central Processing Unit (CPU)** is the heart of the computer, and is inside the system unit.

A computer system may also include a **scanner,** a **modem, speakers,** a **DVD drive** and other hardware devices temporarily attached to it, such as a smart phone or an external hard disk.

An **input device** is for 'putting in' information to the machine. The keyboard is an input device; you type characters in using the keyboard.

The mouse is another input device. The monitor is an **output device.** Your computer uses it to display things to you. Another output device is the printer.

Look at Figure 1.3. The arrows show the direction of data flow. The keyboard sends information *in* to the system, hence the direction of the arrow from the keyboard to the system unit. Copy this diagram and draw in the arrows that are missing from the other lines. The big circles are for you to name some additional devices. Then draw in the arrows for those devices too.

Types of computer

At first, computers were very large, but today a complex circuit can fit on a single chip the size of your fingernail. This means that computers can now be small and yet very powerful. It also means that if someone today builds a large computer, that machine will be really powerful. A computer just as powerful as the original machines can now fit easily into a schoolbag.

Different types of PC

- A **desktop** PC usually has these basic components: a monitor, a keyboard, a system unit and a mouse.
- A **laptop** computer is slightly larger and much heavier than an A4 file (see Figure 1.5).
- A **tablet** computer is a laptop computer with a sensitive touch screen that can be used instead of the keyboard.

Look for these keys on your keyboard:

Space bar	Alt
Ctrl	Del
Shift	Caps Lock
Tab	Enter
Backspace	Numeric keypad

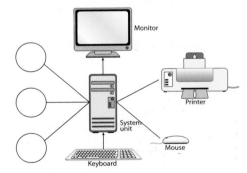

Figure 1.3 *Common computer devices*

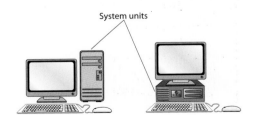

Figure 1.4 *Typical desktop PCs*

Figure 1.5 *A laptop computer*

Figure 1.6 *An Xbox 360 games console*

- A **notebook** computer is a small laptop computer that is about as big as an oversized book. A notebook computer is likely to be half the size of a laptop and is lighter and easier to carry.

- A **netbook** computer is a very small laptop that is optimized for Internet and email access. It is intended to be light and easy to carry and has a long battery life. For example, the Packard Bell Dot S2 netbook has a 10.1 inch screen, weighs 1.25kg and has a 10-hour battery life.

- A **hand-held** computer or **Personal Digital Assistant (PDA)** or **palmtop** can fit in one hand or in your pocket, but it is too small for general work. A PDA usually has a touch-sensitive screen. Although PDAs can be temporarily attached to a keyboard, you cannot comfortably type a long document into a PDA. A **smart phone** is a mobile phone with the functions of a PDA. Hand-held computing devices can perform a range of activities such as personal record-keeping and satellite navigation.

- A **games console** is a PC that is designed specifically for playing games and is likely to have these features:

    - A screen that displays graphics very quickly.

    - A large hard disk for saving games; gamers often have a large number of games.

    - A game pad used to control the games.

    - Possibly an Internet connection for playing online games.

  A desktop PC may have a better specification than a games console but it is likely to be more expensive. Examples of games consoles are: Microsoft Xbox®, Sony PlayStation® and Nintendo Wii®.

- An **embedded computer** is designed for and built into a specific application where it will perform a limited range of dedicated functions. The size and functionality of an embedded computer depends on the application. They may be very small devices built into a single microchip and may control, for example, DVD players and mobile phones.

Processors

A **processor** or microprocessor is built into a microchip that has memory and other components built into it. The microchip itself is often referred to as the 'processor'. If there is more than one processor built into the microchip, then the microchip is referred to as the 'processor' and processors built into it are referred to as **cores**.

The processor accepts input data, this is processed under the control of a stored computer program, and produces the output. A computer program being processed is loaded into the **RAM**. The program instructions are sent to the processor one at a time and the processor carries out the instructions.

An important feature of a processor is the speed at which it can process instructions. It is better to have more and faster cores, which will enable a computer to run applications quickly; however, faster multicore processors are expensive.

The processor speed required depends on what the computer is to be used for. An AMD Sempron or Intel Pentium Dual Core processor might be sufficient for a

Exercise 1.1

1. Daily life can be affected by ICT systems.

A	Listening to the radio
B	Doing the ironing
C	Feeding your pet
D	Watching TV

Put a cross in one box to show which aspect of daily life would not be affected immediately by the failure of an associated ICT system.

☐ A

☐ B

☐ C

☐ D

2. Describe the similarities and differences between data and information.

3. Explain what is meant by hardware.

4. Draw a labelled diagram of a desktop computer system showing the range of hardware devices that could be attached to it.

5. Describe the similarities and differences between a desktop computer and a laptop computer.

6. Describe the similarities and differences between a desktop computer and a hand-held computer.

7. Explain how a PDA user can benefit from having an external keyboard.

8. Figure 1.2 shows the flow of data through the input–output process. If the input was the intake of pupils into a school, describe what would represent the 'PROCESS', the 'INSTRUCTIONS' and the 'FINAL OUTPUT' (see Figure 1.8).

Figure 1.7 *A hand-held computer attached to a larger keyboard*

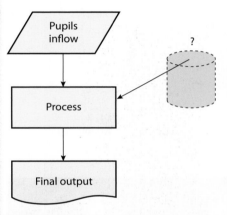

Figure 1.8 *Another form of data flow*

computer occasionally used for word processing, email and web browsing. However, a faster processor is required for a computer also used for playing online multimedia games and making heavy use of multimedia applications; an Intel Pentium Quad Core processor would be suitable.

An example of a microprocessor is the Intel Core 2 Duo E8600 Processor (3.33GHz, 1333MHz FSB, 6MB Cache). This processor has two cores and the speed at which these run is 3.33GHz. The **front side bus** (FSB) is the bus that carries data between the processor and memory and this can transfer data at a speed of 1333MHz. The **cache** is 6MB of RAM memory built into the microprocessor chip. Processing will be faster if there are more processors, running at faster speeds with a larger on-board cache.

Figure 1.9 *An Intel Core 2 Duo microprocessor*

Input and output devices

There are many devices for putting information into a computer, and for displaying the information that is output. The **peripheral** devices attached to a computer system are for input, output or storage.

Input devices

Input devices accept data signals, and translate them for usage and storage in the computer system.

Keyboards

The most widely used input device is a keyboard. There are different types of keyboard and of these the QWERTY keyboard (see Figure 1.10) is the most popular.

Advantages of keyboards:

- Keyboards are almost always available as an input device. They are widely used at work.

- Many people know how to use a QWERTY keyboard, so help is usually available.

Disadvantages of keyboards:

- To use a keyboard efficiently, you need to know the layout and be able to touch-type.

Figure 1.10 *A QWERTY keyboard*

Numeric keyboards only have keys to input numbers and a few special characters. A **QWERTY keyboard** may have a numeric keyboard built into the right-hand side. Some devices have only a numeric keypad – for example, an automated teller machine (ATM), also known as a cashpoint.

Pointing devices

There are many other input devices, including **pointing devices** that are used specifically for pointing to (and selecting) objects that are displayed on the monitor screen.

- The **mouse** is the most widely used pointing device. Some have a ball underneath that moves when you move the mouse, resulting in a similar movement of the pointer on the screen. An optical mouse detects movement using light instead of a ball.

- A **joystick** is a lever that gives you similar control to a mouse but its behaviour is slightly different. Joysticks can be used separately or can be

Did you know?
A QWERTY keyboard takes its name from the first six letter keys in the top left-hand corner.

Figure 1.11 *An automated teller machine (ATM) or cashpoint showing the numeric keypad*

built into a **game pad**, where there are often two simple joysticks, one for each thumb (see Figure 1.12). Suppose you are playing a computer game, where you control a 'car' on the screen. The forward speed of the car may depend on how far forward you push the joystick. Moving the joystick left and right can determine the tightness of your steering turn. Some separate joysticks have handles that can be twisted, and some have 'throttle' buttons as well or these features can be built into a game pad. All of these features can have different effects, depending on the program being used. So the joystick or game pad can be more than just a pointing device.

Figure 1.12 *A game pad with joysticks built in*

- A mouse may have a ball underneath it which rolls as you move the mouse. If you turn it over, you can roll the ball with your finger. A **tracker ball** (see Figure 1.13) is like an upside-down mouse. The ball is on the top of the device and you move it with your thumb.

- A **trackpad** (see Figure 1.14) is a small, flat, square pad below the space bar. As you move your finger across the trackpad's surface, the pointer moves across the screen.

- A **graphics tablet** (see Figure 1.15) or graphics pad is a flat rectangular pad between 6 and 30 inches (15 and 76 cm) wide. It works with a stylus, which you move along the surface of the pad to produce drawings in the computer. There are several types of stylus. One, the puck, is a small rounded device with cross-hairs for tracing lines accurately and with a number of buttons. The stylus can also be pen-shaped. A graphics tablet is used mainly for computer-aided design and drawing.

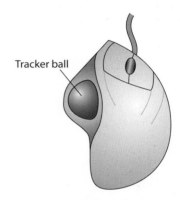

Figure 1.13 *A tracker ball*

Advantages of pointing devices:

- Many people find it easier to point and click than to use a keyboard.

- It is usually easier to access most of the features of the software being used.

Disadvantages of pointing devices:

- A pointing device is not useful unless a graphical user interface is being used.

- Some people find it difficult to control the on-screen pointer using a pointing device.

- It can be much harder to input text with a pointing device than with a keyboard.

Figure 1.14 *A trackpad on a laptop computer*

Scanners

A scanner reads printed data into the computer. A number of different devices are referred to as scanners:

- A **hand-held scanner** reads the image while being dragged over it.

- In the case of a **flatbed scanner,** the image is laid flat on the scanner's surface, and is captured in a similar manner to that of a photocopier.

- A **sheet-fed scanner** feeds the image in through rollers. The scanner reads the image as the paper goes through. The image must be printed on a flexible sheet of paper.

Figure 1.15 *Graphics tablet and puck being used to trace a drawing*

Coda bar

A 1 6 1 1 C 0 6 5 A

Figure 1.16 *A bar code*

Figure 1.17 *A UK National Lottery form. An OMR reader is used to input the information on the form*

There are also systems where the scanner reads a particular type of image, and the computer tries to interpret it as something meaningful. In this case, there needs to be a program to analyse the image. A **bar code scanner** or bar code reader is an example of such a system. This reads a pattern of bars representing the code number of the item on which it is printed. The bar code scanner usually passes a small laser beam over the pattern and reads in the pattern of reflected light. Bar code scanners may be hand-held, but some are built into the surface of a supermarket checkout counter. Many other devices can scan information that has been printed or encoded in some way.

Advantages of scanners:

● Scanners quickly convert printed images on paper to electronic form.

Disadvantages of scanners:

● The accuracy of the data input is unlikely to be verified.

Optical Mark Recognition (OMR)

OMR technology is used to interpret pencil marks on a piece of paper. An OMR reader can recognise the position of a mark or set of marks on paper, because the mark is darker than an unmarked area. The computer then records the mark's position and can analyse it to determine the meaning of the data. Marks made on this kind of form must be very clear, or they may not be properly recognised.

Advantages of OMR:

● There is no requirement to type in the information written on the paper form. Because of this, input is faster and less expensive.

● The person who fills in the form is responsible for the accuracy of the information on it.

Disadvantages of OMR:

● OMR forms must be printed very accurately because the position of the mark on the paper affects the accuracy of the input. Because of this, printing costs more.

● Verification checks on the input are unlikely to be carried out, so mistakes inputting the data are less likely to be detected.

Optical Character Recognition (OCR)

OCR is the identification of printed or written text characters by a computer. Printed text is scanned and input to the computer, which attempts to recognise the characters in it. These are then stored as text that can be word-processed. OCR can also be used to read handwriting. OCR software is often included when you purchase a scanner, so that any office with a scanner has OCR capabilities.

A similar process of character recognition is used to interpret handwriting on the screen of a PDA or tablet computer. PDAs and tablet computers have touch-sensitive screens that accept handwriting as input and have character recognition software that can convert it to text characters that can be word processed.

Advantages of OCR:

● Text printed on paper can be converted to electronic form and edited. This is especially useful for creating electronic versions of books printed before computers were available.

Disadvantages of OCR:

● Character recognition is not always accurate and the electronic text has to be checked carefully.

Magnetic ink character recognition

Magnetic ink character recognition (MICR) identifies data printed using a special magnetic ink. Instead of relying on reflected light to detect a character, it depends on the magnetic behaviour of the ink, which is activated by a magnetic field that can be detected by a MICR reader. Specially shaped magnetic ink characters are used to speed up recognition.

Do you notice the similarity between OCR and MICR? One difference is that one technology uses reflected light, while the other uses magnetic field patterns produced by the characters. Another important difference is that OCR systems can recognise handwriting and different types of text, but MICR needs specially shaped characters.

Advantages of MICR:

● Forms can be pre-printed with data which can be read by a computer. This can save time as otherwise all the data on the form would have to be typed in using a keyboard.

Disadvantages of MICR:

● MICR characters have to be printed in magnetic ink and this is more expensive.

● Characters printed in ordinary ink are not detected.

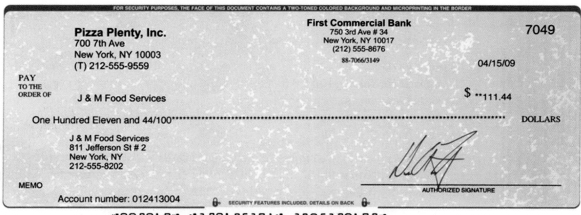

Figure 1.18 *MICR uses uniquely shaped characters, printed in magnetic ink*

Magnetic stripe card

A **magnetic stripe card reader** reads information from a magnetic stripe on the surface of a plastic card (see Figure 1.19) when it is swiped through the reader.

Stripe cards can be used to control access to buildings. For example, to gain access to a building or to leave it, a stripe card is passed through a reader that controls whether a door opens or closes. If the identification number on the card is recognised by the ICT system, the door will open; if not, the door remains closed. As a result, the ICT system knows who is in the building. Such a system could be used for registering school pupils; however, when large numbers of pupils enter a school at the same time, some may not bother to swipe their card through the reader. The ICT system can only know if a particular card is in the building and some pupils will give their cards to others to swipe for them. Such difficulties suggest countermeasures such as turnstiles or very careful supervision but these are often impractical as they can lead to long queues, disorder and the expense of employing supervisors.

Magnetic stripe cards are also widely used as bank or credit cards. In addition to being able to read the magnetic stripe, some devices can also write information to it. The stripe can store a permanent value, such as an account number, or a value that could change, such as the amount of cash you are allowed to withdraw from a cashpoint.

Advantages of magnetic stripe cards:

- They are often used as a form of identification that is small and light and can be carried at all times.
- The data recorded on the magnetic stripe is in electronic form and can be input directly into a computer.

Disadvantages of magnetic stripe cards:

- The data recorded on the magnetic stripe can be affected by electromagnetic radiation, such as that from televisions and computers.
- The data recorded on the magnetic stripe can be copied or edited. This is an opportunity for determined criminals to commit identity theft and fraud.

Figure 1.19 *A magnetic stripe card*

Smart cards

A **smart card** is similar in shape and size to a magnetic stripe card, but has a microprocessor chip embedded in it (see Figure 1.20). The chip can do some processing, as well as storing information. Special devices can communicate with the chip to read and write information on the card. Security features can be programmed into the chip.

Bank and credit cards used to be magnetic stripe cards but are now more usually smart cards or **Chip and PIN** (personal identification number) cards. These cards can be used to withdraw cash at a cashpoint. Cashpoints are specialised computer terminals with a small screen, numeric keyboard and smart card reader. The customer puts their card in the reader and is prompted to enter their four-digit PIN. If the PIN entered on the keyboard matches the PIN read from the card, the customer can proceed; if not, the card is either confiscated or returned to the customer. Most ATMs will dispense cash and display the balance in the customer's bank account. In a similar way, bank and credit cards can also be used to pay for goods in retail stores such as supermarkets.

A Chip and PIN card provides very secure access to a bank or credit card account. The customer should remember their PIN (it should not be written down), and no one else should know it. For this reason, the numeric keyboard is shielded so that it is difficult for anyone other than the person entering their PIN to see what number is entered.

For example, an Oyster® card is an electronic smart card that can be used to pay for travel, as well as in shops, theatres and restaurants and for entry to tourist attractions. It is used very much like a bank or credit card except that it is preloaded with cash credits. This can be done on the Web or in a manner similar to withdrawing cash from a cashpoint. As a result, payments can be made without online access at the time. Payment is made by touching the Oyster card on a reader and the payment is automatically deducted. This speeds up payment. Oyster cards are in widespread use in London.

Advantages of smart cards:

- Often used as a form of identification that is small and light and can be carried at all times.
- The data recorded on the chip is in electronic form and can be input directly into a computer.
- The data recorded on the chip is more secure than data recorded on a magnetic stripe.
- The data recorded on the chip can be updated during transactions.

Disadvantages of smart cards:

- The data recorded on the chip can be affected by electromagnetic radiation; for example, from televisions and computers.
- The data recorded on the chip can be copied or edited by very determined criminals and used for fraud.

Figure 1.20 *A smart card showing the microprocessor chip embedded in it*

Digital cameras, digital video cameras and webcams

Digital cameras store pictures on a memory card in a format suitable for saving and displaying on a computer. Pictures can be transferred from the camera to the computer where they can be edited and enhanced in graphics software or viewed on screen. The pictures can be transferred to a computer directly by connecting the camera to the computer, or the memory card can be removed and read using a memory card reader, which may be built into the computer or connected to it. Television sets can also have memory card readers built in or connected so that several people can view the pictures together on a large screen.

The picture made by a digital camera (as for a printer or a monitor) is formed by a quantity of very small dots of different colours, merging to form a picture. The picture quality is related to the density (or closeness) of the dots making the picture, the accurate placement of the dots and the correctness of the colours being displayed. Thus an 'eight mega-pixel' camera uses eight million dots (the **pixels**) to form a picture, and so would usually produce better output than a 'two mega-pixel' camera.

Digital cameras may have a traditional viewfinder but more usually have a small LCD screen or both. The advantage of having both is that the viewfinder can be used if bright sunlight makes the LCD screen unclear.

A digital video camera or camcorder has similar functions to a digital camera but records moving images with sound. Camcorders can save recordings on a memory card but may also use DVD, miniDV tape or a built-in hard disk. All these formats are transferable to a computer for editing and storage and are likely to be playable on a home entertainment system.

A **webcam** is a type of digital video camera where the image captured is viewed using a computer. Recordings can be made but this is not always done. A webcam can be used to view a remote location. The computer connects to the webcam over the Web and the image is displayed on the computer screen. This has a variety of different uses:

- You could see if the weather is suitable for skiing by viewing the webcam in the mountains above Grindelwald in Switzerland.

- You could install a webcam at home for security and view this when you are out at work.

- You could attach a webcam to your computer and contact a friend who has a webcam so that you could both see each other while you are talking. You could use VoIP (Voice over Internet Protocol) software to do this. You could use a similar arrangement to practise speaking a foreign language.

- You could set up a webcam in a classroom and listen to a teacher from another school. This might be useful if you were learning to speak English and could not find a teacher locally.

Simple webcams have a fixed position and can see only one view; however, some webcams allow the user to turn them so that many different views can be seen.

Advantages of webcams:

- Photos and video can be recorded in a digital form that can be saved on a computer. This makes backup easier, more reliable and more extensive.

- Digital photos and video can be displayed on a wide variety of devices, such as smart phones and television screens. This allows access in a wider range of locations and by several people at the same time.

- Digital photos and video can be sent by email.

- Digital video can be broadcast over the Internet so that TV programmes can be available on demand.

Disadvantages of webcams:

- Users tend to have more photos and longer videos and this creates a need for more backing storage.

- High-quality photos and videos can be in very large files. When these are sent by email or broadcast over the Internet, this uses bandwidth and slows down the network.

Figure 1.21 *A digital camera*

Biometric scanners

A **biometric scanner** is a pattern recognition system which makes a personal identification based on a person's unique physical characteristics. Biometric scanners can use face recognition, fingerprint matching, iris and retinal scans, voice recognition, and hand geometry. Biometric scanners can be built into mobile phones, desktop and laptop computers, and smart cards. They can be used to control entry to buildings, and can even replace keys in cars.

Advantages of biometric scanners:

● There is no need to remember to carry personal identification.

● The person has to be present. This makes identification theft and fraud much less likely.

Disadvantages of biometric scanners:

● Identification using biometric scanners is not yet sufficiently accurate. Permitted users will not be recognised at times, and blocked users will sometimes be permitted.

Figure 1.22 *A biometric scanner using finger prints*

Sensors

Sensors are used to input data about the environment into a computer. There are many types of sensors. They are available in many different shapes and sizes, and they have a wide variety of uses. For example, sensors can be used to record light intensity, temperature and pressure. Sensors usually produce a low voltage which must be converted to a digital signal for the computer using an analogue-to-digital converter (ADC).

Sensors are used extensively for data logging and control applications. They are essential in applications such as the following: automatic washing machines, automatic cookers, air conditioning controllers, central heating controllers, computer-controlled greenhouses, burglar alarm systems, control of factory production lines, robotics, and for monitoring scientific experiments and remote weather stations.

Advantages of sensors:

● Sensors can be placed in dangerous locations where people would be hurt.

● Sensors can continuously and reliably record data whereas to organise this using people could be much more unreliable and expensive.

● Sensors can record data that people do not sense or do not sense accurately, such as humidity.

● The data recorded by sensors can be automatically recorded in a form that can be processed by a computer.

● Data can be collected by a central computer from sensors in remote locations. People do not need to travel and this saves time and allows data to be collected more frequently.

Disadvantages of sensors:

● Sensors cannot interpret the data.

● Sensors detect a very restricted range of the different types of data.

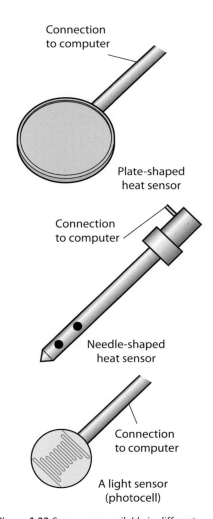

Figure 1.23 *Sensors are available in different shapes and sizes*

Audio input devices and technologies

There are various input devices and technologies relating to computer input from sound.

- A **touch-tone telephone** issues a beep whose frequency depends on the button being pressed. On the other end of the line is a computer with an input device that can analyse the beep to determine which button is being pressed. So your touch-tone telephone functions as an input device. You may then listen to a voice response from the computer.

- A **microphone** can be used to record sounds and voices, to give voice commands and for voice communication over the Internet.

- Your voice carries many tones, all making up the sound that people hear. People can recognise your voice because they can recognise the combination of tones that make up your voice. Computers have also been programmed to do voice recognition. **Voice recognition** software enables the computer to know who is talking but not what has been said.

- **Speech recognition** is often used for **voice command systems.** These require that the voice first be recognised, as above. A microphone is used to input the spoken words, which are then analysed by the program. The sound is compared with other sounds stored in the computer, to find the matching word; this match may be interpreted as a command. This is an unreliable process because a user can make words sound different at different times, and different users will say the same words differently. As a result, the software may have to be trained to recognise a particular user.

- **Natural language processing** is where a computer processes a sequence of instructions or data given in a natural language – for instance, spoken English. You could use natural language processing to dictate a letter or give instructions to a computer.

Advantages of audio input:
- People speak to the computer and do not have to learn how to operate a keyboard or other input device.

Disadvantages of audio input:
- Voice recognition software has to be trained to recognise human speech. This can be a very lengthy process if the computer needs to recognise the full range of words used.

- Voice recognition is not entirely accurate because people pronounce words differently and speak in a wide range of accents and different tones of voice.

Remote Control

Many devices can be operated using a remote control handset (see Figure 1.24). Here are some examples: televisions, video players and recorders, DVD players and recorders, satellite receivers, hi-fi music systems, multimedia projectors, model cars and airplanes, and garage doors.

The main remote control technology used in the home is infrared. The signals between a remote control handset and the device it is controlling are infrared light pulses, which are invisible to the human eye.

The **transmitter** in the remote control handset sends out a pulse of infrared light when a button is pressed on the handset. A transmitter is often a light-emitting diode (LED) which is built into the pointing end of the remote control handset (see Figure 1.25). The infrared light pulse represents a binary code that corresponds to a command, such as 'power on' or 'volume down'. A **receiver** is built into the device being controlled in a position where it can easily receive the infrared light pulses – for example, it is built into the front of a satellite TV receiver. The receiver passes the code to a microprocessor, which decodes it and carries out the command.

The remote control handset will often have two LEDs that light up at the same time when a button is pressed. One LED is the infrared transmitter and the light from this is invisible. The other LED emits a visible light and this is to reassure the user that the remote control is functioning (see Figure 1.25).

Some handsets only work when they are pointing directly at the receiver on the controlled device, while others work when they are pointing generally towards the receiver. This is because the strength of the infrared light pulse varies. A handset with more than one infrared LED or a very powerful LED can produce a stronger, broader signal.

Advantages of remote control:

- Less movement and energy are needed to operate remote controlled devices.

- Inaccessible or hidden devices can be controlled.

Disadvantages of remote control:

- Some devices cannot be operated without the remote control handset. If this is lost or damaged, the device cannot be used.

Output devices

Monitors

Monitors are also known as **visual display units (VDUs).** They come in different styles and quality levels. Screen colour quality, resolution and clarity are just some of the features that affect how desirable a particular monitor is to you.

Picture elements

Although the picture on a computer monitor may look sharp and clear, it is made up of many illuminated dots known as **picture elements** or **pixels.** The dots are usually so tiny that you would not normally notice them individually – you just see the whole picture. If you could actually see the picture elements, the picture would look jagged (see Figure 1.26).

The screen itself may perhaps have 1024 screen dots going across the screen, and 768 from top to bottom. In this case the screen is said to have a **resolution** of

Figure 1.24 *A remote control handset*

Figure 1.25 *The LEDs built into a remote control handset*

1024 by 768. These screen dots are not the same as picture elements, because some software packages use picture elements that are much bigger than the tiny screen dots. For many packages, however, the picture element is as small as the screen dot – this is the smallest possible size for the pixel.

Graphics cards

The graphics card which is also known as the **video card or display card** is housed within the system unit, and controls the signals going to the monitor screen. Higher-quality cards can produce very clear graphics very quickly. Some computer games demand advanced display cards and high-quality monitor screens.

Cathode ray tube (CRT) monitors

Cathode ray tube monitors used to be the commonest type of monitor. CRT monitors can be relatively bulky (see Figures 1.27 and 1.28).

Liquid crystal display (LCD) monitors

Liquid crystal display technology allows the screen to be flat, instead of bulky as with CRT monitors. LCD screens consume less power than CRT displays. An LCD screen is generally more compact than a corresponding CRT display (see Figures 1.27 and 1.28).

LCD monitor screens vary considerably in size and resolution. For example, a typical 15-inch screen might have a resolution of 1024 × 768 pixels and a 30-inch screen 2560 × 1600. Higher-quality screens have more pixels per inch. Small screens built into PDAs and smart phones are likely to have a lower quality display with fewer pixels per inch.

LCD screen technology is currently the most popular for use with PCs. However, there are other alternatives; for example, plasma displays (which are clear and bright) and electroluminescent displays (which have the potential to support very large flexible displays).

Touch screens

A **touch screen** is not just an output device; it is a two-way user interface. You can interact with the computer by touching pictures or words on the screen. Touch screens are widely used with tablet PCs, PDAs and Smart Phones. There are different touch screen technologies. For example, the iPhone uses a capacitive touch screen. This is glass panel with a layer that stores electrical charge on it facing outwards. When you touch the screen, you conduct some of the electrical charge, reducing it at that point. The iPhone knows where you touched the screen because it knows where the charge was reduced. This is why the iPhone works best if you use your finger to operate it. Resistive screens often work best with a stylus because they work by detecting changes in the electrical charge when internal charged and conductive layers are pressed together.

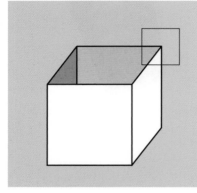

A perfect box

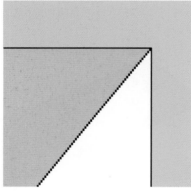

Close-up view of the top right corner, showing the picture elements (pixels)

Figure 1.26 *Picture elements*

Figure 1.27 *Front view of a CRT monitor and an LCD monitor*

Figure 1.28 *Side view of a CRT monitor and an LCD monitor*

Multimedia projectors

A **multimedia projector** or data projector projects an image that would normally be displayed on a computer screen onto a larger, separate screen. This allows the image on the screen to be shared with an audience in a large room. Multimedia projectors are almost always used when giving a computer-based presentation. They can be found in school classrooms, university lecture theatres and commercial training organisations. Multimedia projectors are also used with home entertainment systems, enabling people to watch TV and DVDs and to play computer games.

Interactive whiteboards are large touch sensitive panels used as screens for multimedia projectors. They are operated as touch screens. Some use capacitive or resistive technology but others use an optical 'curtain'. Breaks in this curtain are detected and so the computer knows which part of the interactive whiteboard has been touched.

Advantages of monitor screens:

● Enables the use of a graphical user interface.

● Interactive, on-screen use of a computer is more natural and intuitive than programming.

Disadvantages of monitor screens:

● Screen size can limit the extent and detail of what can be seen. For example, it is possible to refer to several printed pages at the same time. It could be much more difficult to arrange this on a monitor.

● Screen displays can be difficult to read for people who have impaired sight.

Printers

● Printed output is often called a **printout** or **hard copy.** An **impact printer** usually strikes through an inked ribbon, making marks on the paper. A **non-impact printer** uses a non-striking method to form the image on the paper. Examples of non-impact printers are laser printers and inkjet printers.

● **Inkjet printers** use tiny dots of ink sprayed onto the paper, forming the shapes of characters and pictures. Inkjet printers are quiet and produce good quality output. They usually produce colour prints, and are very popular for home and small-office use.

● **Laser printers** use laser light to make patterns of ink on a drum. This drum then transfers the ink to the paper, and finally a heating process fuses the ink to the paper. Laser technology gives excellent quality, and prints quickly. Laser printers are widely used but are more expensive than inkjet printers, and often only print in black and white.

● **Thermal printers** use heated wires to mark dots on the surface of a heat-sensitive paper.

● **Thermal dye transfer printers** use special coloured dyes heated into a gas. This process gives the best quality of colour printing, but is very expensive and requires special paper.

● **Thermal wax transfer printers** use molten wax, forming tiny dots of different colours on the paper. These coloured wax dots blend to produce tones.

Buffers and spooling

Printers (and some other devices) are much slower than the computers and networks that send information to them to be printed. So that the computer does not have to wait for the printer to finish printing, most printers have a **buffer** (a small amount of memory) built into them. A document sent to the printer will be quickly saved in the buffer so that the computer can do other tasks while the printer is printing the document.

A buffer will only hold a few short documents, and on large networks many users may be sharing the same printer. To avoid users having to wait, documents are first put into a queue on a server and then sent for printing in turn. This queuing process is known as **spooling.**

Figure 1.29 *Enlarged dot-matrix printing produced by an inkjet printer showing how the dots form characters*

Did you know?
You can see this process in action. If you are using a computer with a local printer attached, print a long document then turn off the computer but not the printer. The printer will continue printing and will print that part of the document that is in its buffer.

Print quality

All these types of printer use very small dots to produce pictures. The smaller the dot, the better the quality of the picture. An important measure of print quality is the number of **dots per inch (dpi).** The higher the dpi, the better the picture. In addition, for the best-quality output the dots must be accurately placed.

Printers and paper

Printers can use different types of paper.

- Many printers use sheets of A4 paper.

- Some printers have a long stream of **continuous paper** flowing through. Usually the paper is perforated, so that it can be torn easily to produce separate pages of output. There may be several sheets together, either impregnated with carbon or with carbon sheets between them, so that multiple copies are produced at once.

- In pre-printed stationery, certain information – for instance, the name of a company – has already been printed on the paper. This is usually the case with utility bills, which are printed with a high-volume single-coloured printer on forms that already have coloured logos and other symbols printed on them.

Photo-printers

Photo-printers are specially designed to print digital photographs. A memory card storing pictures taken by a digital camera can sometimes be plugged directly into the printer, and the pictures printed. In other cases, the camera can be directly connected to the printer.

Advantages of printers:
- Printed output can be viewed without the need for a computer.

- Many people and organisations still use paper-based communications and similar legacy methods.

Disadvantages of printers:
- Printing is slow and expensive compared with electronic communications and storage.

- Paper is bulky and deteriorates in storage.

- Printed materials are more difficult to access and distribute. For example, printed photographs can be viewed by a limited number of people compared with digital photographs displayed on a TV screen, and it is more difficult and expensive to send copies to others.

Plotters

A **plotter** draws lines on paper using differently coloured pens. In a flatbed plotter, the paper is held still while the pen moves. Other plotters have the pen moving from left to right, while the paper goes forwards and backwards. Yet others use wires to draw charged patterns on special paper, then fuse toner onto the electrically charged patterns. If a job essentially consists of lines – for instance, a graph – a plotter will quickly draw the required lines. An upright plotter can also handle very long sheets of paper, because of the way the paper flows, and can produce long continuous lines. Plotters are frequently used in **computer-aided design.**

Advantages of plotters:

● Much larger and longer sheets can be printed.

Disadvantages of plotters:

● Printing is very slow.

● Plotters are usually more expensive than printers.

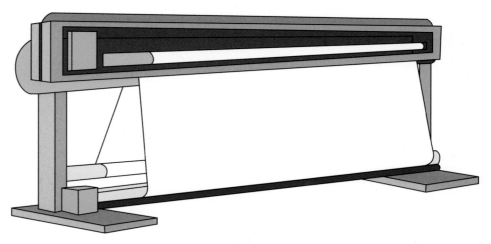

Figure 1.30 *An upright plotter*

Multi-function printers

Printers are now being built in combination with scanners, and sometimes with fax machines. Combining a printer with a scanner produces the effective functionality of a photocopying machine, as well as providing the separate functions of scanning and printing.

Advantages of multi-function devices:

● A multi-function device takes up much less space on the desktop than the individual devices it replaces.

● A multi-function device is usually less expensive to buy than all the individual devices it replaces.

● A multi-function device will be used more before it becomes obsolete.

● A multi-function device can be replaced more frequently, having provided good value, so that more modern technology is available for use.

Disadvantages of multi-function devices:

- If part of the device develops a fault, all the functions may be unavailable.

- Only one person at a time can use a multi-function device.

Speakers

Many computers have two **speakers** which can be used to listen to the sound output by a computer in mono or stereo. Sound systems with more than two speakers are increasingly common. **Headphones** are two small speakers built into a headset. Sound is needed when computers are used to play music, to make telephone calls using VoIP, to listen to voicemail, to play video and DVDs for entertainment or education, and to listen to online TV and radio.

Speakers are also needed for **speech synthesis,** where a computer reproduces human speech. The voice need not be a recording and could be computer-generated. For instance, you can have a text-reading program that takes a word-processed document in electronic form and reads it aloud.

Advantages of speakers:

- They allow computer systems to be used for a wide range of multimedia applications.

- Interaction with a computer using voice recognition and speech synthesis is more natural and intuitive than programming.

Disadvantages of speakers:

- Applications that use speakers can be difficult to operate for people who have impaired hearing.

- Voice recognition systems can be difficult to set up and use.

Sound cards

A **sound card** controls the input and output of audio. Audio input through a microphone and output through speakers are usually analogue and the sound card will handle conversion to and from the digital signals which can be processed by a computer. A sound card will also handle digital audio input from, for example, DVD and the Internet.

The uses of sound cards include providing the sound for multimedia applications such as music, video or audio editing, preparing and giving presentations and playing games.

Sound cards may be:

- Built into the motherboard in a PC and integrated with it.

- Specialised sound cards that plug into the motherboard.

- External devices that plug into the USB or firewire port on a PC. These are often used with laptops which often have a limited integrated sound card.

Sound cards may have features such as:

- **Polyphony**, which is the ability to play more than one sound or voice with each sound being played independently at the same time.

- Output through one or more sound **channels**. For example, mono, stereo (two channels), quadraphonic (four channels) or more. Some sound cards now support up to eight audio channels.

- Recording (input) and playing (output) of different sounds at the same time.

- Surround sound or 3D audio that gives the impression of sound being output from different positions.

- The ability to restore the detail and clarity of compressed files, such as mp3 music files.

- On board memory to help provide faster sound processing.

- USB, firewire, optical and other ports to enable DVD recorders and other devices to be connected.

- **Musical Instrument Digital Interface (MIDI)** support to connect synthesizers or other electronic instruments to the computer.

Control devices

In control applications, computers make events happen using **control devices** or **actuators.** Examples of actuators are valves, heaters, coolers and motors. These can be powered by a range of different sources of energy, including electricity and compressed air. Actuators also include devices such as buzzers and alarms, which can warn us about various events: a burglar has entered through the window, the automatic cooker has finished cooking our pizza, or the microwave oven has defrosted the frozen chicken.

Advantages of control devices:

- Actuators enable a computer to perform physical tasks in the real world. For example, computers can control a central heating system or a mechanical digger.

Disadvantages of control devices:

- Actuators perform physical operations when instructed by a computer. This can be dangerous for people if their presence is not known to the computer.

Exercise 1.2

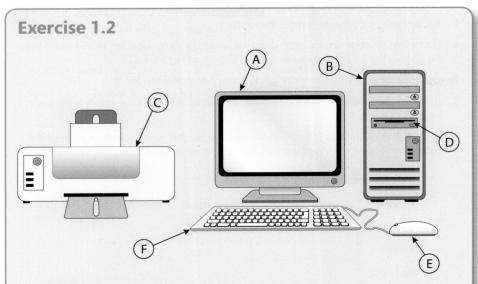

Figure 1.31 *Parts of a computer system*

1. a) Look at Figure 1.31 and complete the table below using words from this list.

Monitor	Word processing sotware	Keyboard
System unit	Network cable	Mouse
Spreadsheet	Printer	Operating system
Email	Scanner	DVD drive

Label	Name
A	
B	
C	
D	
E	
F	

b) Write down the labels of the parts of the computer used for input.

c) Write down the labels of the parts of the computer used for output.

d) Other than the monitor, which parts of a computer would you use:

   ✓ to type a letter
   ✓ to draw a picture on the screen
   ✓ to print a report.

2. Name three input devices that can be used to point on the monitor screen, and explain why different pointing devices are needed.

3. Describe three ways to input data and describe what they are used for.

4. Discuss the advantages and disadvantages of an inkjet printer and a laser printer to a home user.

5. Explain why a computer needs speakers.

6. Name two output devices and describe what they are used for. How would they be connected to the computer system shown in Figure 1.31?

7. Describe one type of pre-printed stationery and one use for it.

8. Is a games console an input device or an output device? Give reasons for your answer.

9. A pelican crossing has input, processing and output. State whether each of the following is used for input, processing or output: button, bleepers and red light.

Pelican crossing	
Device	**Input, processing or output**
Button	
Bleepers	
Red light	

10. Describe the advantages and disadvantages of multi-function printers that combine a printer, scanner and fax compared with using three single-function devices.

1. Computers are now commonplace, and affect our lives in many ways every day.

2. An ICT system carries out a task in three main stages, which may overlap: **input**, **processing** and **output**.

3. A computer is an electronic machine that can follow a set of instructions to input, process, store and output data.

4. **Hardware** is the equipment that makes up the complete ICT system: the components such as the keyboard, the monitor, the system unit and everything inside it, a printer, a scanner and speakers.

5. Input devices include the **keyboard**, pointing devices (such as a **mouse**, **joystick**, **game pad** or **trackpad**), **scanners**, **magnetic stripe readers**, **OMR readers** and **light sensors**.

6. Output devices include **monitors**, **printers** and **speakers**.

7. Printers can be divided into impact and non-impact printers. An **impact printer** strikes an inked ribbon which makes marks on the paper. A **non-impact printer** uses a non-striking method to form the image on the paper. This type includes laser printers and inkjet printers.

8. Printers use different kinds of output medium, such as single A4 sheets of paper, continuous paper and specialist paper for printing photographs or other digitised images.

9. **Multi-function printers** combine a printer, scanner and fax machine. Combining a printer with a scanner produces the effective functionality of a photocopying machine.

Chapter 2: Backing storage and memory

Storage devices and media

You need to store data, even after a computer or other digital device is turned off. While the computer is running, data is kept in its **memory,** but when the computer is turned off, the data stored in memory will disappear. You need **backing storage** (or secondary memory) to save your data after the computer is turned off.

The computer will store your work as a **file**. The size of the file depends on the amount of data in it, and is measured in **bytes**. A byte can store one character of data:

- One kilobyte or KB is 1024 bytes.

- One megabyte (MB) is 1024 KB or 1024 × 1024 = 1 048 576 bytes.

- One gigabyte (GB) is 1024 MB or just over one thousand million bytes.

- One terabyte (TB) is 1024 GB or just over a million million bytes.

The storage **medium** is the actual material object used for storing the data. The storage **device** is the item of equipment that handles the use of the medium. For instance, a DVD is a storage medium. The DVD drive is the device that is used to access data on the DVD. The main storage area in a desktop computer system is the hard drive. USB memory sticks are commonly used for saving and transporting data; DVDs can store around 4.7 GB of data; and hard disks can store a very large amount. Magnetic tapes can also store very large amounts of data. Storage technology is constantly developing.

Hard disks

It is common for the hard disk in a desktop computer to store 500 GB of data or more. Access to the data on a hard disk is very fast.

On a hard disk, the data is stored on multiple disks or **platters,** held vertically above each other (see Figure 2.1). On each individual disk, the data is stored in concentric tracks. For every track of data, there are corresponding tracks above and below it. For instance, the fifth track on the first surface is directly above the fifth track of the second surface, and below that is the fifth track of the third surface. The corresponding tracks form a **cylinder.** The number of cylinders is equal in number to the tracks on each surface of the disk. For each surface (usually at the top and bottom of each platter) there is a **read/write head**, set on the tip of a small arm. These heads move in step with each other, traversing in and out over the spinning disk.

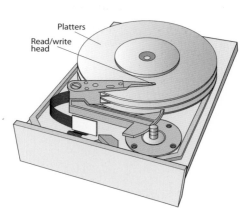

Figure 2.1 *The inside of fixed hard disk with moveable heads*

The total storage space on a hard disk is given by the following formula:

$$\text{Number of readable sides} \times \text{Number of cylinders} \times \text{Sectors per track} \times \text{Bytes per sector}$$

Access time

To reach the correct spot on the disk for reading or writing data, the head must first move to the correct track. Meanwhile, the hard disk spins, maintaining a constant speed. The byte to be accessed arrives under the head as the disk turns. On average, it takes half a rotation for the correct byte to reach the head's position. The total access time on average is then:

Time for head movement to reach track + *Time for half a complete rotation*

If the drive needs to access bytes that directly follow each other on a single track, no further head movement is needed because the head can remain on that same track. Moreover, if the bytes follow each other, it takes very little time for each consecutive byte to arrive beneath the head. So the average access time per byte is far less if a stream of consecutive bytes is being read than it is for one-off access.

Fixed heads and moving heads

Some types of hard disk have a read/write head permanently stationed above each track of the disk. Each surface has many fixed heads instead of a single moving head per surface. This means that no time is needed to reach the correct track: the respective heads are already in place. So access is much faster – on average, the time for a half rotation.

RAID (Redundant Array of Inexpensive Drives)

This storage device essentially carries multiple copies of data, on different hard disk drives. If one fails, the data can still be recovered from the others.

External hard disks

External hard disks are built into a separate case and are robust, small and lightweight. They can be easily and safely carried around, and can usually be connected to any computer with a USB socket (these are very common on PCs). These typically store around 150 GB.

Figure 2.2 *An external hard disk drive*

CDs, DVDs, HD DVD and Blu-ray

Compact discs (CDs)

A typical compact disc (CD) stores around 700 MB of data on one side of the disc. Access time is slower than a hard disk. Although CDs are easily damaged, they are inexpensive.

A CD is a piece of plastic, about $\frac{4}{100}$ of an inch or 1.2 mm thick. During manufacture, a pattern is etched onto the lower polycarbonate plastic layer. This pattern is a single, continuous, extremely long spiral track of data. This lower layer is covered with a thin, reflective aluminum layer. Then a thin acrylic layer is sprayed over the aluminum to protect it. The CD's label is then printed onto the

Figure 2.3 *A compact disc*

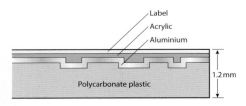

Figure 2.4 *Cross-section of a compact disc*

acrylic. CDs are read using optical technology and the CD drive has a laser beam in the read/write head, which can read the information on the disc.

Digital versatile discs (DVDs)

A digital versatile disc (DVD) looks much the same as a CD. A single-sided, single-layer DVD can hold up to 4.7 GB on one side. In contrast, a dual-layer DVD can carry two layers of data on each of its two sides: this means it can hold up to 18 GB of video, audio or other information.

Types of CD and DVD

Data can be read from but not written to **CD-ROM** and **DVD-ROM.** This type of CD or DVD is used to prevent the deletion or amendment of data. For example, they are used for the distribution of software, music, electronic reference books and encyclopedias. Films are distributed on DVD-ROM.

- **CD-R** and **DVD-R** allow data to be written to them on one occasion only; after this, the data on them can only be read. This enables you to create your own music CDs and record TV programmes on DVD. CD-R and DVD-R are useful for backing up the hard disk on a computer, because once the data has been written it cannot be deleted or changed.

- **CD-RW** and **DVD-RW** can be written to repeatedly up to around 1000 times, and can be used for continuously backing up data or archiving. Data recorded on them can be deleted or replaced by more up-to-date data.

- **DVD-RAM** may be sealed inside a cartridge and can be rewritten more than 100 000 times. Data written to DVD-RAM is expected to last at least 30 years. DVD-RAM drives are used in video recorders, camcorders and computers.

- **HD DVD** is an optical disk format for storing digital information, similar to DVD but with sufficient capacity for high-definition video and movies. Its development was supported by a group of manufacturers led by Toshiba. HD DVD was created to succeed DVD but found competition in Blu-ray, which is a rival format. In 2008, HD DVD marketing and development ceased.

- **Blu-ray** is a high-definition DVD format supported by a group of manufacturers led by Sony. It is intended as a replacement for the current range of DVDs and is used for distributing HD material such as movies. A dual-layer Blu-ray disk can store 50 GB, almost 10 times the capacity of a single-sided, single-layer DVD. It is the same size as a CD.

Compatibility problems

There are many different types of CD and DVD. DVDs may also be described as, for example, DVD-RW and DVD+RW. All these different types of media formats are confusing and there are compatibility problems because a CD, DVD or Blu-ray drive may not play or write all the different formats. In addition, not all drives can read recorded disks. A further problem with music CDs is that not all players will play MP3 files, which is the most common format for music files stored on a computer.

Magnetic tapes

A magnetic tape is wrapped onto a reel and provides a large amount of surface area. This abundance of surface area means that a great quantity of information can be stored on a tape. But tape storage offers only **serial access.** So if you want to access data at the middle of the tape you must start at the beginning, and forward through the tape to reach the part you want. For this reason, accessing data on a tape can be very slow, and so magnetic tape is mostly used for backing up data, not for quick regular access, for which you might use a memory stick, CD, DVD or hard drive. Magnetic tape is available in a variety of formats. One of the most common formats used for backing up PCs and servers is the magnetic tape cartridge.

Figure 2.5 *A magnetic tape cartridge*

Backups

A **backup** is a copy of a file. You should back up all your files regularly so that you always have up-to-date copies of all your work. A backup is more secure if it is stored separately from the computer.

The data stored on backing storage could be very important to you. For a business, there are costs involved in collecting the data. However, the data could be lost if the media is damaged; for example, because of a hard drive crash, power supply failure or fire. A backup is a way of trying to make sure that you do not lose your data. Ways of doing this can be simple or very elaborate.

Personal backups should be done systematically:

- You could back up a file after every session in which you edit it.

- You could back up every time you create an important piece of work.

- You could back up all your data files every day, week or month.

When making a backup you should:

- Arrange for a backup of all your data files to be done automatically so that you do not forget to do it. Make more than one copy of this backup.

- Save more than one copy of files created or changed between major backups, and keep copies of any data used to change files.

- Keep a backup on hand so that you can conveniently use it if a file is lost.

- Keep a backup on hand in a fireproof safe so that if the building burns down you still have a copy.

- Keep at least one backup in another location so that if all your local backups are destroyed you have a copy elsewhere.

Backing up a home computer

You might back up all the data saved on the hard disk of your home computer onto a DVD-RW every month. If you create any important work in between these major backups, you could save it on the hard disk and make a copy on an external portable hard disk. If you keep the DVDs, eventually you will have copies of your work going back over several months or years. You might store some of these in a safe place away from your home, so that if it burnt down you would still have a copy of your work. A DVD-RW will probably be big enough to store all your work if this is only word-processed documents, spreadsheets and database files. If you start storing pictures and graphics you could use several DVDs or you could **compress** your files.

If you kept backups in this way, if a file became lost or corrupted you could recover it by looking for a copy on the external portable hard disk, and then on the most recent DVD. If you could not find a good copy then you would work back through the DVDs until you found one. If the backup file was compressed, you would have to **decompress** it before you could use it.

Backing up a network

Networks can be automatically backed up as frequently as required – it is usual to do this at least once every day. The backup may be a copy of an entire hard disk or of several hard disks. Backups can be made using the network so that a backup can be made locally and saved onto backing storage media attached to the network anywhere in the world. Backup copies are often made onto other hard disks because this speeds up the copying. If the speed at which the backup is made is not important, magnetic tape cartridges are often used as these are cheaper. Some of the backups could be onto backing storage devices and media that are enclosed within containers that are fireproof, waterproof and bombproof.

The software that is used to organise automatic backups will keep track of when they were taken and where they are stored. When a file is lost and needs to be recovered, the backup software will search back through all the copies of the file to find the most up-to-date version.

Memory

Main memory

The computer's **main memory** may be **random-access memory** (**RAM**) or **read-only memory** (**ROM**). Random-access memory can be written to, read from and edited. The data in it can be accessed in any order (hence the use of the word 'random'). Read-only memory can also be accessed in random order, but the data in it cannot be changed. ROM is intended for permanent data, necessary for the operation of the computer system. RAM is **volatile** memory, which means that it is cleared when the computer is switched off; ROM is **non-volatile,** which means that it retains what is stored in it when the computer is turned off. Both ROM and RAM are made in the form of microchips. RAM is now supplied in **modules** comprising a number of chips together on a small board. When the memory of a PC is upgraded, more memory modules are installed in the system unit.

The computer uses RAM to store data and programs in memory while it is running. This is why computer scientists refer to the RAM as the **main memory** (or **primary memory**). Main memory holds the programs currently running, and the data being used by the programs that are running. Memory sticks and hard drives are called **backing storage** (or **secondary memory**).

The term **immediate-access store** (**IAS**) means the memory immediately available to the CPU – which includes both RAM and ROM.

Types of ROM

Programmable read-only memory (**PROM**) has no data locked into it when first manufactured. But later, a company using PROM chips to make a computer can put in its own information. The data would then be locked in place, so the memory can no longer be changed. **Erasable programmable read-only memory** (**EPROM**) gets its original data in the same way as PROM does. But, if necessary, the data can be erased using a special light shining on a 'window' on the chip, or by using a special electric charge (**electrically erasable programmable read-only memory – EEPROM**). This means that the data can be used in read-only mode, but that the memory can also be reset as required.

Flash memory

Flash memory is a type of EPROM. The memory can be reset quickly and easily so that it can be written to, read from and edited. It retains what has been stored without a power source.

A common use of Flash memory is for the **basic input/output system** (**BIOS**) of your computer. On virtually every PC available, the BIOS makes sure the computer starts up as it should and that all the parts of the computer work together.

Flash memory is often removable. Popular forms are the Compact Flash memory card (see Figure 2.6) and the USB flash pen device. These can be moved easily from one device or computer to another and can be used as backing storage.

Memory cards are removable and are used in video game consoles, digital cameras, mobile phones, PDAs and other portable devices. PCs often have card slots. Memory cards can store up to 32 GB of data. There are many types of memory card, including Compact Flash (CF), Secure Digital (SD), mini and micro SD, xD cards, SmartMedia and MultiMedia cards.

Flash pen devices or **memory sticks** (see Figure 2.7) usually plug into the USB port on a computer. They are lightweight and fit easily into your pocket so they are a convenient way of moving data from one computer to another. They have a storage capacity of up to 32 GB. They are used by teachers and lecturers to store presentations and other files, because they can be easily moved from one classroom to another. They can be incorporated into other mobile items; for example as a key ring fob. They often have a clip or cord for attaching them to clothing. They are robust and not easily damaged, and are a relatively inexpensive storage medium.

Addresses and locations

Memory is divided into many different locations, each of which can store one byte. The computer can find a specific location in memory using its **address,** which is a unique number referring to that location. Having *addressed* a particular location in memory, the computer can read or change its contents.

Words, bits and bytes

A **word** is the amount of data that a computer can directly access at one time. Different computers can access one, two, four or more bytes of data at one time. Each byte is a combination of eight signals, each of which can be either off or on (0 or 1). Each of these signals is a **B**inary dig**IT** or **bit,** so each byte has eight bits. We

Figure 2.6 *A Compact Flash memory card*

Figure 2.7 *A memory stick*

Quick question
- What is the word size in bits if the computer reads one byte at once?
- What is the word size in bits if the computer reads two bytes at once?
- What is the word size in bits if the computer reads eight bytes at once?

say that the computer has a word length of that many bits. The word size is always stated in terms of the number of bits, and not the number of bytes. For example, if the computer reads four bytes at once then its word length is 32 bits.

Exercise 2.1

1. Put a cross in one box to show the number of 700 MB CD-Rs needed to store 1 GB.

    ☐ A   5

    ☐ B   3

    ☐ C   1

    ☐ D   2

2. A memory stick stores 8 GB of data. Put a cross in one box to show the number of DVDs that would be needed to store 8 GB of data.

    ☐ A   5

    ☐ B   3

    ☐ C   4

    ☐ D   2

3. Describe the differences between a storage device and a storage medium. Give an example of each.

4. Describe the similarities and differences between a USB memory stick and a hard disk.

5. Describe the similarities and differences between a DVD and a hard disk.

6. A magnetic tape provides serial access. Explain why this can be a disadvantage. Describe one use for tape.

7. Explain the need for backup procedures. Describe suitable backup procedures for a small business, including how often backups should be taken and where they should be kept.

8. Describe the similarities and differences between main memory and a hard disk.

9. Describe the similarities and differences between main memory and flash memory.

10. Explain the difference between a word, a byte and a bit.

1. A **byte** is 8 bits, each of which can be either 1 or 0 (on or off). The **bit pattern** represents the piece of data in that byte of storage.

2. 1 kilobyte = 1024 bytes; 1 megabyte = 1024 kilobytes; 1 gigabyte = 1024 megabytes; 1 terabyte = 1024 gigabytes.

3. You need **backing storage** (or secondary memory) to store your data after the computer has been turned off. The computer will store your work as a file. Its size depends on the amount of data in it, and is measured in bytes. A byte is one data character.

4. Backing storage media includes hard disks, CDs (compact discs), DVDs (Digital Versatile Discs), magnetic tapes, memory cards and USB memory sticks.

5. A **magnetic tape** can store a very large amount of information but there is only **serial** access to the data – you must start at the beginning, and go through the tape to reach the part you want. For this reason, magnetic tape is mostly used for backing up data.

6. To avoid the loss of data stored on backing storage, a **backup copy** is made. Backups should be made frequently and automatically. Backups should be kept in three places: on hand, in a fireproof safe, and in another location. The schedule of backups is adjusted to suit the circumstances in which the computer system is being used.

7. While the computer is running, data and running programs are held in **main memory**, but the contents will be lost when it is turned off. This type of memory is **random-access memory (RAM)**, which can be read from, written to and edited while the computer is running. This memory can be accessed in any order (hence 'random').

8. **Read-only memory (ROM)** is intended for permanent data, necessary for the operation of the computer system. It can also be accessed in any order, but the data stored in it cannot be changed.

9. **Erasable programmable read-only memory (EPROM)** is a type of ROM where the data stored on it can be changed.

10. **Flash memory** is a type of EPROM. In a computer, flash memory is used to store the **BIOS (basic input-output system)** which makes sure the computer starts up as it should and that all the parts of the computer work together. Portable Flash memory is used as backing storage and is available as, for example, Compact Flash memory cards for digital cameras and as pen devices or USB memory sticks, for storing and transferring data between computers.

Chapter 2: Backing storage and memory

Chapter 3: Software

Types of software

Software is another name for the programs that run on a computer. A **program** contains a series of instructions to the computer. When a program is run or **executed,** the computer goes through these instructions one by one, and so accomplishes its tasks.

There are different types of software. **Operating system** (**OS**) software controls the hardware to give you full use of the computer, and prepares it to run other software. The operating system is **system software.** To actually carry out your tasks on the computer, you need to use **application software** – programs that relate to the things you want to do.

Application software

Office productivity software

Office productivity software helps you work more efficiently when doing tasks in the office.

Word processing is the preparation of typed documents that contain mainly words and some pictures. **Word processing software** enables you to manipulate text. You can move whole blocks of text around. You can set the size and shape of your text. You can let the word processing software check your spelling and grammar. And you can save and keep a document that you have prepared on the computer. An example of word processing software is Microsoft Word.

Desktop publishing (DTP) is like word processing but text and pictures are managed in columns as in a newspaper. Most word processing software has features similar to DTP software but often does not handle columns as well as DTP software, which is designed to do this. An example of desktop publishing software is Microsoft Publisher.

A **spreadsheet** is a table of numbers (mostly) arranged in rows and columns with related charts and graphs. Some of the numbers may have been calculated using others in the table, so if you change any them, a **spreadsheet** will automatically redo the calculation. An example of spreadsheet software is Microsoft Excel.

Database software is used for managing records. Even people who never use a computer are affected by the use of this kind of software, because database software is used to keep records that relate to people. For example, a supplier of domestic electricity will have at least the name, address and meter reading of all its customers. A database stores the records, and also provides many tools for handling and investigating the data it contains. An example of database software is Microsoft Access.

Web browser and communications software

Web browser and communications software helps you use the web and collaborate with others.

In order to access the Web you must have **web browser** software running on your computer. When you are connected to the Internet and you start up your web browser, the home page will be displayed. You can now surf the Internet by using your mouse to click on links or you can enter the web address or uniform resource locator (URL) of the website you want to access. A **search engine** enables you to search the Web by entering keywords that describe the information you are looking for. Microsoft Internet Explorer, Mozilla Firefox and Google Chrome are commonly used web browsers, and Yahoo and Google are popular search engines.

Email can be accessed by using either an email client running on your own computer, or webmail (that is, email software running on a website that is accessed using a web browser). Using these you can send and receive emails. You can filter the incoming email so that unwanted emails (spam) are removed. An example of email client software is Microsoft Outlook.

Presentation software

Multimedia presentation software helps you prepare for and deliver a talk to an audience. The monitor display is projected onto a very large screen during the talk. A presentation will consist of a series of slides with mainly text and graphics, and notes for the speaker. Presentation software is widely used throughout education and in business and commerce. An example of multimedia presentation software is Microsoft PowerPoint.

Image and sound editing software

Image and sound editing software helps you prepare and edit pictures, photographs, video and music.

Graphics software is used to manipulate pictures, drawings and photographs. Graphics software enables you to produce original art on the computer. You can also open existing pictures and photographs and change them. You can add, distort or erase parts of a picture, and resize it. Examples of graphics software are Microsoft Paint and Adobe Photoshop.

You could create a video on a camcorder, copy it to your computer and use **video editing** software to edit it. You can insert titles and other text, rolling credits, use transitions (fades, blurs and wipes) between different scenes add sound tracks and other effects, change backgrounds, adjust the playback speed, change the brightness and contrast, and delete sections of the video. You can play back the video as you edit it and save it in a variety of formats, for example as mp4. Examples of video editing software are Microsoft Movie Maker and Avid Pinnacle Studio Plus.

Audio editing software is used to create and edit music and other sounds. You can write musical notation, record live music, input music and sound files, edit tracks of individual instruments, insert sound effects and voiceovers, change pitch, change tempo, apply noise reduction and filtering, and adjust the volume. Examples are Audiacity and Goldwave.

Web authoring software

Web authoring software is used to create a website. A website is a structured collection of web pages that is accessible via the Internet. Web pages usually include text and graphics, and are written using Hypertext Markup Language (HTML) or software that generates HTML. Most software, including word procesing software, spreadsheets and databases, will allow you to save your work as a web page, but web authoring software gives you more control over this. Web authoring software may also include facilities to manage your website. Examples of web authoring software are Arachnophilia and Adobe Dreamweaver.

Project management software

Project management software can be used to track and chart the timelines of the individual tasks or events that have to be completed in order to complete a project. A project could be, for example, the construction of a large building. People and resources are allocated to each task. Some events will depend on completing other tasks and these must be scheduled in order. The critical path is the longest sequence of dependent events. Management of a project will focus on ensuring that the tasks that make up the critical path are completed on time. Project management software that is used to schedule tasks is likely to produce a Gantt Chart. For example, Microsoft Project can be used to track and chart timelines and has a Gantt Chart view.

Educational software

There are many **educational software** packages. A particular package might, for example, teach you how to type. It could record the keys you press, to measure your speed and accuracy, and could set up personalised typing lessons to help improve your typing. There is also educational software to help you learn, for example, English and Mathematics and revise for your examinations.

Quick question
Which educational software packages have you used?

Other application software

Integrated software packages have many applications bundled into one package (e.g. Microsoft Office or Star Office), or a single program for many general purposes (e.g. Microsoft Works or Claris Works). The software is designed so that data can be transferred easily between different parts of the package. For example in Microsoft Office, a spreadsheet prepared in Excel can be copied and pasted into a Word document.

Specialist application software provides the tools for a specific task, rather than for a broad application area. An example of this would be a program especially for preparing and printing DVD labels. Such software provides limited word processing and drawing facilities but would not be suitable for general-purpose typing or drawing.

General-purpose software, in contrast to **specialised software,** can be used for a variety of tasks but must be set up or customised before use. It is usually **off-the-shelf** software – you can walk into a shop and buy it off the shelf.

Custom-written or bespoke software

Bespoke software is software that has been uniquely created only to meet the needs of a particular business or individual. There are advantages and disadvantages to using custom software.

Advantages of bespoke software:

- You get what you want. Whereas off-the-shelf software may not encompass all your needs, bespoke software is tailored just for you or your business.

- You have closer control over revisions made to the software. A company that owns the original **source code** for the program can change it as needed.

- A program written for a specific purpose may run faster, because its code is optimised to serve that one purpose only.

Disadvantages of bespoke software:

- Custom software takes time to develop. If the business used an easily available software package instead, it could be off to a quick start in computerising its activities.

- The cost of development for custom software could be higher than the price of off-the-shelf software. This is because you must pay an ICT specialist to design and produce the software.

- A custom package is essentially new, since it has only just been produced. An off-the-shelf package may have been around for some time – other people will have used it, so you can learn from them about its strengths and weaknesses. You cannot fully assess a custom package beforehand.

- General-purpose packages tend to be widely used, so there may be many people who are already familiar with them. People who are looking for a job will even train themselves to use such software. This means that even new employees may already be familiar with the software.

- You may have to spend some time training staff to use custom software as it will not be like other software. In contrast, general-purpose software is usually designed to be easy to use, so you do not need long training periods to prepare staff to use it.

Customised software

An alternative to purchasing specialised software or using off-the-shelf general-purpose software is to **customise** off-the-shelf software. This should let you maintain the familiarity of general-purpose software, while allowing you to add other features that are important to you. It still takes some time to develop, but not as much as developing custom-written software from the very beginning. Many general-purpose software packages are customisable. Customisation may enhance the performance of the software, and enable you to carry out some tasks automatically.

Exercise 3.1

1.

	Type of software
A	Database
B	Spreadsheet
C	Desktop Publishing
D	Email

Put a cross in one box to name the type of software used to write a newsletter.

☐ A

☐ B

☐ C

☐ D

2. Name the type of software that would help you do these tasks. One has been done for you.

Task	Type of software
Write an essay for homework	Word processing
Send an email to a friend	
Look for information about mobile phones on the Web	
Remove the buzzing at the start of some music you have recorded	
Make a film about your holidays	

3. Name an example of graphics software and describe what you can do using this software.

4. Name an example of multimedia presentation software and describe what you can do using this software.

5. Name three types of software and give an example of another task that you could do with each of them.

6. State the name of an integrated software package. Name and describe the different applications that are integrated within the package.

7. Explain what is meant by general-purpose software.

8. Explain what is meant by off-the-shelf software.

9. Discuss the advantages and disadvantages of buying custom-written software compared with off-the-shelf software.

10. One example of specialist application software is a program for preparing and printing DVD labels. Name and describe another example of specialist application software.

Operating System (OS) software and Graphical User Interfaces (GUIs)

The **operating system (OS)** controls the computer; you could not use the computer without it. The operating system is software that runs between the hardware and application software. It enables application software to use the computer's hardware and other resources. The OS has many functions, including the following:

- input and output control
- error handling
- resource allocation
- providing a user interface
- allowing users to give commands to the computer
- file handling.

Input/output control

The operating system controls all input and output and the transfer of data within the computer. It manages the interfaces with the various devices that make up a computer system, and controls their behaviour so that application software functions smoothly.

Error handling

The operating system manages error handling. For example, when you are printing something, you might get the message in Figure 3.1. The printer has sent a signal to the computer telling it that it is out of paper. The operating system receives this signal, interprets it and displays a message on the screen that you can understand. Errors that arise while a program is running are known as **run time errors**.

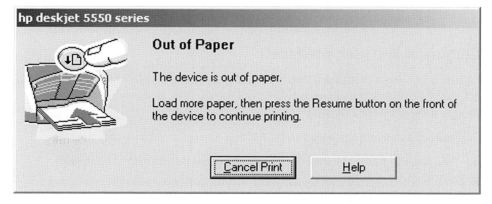

Figure 3.1 *An error message displayed when the printer is out of paper*

Resource allocation

The operating system ensures that all the software has access to the different resources it needs to run successfully. The programs running on a computer are broken up into **processes** that need different types of resources in order to run.

For example, if you want to print a document you must have the use of the printer. The operating system controls the running and scheduling of all these processes and manages the share of the CPU's processing time that is used by the different processes. If you only have one processor you can only run one process at a time, but you can interleave different processes that need different resources. If you have a dual- or multi-processor computer, you can run more than one process at the same time – this is **parallel processing.**

The operating system manages the use of shared resources on the computer. With more than one process running at the same time, it may well happen that two processes try to use a single resource, for example a printer, at the same time. In this case, the operating system will place the jobs into an orderly queue, and will control the way in which the output gets to the printer. In fact, the operating system has the task of controlling the use of any device that several programs might be trying to use at the same time.

The operating system controls communications between the various devices that make up the computer system. For example, when you move the mouse, you expect the mouse pointer to move on the screen. What actually happens is that a part of the operating system will display a mouse pointer at a particular location on the screen, and will control its movement as the actual mouse moves and sends signals to the computer.

On a PC, the operating system will handle resource allocation during **multitasking** (when one user is using more than one piece of software at a time). For example, when a user is running Word and Excel at the same time.

Commands and User Interfaces

The operating system enables you to give commands to the computer. You could give the computer commands in different ways. You could do any of the following:

- Type in commands on a command line.
- Select an option from a menu-driven system.
- Use a graphical user interface (GUI), and navigate and select using a mouse.

The operating system interprets these commands however they are given to it, and controls the computer so that it carries out the task you have commanded.

Command line user interfaces

Figure 3.2 shows a command line user interface. The example used here is from Microsoft DOS (disk operating system), that is, MS-DOS. It shows a listing of the files on a memory stick in drive L:.

Command line user interfaces can be difficult to use for various reasons:

- You have to know the exact instruction to type in.
- You have to type in exactly the right instruction otherwise the operating system will reject it.
- To make full use of the operating system, you need to know all the instructions available.
- If you don't know what instruction to use, you have to look it up in the documentation and this could be very time consuming. However, if you can do this, then command line user interfaces are straightforward and quick to use.

```
C:\ Command Prompt                                    _ □ X

Microsoft Windows XP [Version 5.1.2600]
<C> Copyright 1985-2001 Microsoft Corp.

L:\>dir
 Volume in drive L has no label.
 Volume Serial Number is D40D-DFE8

 Directory of L:\

19/03/2010  16:32            79,360 letter.doc
14/03/2010  06:49           290,427 report.doc
14/03/2010  06:28           301,677 essay.doc
              3 File(s)         671,464 bytes
              0 Dir(s)      129,073,152 bytes free

L:\>
```

Figure 3.2 *A command line user interface*

Menu-driven user interfaces

Figure 3.3 shows a menu-driven user interface that maybe displayed when starting up a computer. The user can choose any option from the menu by typing in the number next to the menu option and pressing **Enter**. Often, menus are hierarchical and one menu leads to another menu, which leads to another menu.

A menu-driven user interface can be easier to use than a command line interface because you don't have to remember the commands. However, they can be irritating if there are too many levels of menus to move through. It may not be as easy to move through the levels of menus on a menu-driven user interface as it is using a GUI. If you know the right command and you are using a command line interface, you can run the required option immediately.

Graphical User Interfaces (GUIs)

A graphical user interface (see Figure 3.4) will have a desktop on which windows, icons and menus are displayed. The user controls the GUI using a pointing device such as a mouse. Menu options and icons are selected by pointing (see Figure 3.6) and clicking the left mouse button. Other features of a GUI are as follows:

- A **menu bar,** which is a rectangular strip, usually horizontal and near the top of a window, containing the names of menus relevant to the program's operation. An example is the **My Computer** window shown in Figure 3.4 which includes the **File**, **Edit**, **View**, **Favorites**, **Tools** and **Help** menus.

- A **drop down** menu is one that opens immediately below the position of your mouse. You move the mouse downwards to go through the items in the menu list. The **View** drop-down menu is shown in Figure 3.4.

- A **sub menu** opens when you point at some menu items. For example, in the **View** menu, a sub-menu would appear if you pointed at **Toolbars**.

- A **toolbar** is a group of screen buttons equivalent to a menu which represents the tools available, that is, the actions that can be carried out within the software. The set of tools in a toolbar is often called a **toolbox**.

Figure 3.3 *A menu-driven interface*

● A **scroll bar** enables the user to look at content that is not shown in a window. For example, in word processing software, the user moves a slider up or down a vertical scroll bar in order to see text that is above or below that displayed on the screen. A horizontal slide bar works in the same way but moves the view of the content to the left and right. The vertical scroll bar is usually on the right of the screen and the horizontal scroll bar is usually at the bottom of the screen (see Figure 4.1).

● A **dialog box** (see Figure 3.5) conveys messages to you and invites a response.

Figure 3.4 *A graphical user interface (GUI)*

Using a mouse with a graphical user interface, you can do the following:

● **Open** (or activate) a process; for example, in Windows, by pointing at an icon and double-clicking on the left mouse button.

● **Move** an icon or a highlighted area; for example, in Windows, by pointing at it, holding down the left mouse button, dragging it to the required location and releasing the mouse button.

● **Close** a process; for example, in Windows, by selecting **Exit** in the **File** menu or by clicking on the **Close** button in the top right corner of a window.

For example, in Windows, you could open 'My Computer' by double-clicking on its icon on the desktop. A window opens with the words 'My Computer' in the title bar. You could move the window by pointing at the title bar and dragging the window to the required location. You can close the window by clicking on the **Close** button at the top right corner of the window.

How a GUI is operated can often be customised to suit the preferences of the user. For example:

● The **window size and position** can be adjusted. For example, in Microsoft Windows you can drag the bottom right-hand corner of a window to change

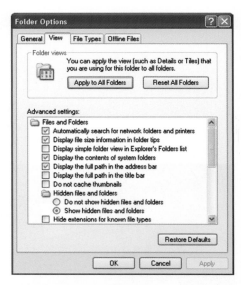

Figure 3.5 *A dialog box*

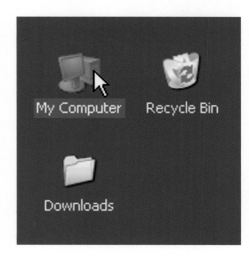

Figure 3.6 *Using the mouse pointer to select an icon*

The Close button

its size. Dragging the title bar at the top moves the window around the screen. The **minimize** button removes the window but does not close it so that it can be reinstated later; the **maximize** button makes the window occupy the whole screen.

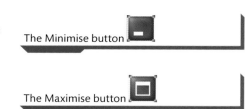

The Minimise button

The Maximise button

- **Mouse settings** can be altered, for example to switch the mouse buttons so that the left-hand button has the original functions of the right-hand button and the other way round. This could be helpful to left-handed people. The speed at which the pointer moves across the screen can be changed and pointer trails can be displayed. This could be helpful to those with partial vision. To do this in Microsoft Windows, in the Control Panel select **Mouse** and use the **Buttons** and **Pointers** tabs.

- **Sound volume** can be adjusted or turned off. For example, in Microsoft Windows there may be a volume icon in the task bar which allows you to turn the speaker volume up or down, or turn mute on or off. If you right-click on the volume icon, you can access the Master Volume controls which allow you to change the volume of other devices, for example, the microphone.

- **Icon size** can be adjusted. For example, in Windows Explorer right-click on the toolbar and select **Customise**. In the **Customise Toolbar** dialog box in the **Icon** options you can choose between large and small icons.

- **Display Properties** can be adjusted. For example, in Microsoft Windows, right-click on the desktop and select **Properties**. The **Display Properties** dialog box allows you to change the desktop theme, background colour, background image, colour scheme, font size and many other features. This can be helpful to users with a range of visual needs.

A graphical user interface has these advantages:

- GUIs are thought to be more **user-friendly** than command line and menu-driven user interfaces; that is, they are easier for users to operate and understand.

- Using the mouse to select things enables you to carry out operations without having to remember complex commands. The icons and menus soon become very familiar.

- The GUI displays all the options available to you, and you can explore the menus using the mouse. The entire screen can be used to inform you (and to entertain and interest you) whereas a command line interface requires you to remember and accurately enter the particular command that you are typing in. Even entering a number and pressing the **Enter** key on a menu-driven interface is not as easy as using a mouse.

- Keyboard shortcuts allow you to bypass the menu structure and run a command directly as you would when using a command line user interface. However, you do need to know these keyboard shortcuts beforehand.

- A GUI can be customised to suit the user's preferences.

File handling

The operating system handles files, allowing you to name them and save them on backing storage. It provides tools so that you can manage these files; for example, it

File Extension	Association
.doc or .docx	Document files associated with word processing software; e.g. Microsoft Word
.txt	A text file associated with a basic text editor; e.g. Notepad
.rtf	A rich text file may include formatting features not included in a .txt file
.htm or .html	A file containing hyper text mark-up language associated with a web browser
.bmp or .gif or .jpg	Graphic files
.mp3	A sound file format often used for music
.mp4	A video file format. It is a popular format and is used by Apple for video playback on iPod® Video Player
.exe	An executable or program file
.hlp	Help files associated with help documentation built into a program
.csv	A .csv file is a text file containing comma-separated variables. This type of file is often associated with spreadsheets. Stored data items are separated by commas and stored in a text file instead of being stored in a spreadsheet. The advantage of a .csv file is that it can be opened in different spreadsheets
.bat	A batch file containing a series of commands to the operating system
.sys	System files

Figure 3.7 *Some specific file extensions and their associations*

allows you to rename, delete and move them to different locations on a disk or to copy them to different backing storage media.

Filenames

A file is given a name to identify it. A complete filename has two parts: the **name** and the **extension.** The name identifies the file and the extension identifies the nature of the file. For example, the filename **study.doc** has the name 'study', and the extension 'doc'. The extensions bat, com and exe are used by the operating system. Other extensions such as txt, doc and htm are usually associated with particular software (see Figure 3.7).

In the early Microsoft DOS operating system, a name could have between one and eight characters, and the extension up to three characters. Consequently, filenames had to be abbreviated. For example, a word-processing file containing a list of printers might be named **prntlist.doc.** In Windows, filenames can be more descriptive. You could name the file **list of printers.doc** using more characters and spaces in the filename. Windows allows filenames with up to 255 characters, including spaces, but disallows some characters (for example: \ / : * ? " < > |).

Directories and folders

A new USB memory stick or other new storage medium will have only one folder called the **root** folder. You can store your files in this. If you use your memory stick to save a large number of files, it becomes harder and harder to find a particular file as all the filenames will be displayed in one long list.

It is easier to find a specific file if you group your files into separate **directories** - also called **folders.** Figure 3.8 is an example of how folders could be arranged. The route to a file is called its **path.** For example, the file **sermon.doc** is in the folder **church** which is a **sub folder** of the folder **mother.** If these folders were on a memory stick identified as drive **E:,** this would have the path **E:\mother\church\sermon.doc**.

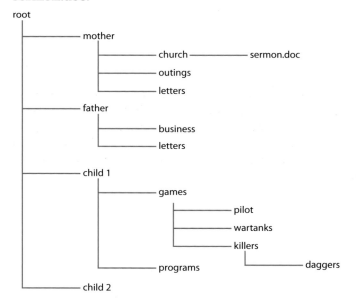

Figure 3.8 *A tree structure of folders*

A modern GUI will have file-handling software that enables you to look at the files and folders on your computer; for example, Windows Explorer (often referred to simply as *Explorer*). It can display the entire branching structure of your folders, and can show what is inside each folder (see Figure 3.9).

The Explorer window has two panes. The left-hand pane shows the branching structure of the folders. This is a tree structure, which shows how folders and files are organised from the root downwards. The right-hand pane shows what is in a particular (selected) folder.

Quick question
- What sub folders does the folder **games** have?
- Suppose **tanks.exe** is a game stored in the **wartanks** folder. What is the path of **tanks.exe**?

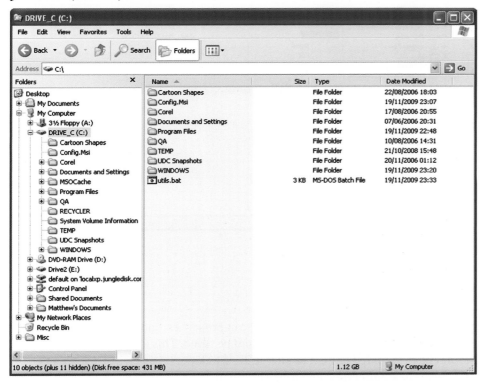

Figure 3.9 *Windows Explorer has two panes in a single window*

Moving, copying and deleting files

In Windows Explorer, you can **move** or **copy** a file by drag and drop. That is, you highlight the file, drag it over another folder and drop it. If the folders are on the same disk then the file is moved; if they are on different disks then the file is copied. Alternatively, you can use copy or cut and paste. To **delete** a file, right-click on the filename (see Figure 3.10) and select **Delete**. A dialog box will ask you to confirm that you want to delete the file.

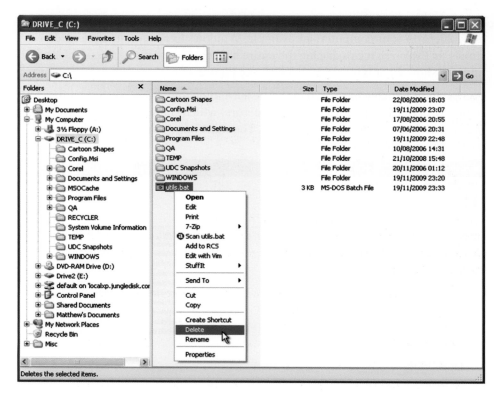

Figure 3.10 *A right-click menu for the selected file*

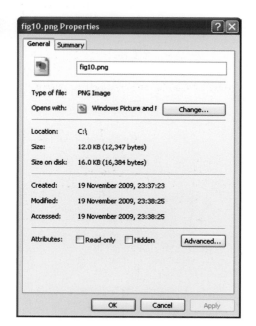

Figure 3.11 *The File Properties dialog box*

Properties

You can set files so that they have important properties, such as being read-only. A read-only file can only be opened; it cannot be saved. This allows others to share a file you have prepared but not to alter it. In Windows, if you right-click on a file, and select the **Properties** item from the menu, it brings up a **Properties** dialog box, which will be similar to the one in Figure 3.11. If the **Read only** attribute is ticked, then no changes can be saved to the file. If the **Hidden** attribute is turned on, the file will be invisible to some operations.

Formatting

The data on a hard disk is stored in **tracks** that run in rings around the surface. Formatting prepares a disk for use by setting up the tracks and dividing them into **sectors,** and setting up an index that lists the name and location of every file on the disk.

In Windows, if you right-click on a disk icon in My Computer, one of the options is **Format.** If you select this, a dialog box appears that will guide you through formatting the disk (see Figure 3.12).

Utilities

Utility software does tasks that help you maintain your computer, making other applications run better. They are often included as a 'bundle' along with the operating system. **Disk defragmenter** and **disk cleanup programs** are examples of utilities.

- When a file is saved on a hard disk the file may be fragmented with different parts saved in different locations on the disk. Access speed to files on the hard disk will get slower as more files become fragmented into more parts. A **disk defragmenter** will reassemble all the different parts of all the files.

- **Disk cleanup** frees up space on the hard disk by, for example, removing temporary Internet files, programs that are no longer used, and emptying the Recycle Bin.

Help and documentation

Even if software provides a good user interface that is easy to use, you may find it useful to also have access to clear and informative help.

Help can be provided in various ways:

- a printed manual
- help within the software
- online help accessible via the Web
- an email help service
- a telephone help line.

Such help should show you:

- how to use the program
- any hardware requirements
- how to get more information and further help if you need it
- how the software is structured, to make it easier for you to configure it.

Documentation is often categorised as user documentation and technical documentation. **User documentation** has simple instructions to get you started and to help you use the software. **Technical documentation** will have more in-depth information about how the software works and will help programmers reconfigure the software.

Did you know?
If a disk already has information on it, formatting will destroy its contents. For this reason, you should not normally format the hard disk built into your computer's system unit.

Figure 3.12 *A dialog box for formatting a memory stick*

Did you know?
Utility software often begins life as an add-on to the operating system, but can be later integrated with the operating system so that it becomes a part of it.

Software licensing

When buying software, purchasers may acquire some or all of the following:

- A copy of the software on a CD-ROM, or access rights to a website to download the software so that the purchaser can install the software.

- A manual explaining how to use the software. This could be printed or available as help files with the software, or as a documentation file on the CD-ROM or downloadable from the Web.

- A licence to use the software.

A software **licence** gives users rights to use the software under the specific conditions and restrictions stated in the licence. The distribution and use of software is restricted.

If a user does not have a software licence then it is illegal for them to use the software. It is assumed that if software is installed on a hard disk, or there is a copy of it on another backing storage medium, then it is in use. Using software without a licence is known as **software piracy.**

There are general categories of software with distinctive licensing arrangements:

- Licensed software

- Public domain software

- Open source software

- Shareware

- Creative Commons.

Licensed software is sold. Purchasers buy the rights to use the software. These rights are typically one or more of the following:

- The right to use the software on one or more standalone computers

- The right to distribute the software over a network for use on a specified number of network stations

- A site licence, giving the right to distribute and use the software on any computer on a particular site.

Public domain software is free software. The owners of the software make it available to anyone who wants to use it, or to specific groups of users, at zero purchase cost. Software producers may place any restriction on the use of the software that they wish. Even so, most public domain software carries no restrictions on its use.

An **open source** software licence makes the source code available for everyone to modify and reuse. Open source licences are usually free and allow users to modify and distribute the software. In contrast, you might not be given the source code of public domain software.

Shareware is licensed software that is initially distributed freely in the manner of public domain software. Users may install the software and try it out. However, if they decide to make regular use of the software, they must pay a licence fee. Users sometimes receive improved versions of the software when a licence fee is paid. Where the licence fee is not paid, continued use of the software is illegal.

Creative Commons licences help those who produce software communicate to users in a straightforward way the rights they keep for themselves and the rights they give others. Different licences are available. For example, an Attribution license lets others copy, modify and distribute your copyrighted work and other work based on it, even for commercial gain, provided you are credited with this in the way you ask.

A **demonstration disk** is a disk containing a demonstration version of software. Demonstration disks are often sent to intending purchasers so that they can evaluate software for themselves. The software on a demonstration disk may be complete but often there is some essential feature, such as printing, omitted. This is to encourage potential purchasers to buy a licensed copy of the software.

Exercise 3.2

1.

	Type of software
A	Database
B	Spreadsheet
C	Desktop Publishing
D	Web browser

Put a cross in one box to name the type of software that would use a file with this filename: balance.xls.

☐ A

☐ B

☐ C

☐ D

2. Name the type of software you would expect to use these files. One has been done for you.

Filename	Type of software
agenda.doc	
index.htm	Web browser
myfamily.jpg	
song.mp3	
holiday.mp4	

3. Look at Figure 3.8. The file council.doc is stored in the business folder on a memory stick in drive G:. What is the full path name of council.doc?

4. Design a file structure to store all the files you might create for your work and leisure activities.

5. Figure 3.1 shows an error message displayed when the printer is out of paper. Describe another error message.

6. Describe what the operating system could do if two programs wanted to print at the same time on the same printer.

7. Figure 3.5 shows a dialog box. Identify a different dialog box and describe what it is used for.

8. Describe how you could format an external hard disk using a GUI.

9. Describe how you would copy a file on the hard disk to a memory stick using a GUI.

10. Describe what is meant by the following:

✓ Licensed software
✓ Public domain software
✓ Shareware.

End of Chapter 3 Checklist

1. **Software** is another name for the programs that run on a computer.

2. To carry out tasks on a computer, you use **application software** – programs that relate to the things you want to do.

3. **Office productivity software** helps you to carry out office-based tasks more efficiently.

   ✓ Word processing software enables you to prepare typed documents that contain words and pictures. An example is Microsoft Word.

   ✓ Desktop publishing (DTP) is like word processing but text and pictures are managed in columns as in a newspaper. An example is Microsoft Publisher.

   ✓ A spreadsheet is a table of (mostly) numbers arranged in rows and columns with related charts and graphs. Some of the numbers may have been calculated using others in the table, so if you change any of them, a spreadsheet will automatically redo the calculation. An example is Microsoft Excel.

   ✓ Database software is used for managing data records, and provides tools for searching these and producing reports. An example is Microsoft Access.

4. **Web browser and communications software** helps you use the Web and collaborate with others.

   ✓ You must have web browser software to access or surf the Web.

   ✓ A search engine allows you to search the Web by entering keywords that describe the information you are looking for.

   ✓ Using email software you can send and receive emails.

5. **Multimedia presentation software** helps you prepare for and deliver a talk to an audience. A presentation will consist of a series of slides with mainly text and graphics, and notes for the speaker.

6. **Image and sound editing software** helps you prepare and edit pictures, photographs, video and music.

   ✓ Graphics software is used to manipulate pictures and drawings. You can add, distort or erase parts of a picture, and resize it.

   ✓ You could create a video on a camcorder, copy it to your computer and use video editing software to edit it. You could insert a title, transitions between scenes and rolling credits.

   ✓ Audio editing software is used to create and edit music and other sounds.

7. **Web authoring software** is used to create and manage a website.

8. **Project management software** can be used to track and chart the timelines of the individual tasks or events that have to be completed in order to complete a project.

9. Many **educational software** packages exist that can help you develop and practise new and improved skills or acquire knowledge.

10. **Integrated software** includes many single-purpose applications. These are usually general-purpose, off-the-shelf software packages. For example, Microsoft Office is an integrated suite of software that includes several single-purpose applications, such as Word and Excel.

11. **Custom-written software** is created specially to meet the needs of a particular individual or company.

End of Chapter 3 Checklist

12. Without an **Operating System (OS)** you could not make use of the computer.

✓ The OS controls all input and output and the transfer of data within the computer.

✓ The OS manages errors.

✓ The OS allocates resources to the software running on the computer.

✓ The OS provides a user interface so that the user can control the computer. Different types of user interface include **command line**, **menu-driven** and **graphical user interface** (**GUI**).

✓ The OS stores files and manages the file storage system.

13. Utility software does tasks that help you maintain your computer, making other applications run better. They are often included as a 'bundle' along with the operating system. Disk defragmenter and disk cleanup programs are examples of utilities.

14. The most common OS for PCs today is Microsoft Windows, which has a graphical user interface (GUI). With a GUI, you can use the mouse to select the operations you want to perform, using windows, menus and icons.

15. A file is given a name to identify it. A filename has two parts – the name and the extension. The extension indicates the nature of the file, and is often associated with particular software. For example, **letter.doc** is a document and **budget.xls** is a spreadsheet.

16. You can put your files into separate **folders**. A folder within another folder is called a **sub folder.**

17. To describe the location of a file or folder on a disk you use a **path name**. For instance, the path *C:\mother\church\agenda.doc* indicates that on drive C: (the hard disk), in the root directory there is a folder named 'mother', containing a sub folder named 'church', which has in it a document called 'agenda' which was created in word processing software.

18. Help can be provided in a printed manual, within the software, via the Web, by email and by telephone. Help should show you how to use the program, what the hardware requirements are, how to get help if you need it and how to customise the software.

19. A **software licence** gives users rights to use the software under the specific conditions and restrictions stated in the licence. If a user does not have a software licence, it is illegal for them to use the software.

20. There are general categories of software with distinctive licensing arrangements:

✓ **Licensed software** – you pay for a license for each copy of the software.

✓ **Public domain software** – this is free to use.

✓ **Shareware** – this is available to download and try out but you must pay for a licence if you decide to use the software in the longer term.

✓ **Open source software** – the source code is made available for everyone to modify and reuse.

✓ **Creative Commons** – these licences help those who produce software communicate to users in a straightforward way the rights they keep for themselves and the rights they give others. Differents licences are available.

Chapter 4: Word processing and desktop publishing

Word processing

Word processing software is used to prepare letters, reports, memos, books or any type of correspondence. These documents can be edited, printed and saved for use at a later date. Some of the various features available in word processing software are described below.

Different word processing software is created and sold by different software companies but they all have many similar features. Examples of word processing software are Writer, which is a part of OpenOffice, and Microsoft Word, which is a part of the Microsoft Office suite of software. The examples given in this chapter and elsewhere in this book are based on Microsoft Office 2007 running on Windows XP operating system unless stated otherwise. There maybe some differences from other versions of Office.

In this chapter you will learn about word processing and desktop publishing software; tools that enable you to prepare essays and newsletters.

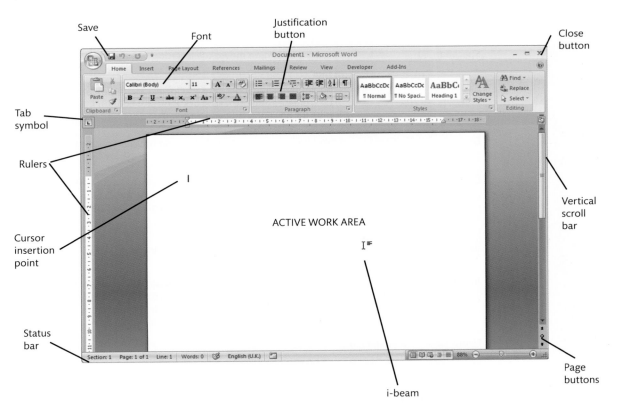

Figure 4.1 *Microsoft Word window elements*

Entering text

When you start up word processing software, usually a new document window opens. This is similar to a clean sheet of paper. You can start typing immediately, and what you type will appear on the screen.

Figure 4.1 shows important features of the opening screen of Microsoft Word, which are typical of most word processing software:

- The **insertion point** is a flashing vertical line, which indicates the position where the next character will be inserted. This is where text appears when you type on the keyboard.

- The **I-beam** or mouse pointer allows you to move the insertion point to a specific position in a document by positioning the I-beam there and clicking on the left mouse button.

- **Vertical scroll bars** allow you to scroll up or down a document.

- **Horizontal scroll bars** allow you to scroll from left to right or from right to left in a document.

- **Page buttons** allow you to move up or down a document a page at a time.

You enter text through the keyboard, and many word processing functions can be controlled using the keyboard. Figure 4.2 shows some of these.

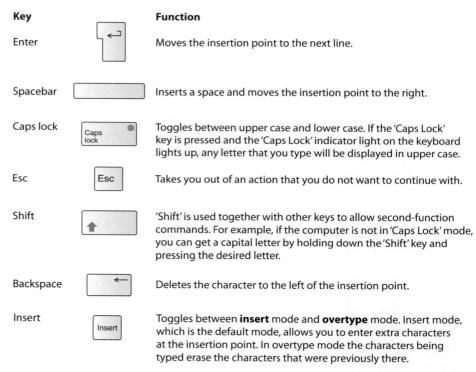

Key		Function
Enter		Moves the insertion point to the next line.
Spacebar		Inserts a space and moves the insertion point to the right.
Caps lock		Toggles between upper case and lower case. If the 'Caps Lock' key is pressed and the 'Caps Lock' indicator light on the keyboard lights up, any letter that you type will be displayed in upper case.
Esc		Takes you out of an action that you do not want to continue with.
Shift		'Shift' is used together with other keys to allow second-function commands. For example, if the computer is not in 'Caps Lock' mode, you can get a capital letter by holding down the 'Shift' key and pressing the desired letter.
Backspace		Deletes the character to the left of the insertion point.
Insert		Toggles between **insert** mode and **overtype** mode. Insert mode, which is the default mode, allows you to enter extra characters at the insertion point. In overtype mode the characters being typed erase the characters that were previously there.

Figure 4.2 *Some keyboard functions*

Word wrap

When you are entering text and are nearing the end of a line (i.e. you are approaching the right-hand margin), if the last word is too long to fit on the line, word processing software will automatically move to the next line. This is called **word wrap.**

You should not press the **Enter** key to move from one line to the next, unless one of the following is true:

- You have reached the end of a paragraph
- You want to create blank lines
- You have reached the end of a line that you want to keep short in appearance.

Saving a document

When you have typed in a document, you should save it so that it is available later. To save a document for the first time you can use either the **Save As** or the **Save** command. When either of these commands is used to save a document for the first time, the **Save As** dialog box appears, as shown in Figure 4.3. You select the backing storage on which you want to save the document, a filename and a file type. You have to give each document a different filename so that you can identify it. Filenames should be meaningful; for example, a letter you wrote to your friend John in May 2010 could be given the filename 'letter to John May 2010'.

Once you have saved a document, you can use the **Save** button to save it again when it has been updated. However, if you use **Save As,** the **Save As** dialog box will appear. You can then either save changes using the same filename, or make another copy of the document by saving it under another filename or storing it in another location. This is a good way to make a backup copy.

The Save button

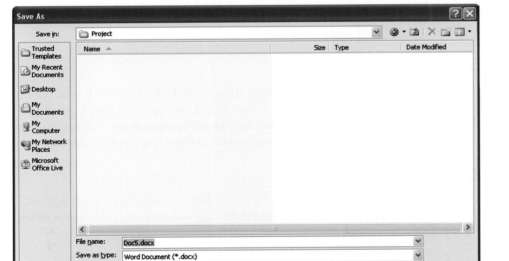

Figure 4.3 *The Save As dialog box*

Saving a document to a memory stick

The procedure for saving documents in Word is similar to that for most word processing software:

- Insert the memory stick into the USB port. This could be, for example, drive K:.
- Click on the Office Button.
- In the **File** menu select **Save As.** The **Save As** dialog box appears (see Figure 4.3).
- Select drive K:.
- Type in a name for the document in the box labelled **File name.**
- Click on **Save.**

Saving a document to the hard disk

Follow the same method used for saving a document to a memory stick disk in drive K: (see above) but select drive C: instead of drive K:.

Saving changes to an open document

If you save an open document, it will save with the original filename on the same disk.

In Word, you can do this very quickly by clicking on the Save icon in the toolbar.

Printing a document

When you have created a document, you will want to print it. For example, in Word, click on the Office Button, then in the **Print** menu select **Print.** The **Print** dialog box will appear (see Figure 4.4).

Print Preview

Before you print a document, you can see what it will look like when it is printed by using Print Preview. For example, in Word, click on the Office Button, then in the **Print** menu select **Print Preview.** The **Print Preview** dialog box will appear, and you can change the margins and orientation before you print the document.

Closing a document

When you have finished you will want to close the document you have produced. This removes it from your screen. In Word, to close a document, click on the Office Button then select **Close.**

Opening a document

When you want to edit or update a document you have previously saved, you will have to open it first. In Word, click on the Office Button then select **Open,** find the file and double-click on it.

Opening a document places a copy of the original document that is saved on backing storage in a document window, and you can see this on the monitor screen. The original is left intact on backing storage. You edit the document you can see but, until you save it, the original document on backing storage is unchanged. As a result, if you mess up your editing and want to return to the original document, you close the document without saving it.

Hint!
You should always save a document before printing it. Printing can cause problems, which could lead to your work being lost if you do not save it beforehand.

Did you know?
When you tell word processing software to print a document, it may take some time before the printer starts to print it. You will not speed up this process by telling the word processing software to print the document again!

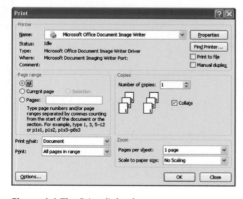

Figure 4.4 *The Print dialog box*

Exercise 4.1

1. State the name of the word processing software you use.

2.

A	Centre
B	Bold
C	Autoshape
D	Primary key

Put a cross in one box to show a software feature that is not usually associated with word processing software.

☐ A

☐ B

☐ C

☐ D

3. Explain why you should give a document a filename before you save it. What happens if you don't do this?

4. Explain the difference between the **Save** and **Save As** operations.

5. Type in the Toobago document below exactly as it appears. You will correct it in Exercise 4.2.

Toobago

Toobago is a small island located approximately 22 miles north east of Trinidad. The population is about 50 000 and consists mainly of descendants of African slaves brought to work the sugar plantations in the 17th century. The native language is English and the majority of the inhabitants are Christians. The people of Toobago are warm and friendly.

Toobago is considered one of the jewels of the Caribbean. Nature lovers and visitors alike can experience the unspoilt lush tropical vegetation that abounds on the island, which is also filled with a wide variety of birds and wildlife.

The surrounding white sandy beaches with their blue Caribbean waters are ideal for relaxation and bathing. For the adventurous at heart there is an abundance of water sports such as surfing, scuba diving and kayaking, just to name a few. The famous Nylon Pool is found in the waters off Store Bay. This is a safe bathing area with clear blue water and is located on a sand bank about a mile from the shore. Not too far off is one of the largest barrier reefs in the world, filled with a wide variety of colourful tropical fish.

a) Save the document on backing storage, for example, on the hard disk. Give it the filename *Tobago*.

b) Print the document.

c) Close the document.

d) Open the document; create a backup copy on different backing storage (for example, save the document on a flash memory stick); then close it.

Editing text

Word processing software provides editing features that enable you to make changes to a document.

Here are some useful keys for editing the text in a document:

- The **Backspace** key deletes text to the left.

- The **Delete** key deletes text to the right.

- The **Insert** key turns on and off the Insert feature. If Insert is on, when you type in new text it does not overwrite the existing text, but when Insert is off, new text being entered overwrites the existing text.

You can move text around in a document (and to other documents or applications) using drag and drop, or cut or copy and paste.

Drag and drop

The easiest way to move text within a document is to highlight, drag and drop.

To move text using **drag and drop:**

- Highlight the text. To do this, drag the mouse pointer over the text – position the pointer to the left-hand side of the text to be highlighted, press the left-hand mouse button and keep it pressed, move the mouse over the text, then release the left-hand mouse button.

- Drag the text to its new position – point at the highlighted text, press the left-hand mouse button and keep it pressed, then move the mouse pointer to where you want the text.

- Drop the text in its new position – release the mouse button to insert the text in its new position.

Cut, Copy and Paste

Cut and Paste

> **Did you know?**
> In Word, the Cut, Copy and Paste commands are on the Home tab.

Another way to move text within a document is to **cut and paste** it. Cut means to remove and temporarily store in the clipboard. Paste means to insert the contents of the clipboard in the document.

You could cut a character, a word, a line or a block of text. To use Cut, you must first highlight the piece of text. There are many ways to select text; for example, you could select the text using the mouse by dragging the mouse over the text you want to highlight.

When the 'Cut' command is used, the piece of the document that is removed is placed in a temporary storage area called the **clipboard.** A copy of the contents of the clipboard can be inserted anywhere in any active document and as many times as you like. This process is called **pasting.** You need to make sure that the insertion point is where you want to put the text you have cut.

Copy and Paste

The copy and paste feature allows you to make as many copies of a block of text as you want. The original block of text remains in position in the document. A copy of the block of text is placed on the clipboard. This copy can then be inserted anywhere, as many times as you wish, into any open document. You use the same method as cut and paste but you choose **Copy** instead of **Cut.**

Moving text from one document to another, or from one application to another

You can use cut and paste, or copy and paste, to move text from one document to another, or from word processing software to another application. Similarly, you can do this from another application into word processing software. This is a very useful feature when you are producing a report or essay and need to include statistics produced in a spreadsheet. You can copy graphs produced in a spreadsheet and paste them into a word processing document.

Spelling and grammar checks, and proofreading

Errors in spelling and grammar can undermine the professional look of a document. To help create more accurate and professional looking documents, word processing software contains tools that check documents for possible spelling and grammatical errors. Words that are spelt incorrectly, grammatical errors or inaccurate spacing between characters can be identified. If a spelling checker does not recognise a word, it identifies the word and displays a list of suggested alternative spellings for you to choose from. A grammar checker will identify possible grammatical errors and suggest how these can be corrected. Spelling and grammar checkers can check your English as you type and will help you correct your spelling and grammar.

Spelling and grammar checkers will detect most but not all errors of this type, and you should carefully proofread your work.

For example, they are unlikely to discover the errors in this sentence:

- The house is over their. They have a big garden with has a large beach tree growing in it.

The correct version is:

- The house is over *there*. *It has* a big garden *which* has a large *beech* tree growing in it.

Proofreading is a careful reading of text. During proofreading you should:

- Look for errors in spelling and grammar that have not been found by spelling and grammar checkers. Make a particular effort to check words that you know you find hard to spell correctly.

- Look for missing words and letters. For example: *a, the, and* and *it* are often omitted.

- Look for transposed words and letters. For example, *friend* not *freind.*

- Check the correct use of capital letters and punctuation marks (such as question marks, apostrophes, commas and full stops).

- Check homophones are used correctly. These are words that sound the same but are spelt differently and have different meanings. For example: *their* and *there; weather* and *whether.*

- Check the spelling of words ending in 'ing'. For example, check that you have used *making* not *makeing* and *trimming* not *triming.*

- Make sure that sentences are meaningful.

- Make sure that in every sentence the verb and subject agree. For example, 'she was going to the cinema' not 'she were going to the cinema'.

- Make sure that paragraphs are well structured. That is, they start with a sentence which tells you the topic of the paragraph, and this is followed by further explanation, supporting argument, or examples.

Extension activity
Produce a word processed report on your weekly spending. Include in it part of a spreadsheet table and a graph that shows how much you spend each week over one year.

Here are some useful proofreading techniques:

- Don't rush. If you do, you could miss obvious mistakes.

- Check the first sentence and the first paragraph very carefully. You may have read this several times and see what you think you have written rather than what you have actually written.

- Check a printout, because it can be harder to find errors when reading text on the screen.

- Have a reliable spelling checker or dictionary on hand to check the spelling of unfamiliar words.

- Read the text to yourself. This will help you spot missing words and meaningless sentences.

- Get someone else to check your writing. They may notice errors you have overlooked.

- Double-check any facts or other information that needs to be accurate, such as web addresses.

Undo and Redo

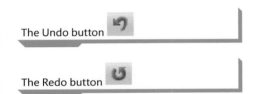

The Undo button

The Redo button

If you intentionally or unintentionally change a document, you can reverse the changes using the 'Undo' function. You can undo more than one previous action and you can select these from a list of earlier actions. In case you then decide your editing really was better than the original, you can use the 'Redo' function, which allows you to undo an undo!

Find and Replace

Find is used to search for a word or phrase in a document. **Replace** is used to replace one word or phrase with another word or phrase.

For example, in Figure 4.5, the **Find and Replace** dialog box has been set up to find the word *change*. When this is found, it is highlighted. You can then choose what to do:

- Do nothing. Click on **Find Next,** and the next occurrence of *change* is highlighted leaving the original unchanged.

- Replace *change* with *alter*. Click on **Replace** and *change* is replaced with *alter*, and the next occurrence of *change* is highlighted.

- Replace all occurrences of *change* with *alter*. Click on **Replace All** and wherever *change* occurs in the document it is replaced by *alter*.

It is risky to use the **Replace All** option. In the text in Figure 4.5, replacing *change* with *alter* leaves the meaning unchanged. However, the word *change* could have other meanings. For example: 'I paid for the newspaper with a $10 note but when I received my change it was incorrect.' Here *change* refers to money and to replace it with the word *alter* would make the sentence meaningless.

Figure 4.5 *The Find and Replace dialog box*

Exercise 4.2

1. Open the document **Tobago** which you saved during Exercise 4.1.

2. Move the lines beginning with *Toobago is a small island* and ending with *The people of Toobago are warm and friendly* so that they come after the paragraph that begins with *Toobago is considered one of the jewels of the Caribbean.*

3. Insert the following piece of text, without the quotes, as a new paragraph at the end of the document:

   The local cuisine in Tobago is truly delightful. A visitor can choose from a wide variety of local and international dishes. Some of the favourite local dishes are curried crabs and dumpling, curried goat and the ever popular bake and fry fish.

4. Find all occurrences of the word *inhabitants* and replace them with the word *population.*

5. Find all occurrences of the word *Toobago* and replace them with *Tobago.*

6. Check your work using the spelling and grammar checker.

7. Type in your name and the date at the bottom of the document.

8. Save the document as 'Tobago *your name*'.

9. Print the document.

10. Proofread your work and, if necessary, save and print it again.

Formatting

The final appearance of a document depends to a large extent on how effectively you can use the many formatting features that are available. We will consider formatting applied to characters, paragraphs and pages. You can change formatting even after text has been typed in.

Character formatting

Many of the features of text that affect its appearance can be changed. A **font** is a complete set of consistently shaped characters; for example, the Times New Roman font. You can change the font type and size; font style (normal, bold, italic, underline - see Figure 4.6); font colour; and font effects (strikethrough, superscript, subscript, shadow, outline, emboss, engrave and caps). In Word, to make these changes you can use the **Home** tab or the **Font** dialog box (see Figure 4.7).

Fonts

A **Font** is a complete set of consistently shaped characters. There are many different fonts, for example: **Arial, Comic Sans** and **Times New Roman.**

The **Times New Roman** font has serifs (see Figure 4.8). Serifs are short extensions of a character. Other examples of fonts with serifs are Courier, Palatino and Century Schoolbook.

Arial and **Comic Sans** are sans serif fonts, which means they do not have serifs. Other examples of sans serif fonts are **Tahoma** and **Univers.**

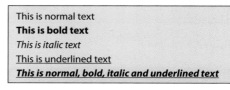

Figure 4.6 *Normal, bold, italic and underlined text*

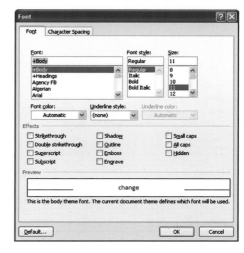

Figure 4.7 *The Font dialog box*

Font sizes

The size of the text in a font is measured in **point size.** The larger the point size, the larger the character. The font size can be changed after you have typed in your text. This means you can experiment to find the most attractive font for your document. As a general rule, point sizes 11 and 12 are easily readable (see Figure 4.8).

The Arial font in point size 8.
The Arial font in point size 10.
The Arial font in point size 12.
The Arial font in point size 14.

The Comic Sans font in point size 8.
The Comic Sans font in point size 10.
The Comic Sans font in point size 12.
The Comic Sans font in point size 14.

The Times New Roman font in point size 8.
The Times New Roman font in point size 10.
The Times New Roman font in point size 12.
The Times New Roman font in point size 14.

Figure 4.8 *Different fonts in different point sizes*

Font effects

There are many font effects but some of these will be more useful to you than others.

A **superscript** character is one that is raised above the normal line. For example, in the mathematical expression $4x^3 + 5x^2 + x$, the numbers 3 and 2 are superscript characters.

Subscript characters are placed below the normal line. For example, the chemical representation of sulphuric acid is H_2SO_4. The numbers 2 and 4 in the formula are subscript characters.

There may also be a range of **WordArt** effects (Figure 4.9).

Figure 4.9 *WordArt*

Paragraph formatting

A document is made up of a number of paragraphs. The format of these can be altered to improve appearance and readability. For example, you may be able to vary the line spacing, indentation and justification, or add bullets, numbering and sub numbering. In Word, you can adjust line spacing and indentation using the **Home** tab or the **Paragraph** dialog box (see Figure 4.10). To use this, click the little box in the bottom right of the **Paragraph** area on the **Home** tab.

Line spacing

Line spacing is the distance between lines of text. Appropriate line spacing can improve the appearance and readability of a document. Line spacing options include single, 1.5 times and double. Other line spacing may be available; for example, you could alter the spacing between paragraphs, and before and after headings (see Figure 4.11).

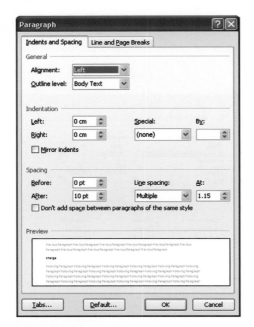

Figure 4.10 *The Paragraph dialog box*

This text has been typed in with **single line spacing**. Notice how close together the lines are. With double line spacing the lines are much wider apart and you will get less in the same space although it may be more readable.

This text has been typed in with **1.5 lines line spacing**. Notice how wide apart the lines are. With single line spacing the lines are closer together and with double line spacing they are further apart.

This text has been typed in with **double line spacing**. Notice how wide apart the lines are. With single line spacing the lines are much closer together and you will get more in the same space although it may be less readable.

Figure 4.11 *Single, 1.5 times and double line spacing*

Indents

When you **indent** a paragraph (see Figure 4.12) you move the vertical edge of it inwards from the left or right margin towards the centre of the page. The size of an indent is the distance between the margin and the text.

You can also have special indents:

- A 'first line' indent is one in which the first line is shorter than the rest of the paragraph.

- A 'hanging' indent is exactly the opposite. The first line is indented less than the rest of the lines in the paragraph, so that it appears to be hanging to the left.

Tabs

With tabs you can easily create columns of text. Put the cursor in front of the text you wish to align into columns and press the **Tab** key on the keyboard. You can use **Tab** several times on one line (see Figure 4.12).

> **This text in bold italics has been indented from both the left and right margins.**
>
> This paragraph has a **first line indent** where the first line is shorter than the rest of the paragraph. This paragraph has a 'first line' indent where the first line is shorter than the rest of the paragraph. This paragraph has a 'first line' indent where the first line is shorter than the rest of the paragraph. This paragraph has a 'first line' indent where the first line is shorter than the rest of the paragraph.
>
> This paragraph has a **hanging indent** where the first line is indented less than the rest of the lines in the paragraph, so that it appears to be hanging to the left. This paragraph has a 'hanging' indent where the first line is indented less than the rest of the lines in the paragraph, so that it appears to be hanging to the left.
>
> The Tab key has been used to produce columns of text:
>
> | First column. | Second column. | Third column. |
> |---|---|---|
> | First column. | Second column. | Third column. |
> | First column. | Second column. | Third column. |

Figure 4.12 *Indentation and tabs*

Justification

A paragraph or an entire document can be **left aligned,** which means that the text is lined up with the left margin (see Figure 4.13). Similarly, text can be **right aligned.** Text which is **justified** is both left and right aligned and is stretched across the page, possibly with more than one space between words. This makes paragraphs look neater but the text can be more difficult to read. You can also **centre** text so that it appears in the middle of the line. Headings are sometimes centred. In Word, text can be aligned and centred by highlighting it then clicking the appropriate buttons (see Figure 4.14).

This Heading is Centred

This paragraph is **left justified** which means that the text is aligned with the left margin. This paragraph is left justified which means that the text is aligned with the left margin.

This paragraph is **right justified** which means that the text is aligned with the left margin. This paragraph is right justified which means that the text is aligned with the left margin.

This paragraph is **both left and right justified** which means that the text is aligned with both margins. This paragraph is **both left and right justified** which means that the text is aligned with both margins.

Figure 4.13 *Justification and centring*

Figure 4.14 *The buttons used to justify and centre text*

Bullets, numbering and sub numbering

Bullets and numbering are useful for organising text where you want to emphasise several short points (see Figure 4.15). In Word, to add **bullets** or **numbering**, highlight the text and click the appropriate button in the **Home** tab (see Figure 4.16).

To use **sub numbering**, highlight the text and click on the **Multilevel List** button so that the **List Library** appears. From this, select the style of sub numbering you want (see Figure 4.16). The sub numbers are applied at an appropriate level when you indent the text.

- This is a bulleted list
- This is a bulleted list
- This is a bulleted list
- This is a bulleted list

1. This is a numbered list
2. This is a numbered list
3. This is a numbered list
4. This is a numbered list

1) This is a numbered list with sub numbering
   a) This is sub numbering
      i) This is sub numbering
   b) This is sub numbering
      i) This is sub numbering

Figure 4.15 *Bullets, numbering and sub numbering*

Figure 4.16 *The buttons used to add bullets, numbering and sub-numbering*

Exercise 4.3

1. Type out the document shown below. The number of words per line may differ in your copy, but keep the paragraph structure.
2. Use WordArt effects (or similar) on the heading *The Zenith Oil Company*.
3. Make Sports and Culture Club the second line of the document and change the font size to a size larger than the rest of the document.
4. Change the font type of the second line of the document to Comic Sans.
5. Place a blank line between the first two lines of the document and the date.
6. Centre the first two lines of the document.
7. Indent all the text between the first and last paragraphs.
8. Use bold for the words *Cash List Form*, *Fund Raising Form* and *Approved Budget 2010/2011* and put a blank line above them and below the words *Fund Raising Form*.
9. Use bullets to emphasise the items approved for the budget.
10. Change the line spacing in the document to 1.5.
11. Check for errors in spelling and grammar.
12. Save the document as 'new procedures'.
13. Print the document.

Here is the document for you to type:

The Zenith Oil Company Sports and Cultural Club 13th December 2009

The Manager,

Zenith Oil Company Sports Club

As you are aware the present executive has reviewed the accounting and budgeting procedures. In order to promote transparency and proper accounting and record keeping, the following systems will now be implemented.

Cash List Form

This form will be used to record all petty cash transactions.

Fund Raising Form

This form will be used to inform the exxecutive of all fund raising details.

Approved Budget 2010/2011

The items listed below been have approved for the 2010/2011 budget:

Cricket bats

Pair Cricket pads

Table Tennis Rackets

Soccer Balls

Twenty Football Shirts

If there are any questions concerning the new forms please contact the assistant treasurer. We look forward to your continued support.

Treasurer

Figure 4.17 *The Page Setup dialog box*

Exercise 4.4

Type out the following, print and save to a single file called 'Practice':

$$40x^2 - 20x + 25$$

$$C_6H_{12}O_6$$

Page setup

A new, blank word processing document already has a default page setup which is satisfactory for most documents you will produce. It is set to print on a standard A4 sheet of paper (210mm × 297mm). However, you may wish to make modifications:

- Change the width of the **margins,** perhaps because you are putting your work in a ring binder and want space for the holes on the left-hand side of the page.
- Change the **page orientation** from **portrait** to **landscape** (see Figure 4.17); for example, so that you can print a spreadsheet that is wider but shorter than a standard A4 sheet of paper.
- Change the paper size, perhaps because you want to print addresses on envelopes.
- Add a header or a footer; for example, so that every page is numbered.
- Start a new page.

In Word, you can make changes to the margins, page orientation and paper size using the **Page Layout** tab or the **Page Setup** dialog box (see Figure 4.17).

Headers and footers

A header is the text or graphics that appears across the top of a page, and a **footer** is the text or graphics that appears across the bottom of a page.

Headers and footers are commonly used to show information such as the filename, chapter title, author's name, page number, date and time. Different headers and footers can be used for odd and even pages. In Word, the header and the footer can be accessed from the **Insert** tab. You can type in text or insert items such as page numbers and the date.

You type in the text you want at the top of each page here

Header

Figure 4.18 *A header*

Page breaks

Word processing software automatically ends each page and breaks up the text from one page to the next. However, you may want to insert a **page break** before the normal end of a page. In Word, you can do this using the **Page Break** button on the **Insert** tab.

Section breaks

It is sometimes useful to divide a document into sections so that there can be different formatting in each section. For example, you may want one or two pages orientated to landscape in a booklet which is mainly in portrait. You would put a section break before the change of orientation from portrait to landscape, and another section break when you change back to portrait.

In Word, to change from portrait to landscape, do the following:

- On the **Page Layout** tab, select **Breaks** then **Next Page.**
- Then click on the **Orientation** button and choose **Landscape.**

To change back to portrait, insert another section break and repeat the same process but select **Portrait.**

Tables

One method of improving the layout of documents is by using tables. Tables are very useful for displaying statistical and numerical data and can also be used for keeping text aligned.

Rows, columns and cells

A **table** is made up of **rows** and **columns.** The intersection of a row and a column is called a **cell** (see Figure 4.19). You can choose the number of columns and rows when you insert a table. In Word, click on the **Insert Table** button (see Figure 4.20) and drag the mouse to set the number of columns and rows.

To add a row to an existing table in Word, do the following:

- Highlight a row by left-clicking to the left of it.
- Right-click to display a menu.
- From the menu, select **Insert** then choose from **Insert Rows Above** and **Insert Rows Below.**

Inserting a column is similar but you must click above the column to highlight it.

To delete rows and columns in Word, follow the same process but select **Delete Row** or **Delete Column** from the menu.

You can change column widths and row heights by dragging the frame.

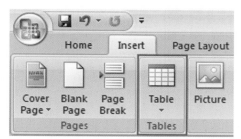

Figure 4.20 *The Insert Table button*

Figure 4.19 *A table with four columns and five rows*

Cell contents and formatting

You can type in text or insert graphics or other objects in a cell and you and can apply formatting such as bold, italic, underline, bullets, and horizontal cell alignment (left, right, centre and justified) to the cell. In Word, highlight the cell and apply the formatting as you would if the text or other objects were not in a table.

Borders and shading

The lines that outline the table are visible in Draft view, Print Layout view and most other views of the document. However, if they are faint, they will only show on screen not when the document is printed. If you want borders to show when you print the document, you could use the **Table Tools Design** tab or the **Borders and Shading** dialog box to set these (see Figure 4.21). In Word, to display the **Borders and Shading** dialog box, right-click on the table and select **Borders and Shading.**

To alter the borders, select the **Border** tab, then choose whether you want none, box, shadow, 3-D or custom borders. Select the line style, colour and width, and use the buttons around the preview to add or remove the top, bottom, left or right border. To apply the borders, click on **OK.**

You can also shade in rows, columns and cells in a variety of colours:

- Highlight the rows, columns or cells you want to shade.
- Display the **Borders and Shading** dialog box and click on the **Shading** tab.
- Choose the fill colour you want to use.
- Use the **Patterns** drop-down menu to select the intensity of the fill; for example, clear, solid, 5%, 10%, etc.
- Click on **OK.**

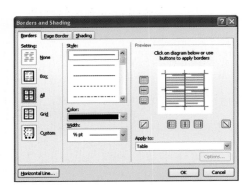

Figure 4.21 *The Borders and Shading dialog box*

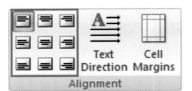

Figure 4.22 *Text directions*

Figure 4.23 *Vertical alignment of text*

Text direction in a table cell

You can change the direction of text in a table cell. To do this in Word, highlight the cell, and in the **Layout** tab select **Text Direction** (see Figure 4.22). This cycles through the available text directions.

Vertical alignment within a cell

You can change the vertical alignment of text within a cell (see Figure 4.23).

To do this in Word, highlight the cell, and on the **Layout** tab select the option you require.

Merge and split cells

The table in Figure 4.19 has four columns and five rows. You might want only one or two cells on one row, for example for headings. You can merge several cells to make them into one cell. Select the cells and in the **Layout** tab in the **Merge group**, select **Merge Cells.**

You might want more columns under a heading, that is, you would want to split some cells vertically. Select the cells and in the **Layout** tab in the **Merge** group, select **Split Cells**. Enter the number of rows and columns you want, then click on **OK.**

Text wrapping around a table

You can change how text outside a table aligns with and wraps around a table (see Figure 4.24).

To do this in Word, highlight the table, and on the **Layout** tab in the **Table** group, click on **Properties.** Click on the **Table** tab, and select left, centre or right alignment (or none or around-text wrapping), then click on **OK.**

Columns

Text **columns** are a very useful layout feature when you want to produce newsletters, newspaper-style documents, indexes or any text that needs to be in continuous columns - so that when the first column is filled at the bottom of the page, the text is started in the next column at the top of the page.

Generally you will use word processing software to produce text that goes across the whole width of the page. This is the default setting but you can lay out a document in one or more **columns,** similar to a newspaper. Even so, if you wish to lay out a document in columns you should consider using desktop publishing (DTP) software - see the section on DTP later in this chapter. In Word you can alter the number of columns in a document or a section of a document using the **Columns** drop-down list on the **Page Layout** tab (see Figure 4.25). The **More Columns** option opens the **Columns** dialog box (see Figure 4.26).

Figure 4.24 *The Table tab in the Table Properties dialog box*

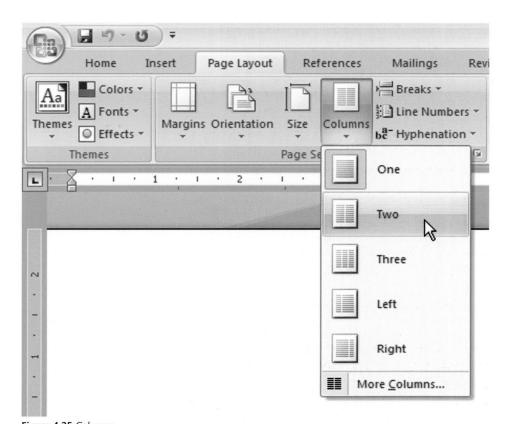

Figure 4.25 *Columns*

Exercise 4.5

1. Here is a list of some food we eat and the approximate amount of energy we get from it, measured in kilojoules.

   ✓ A portion of fish, 363
   ✓ A portion of potatoes, 129
   ✓ One boiled egg, 380
   ✓ A slice of bread and butter, 180
   ✓ One peanut, 25
   ✓ One carrot, 85.

   Using word processing software, do the following:

   a) Create a table with seven rows and two columns.

   b) Put the information above into the table under the column headings 'Food' and 'Energy'. Make these bold.

   c) Save the document with a suitable filename.

   d) Provide evidence that you have done this.

2. Information about the planets in the solar system is listed below, in the following order: planet, diameter (km), distance from the Sun (millions of km) and length of year.

   ✓ Mercury, 4840, 58, 88 Earth days
   ✓ Venus, 12 200, 108, 225 Earth days
   ✓ Earth, 12 800, 150, 365 Earth days
   ✓ Mars, 6750, 228, 687 Earth days
   ✓ Jupiter, 143 000, 778, 12 Earth years
   ✓ Saturn, 121 000, 1430, 29 Earth years
   ✓ Uranus, 47 200, 2870, 84 Earth years
   ✓ Neptune, 44 600, 4500, 154 Earth years
   ✓ Pluto, 6000, 5900, 248 Earth years

   Do the following:

   a) Create a table with ten rows and four columns.

   b) Put the information above into the table with appropriate headings.

   c) Make sure that numbers are right justified and text is left justified.

   d) Save the document with a suitable filename.

   e) Provide evidence that you have done this.

3 This is a list of five students with their name, student number, weight (kg) and height (cm).

   ✓ Adil Mir, 302001,40.5,140.5
   ✓ Mike Johnson, 302002, 45.2, 160.3
   ✓ Julie Maynard, 302003, 50.6, 165.0
   ✓ Brian Taylor, 302004, 48.8, 150.2
   ✓ Andrea Campbell, 302005, 65.0, 166.3

   Do the following:

   a) Put the data in a table with appropriate headings.

   b) Edit the table to improve its appearance.

   c) Save the document with a suitable filename.

   d) Provide evidence that you have done this.

4. The treasurer of the Zenith Oil Company Sports and Cultural Club has prepared a cash listing for the period September 1, 2010 to October 31, 2010. The document is shown below.

   Zenith Oil Company

   Sports and Cultural Club

   CASH LISTING FOR THE PERIOD SEPTEMBER 1 st 2010 - OCTOBER 31st 2010

Date	Description	Receipts	Payments	Cash Balance on hand
	Bal b/fwd			0
Sept 02	Raffle (200 sheets @ $10.00 a sheet)	2000		2000
Sept 06	Breakfast Sale	600		2600
Sept 08	Prizes for raffle		500	2100
Sept 09	Cake Sale	550		550
Sept 15	Cost of prizes for cricket presentation		1200	2650
Sept 20	Cost of refreshments for cricket prize giving function		800	1450
Sept 28	Subscription Fees for September	500		650
	Bal c/fwd			1150
Date: November 05 2010				

   Treasurer

   a) Create the document shown above.

   b) Centre the first two lines of the document and change the font size to one that is larger than the rest of the document.

   c) Right-align the data in the Receipts and Payments columns, and tidy up the table.

   d) Adjust the table so that it takes up the minimum amount of space.

   e) Save the document with a suitable filename.

   f) Provide evidence that you have done this.

The position at the bottom of a column where the text ends and the next column to the right starts is called a **column break.** If a document has two columns and you reach a particular point before the end of the first column where you would like to start in the next column, you can insert a column break. In Word, you can do this using the **Breaks** drop-down list in the **Page Layout** tab.

Templates

If you want to use the formatting and page setup of a document over and over again you could set up the document as a **template.** A business might want to do this so it can have a consistent house style for all the letters and other documents that its staff send to other companies. To use a template, you have to select it when you are setting up a new document. This opens a new document with the formatting and page setup of the template.

To use a template in Word, click on the Office Button and select **New.** The **New Document** dialog box appears (see Figure 4.27). You can then select a template document. Your new document will have the formatting and page setup of the template.

To set up a template in Word, you produce a document with the formatting and page setup you want, and then save the document as a template not as a word processing document.

It is often quicker to start with an existing template and edit this to your requirements. To do this in Word, follow these steps:

● In the **New Document** dialog box, click on **My Templates** and highlight the template you wish to edit.

● Under the heading **Create New,** select **Template** and click on **OK.**

● A new document will open which will have your chosen template. Edit this, then save it with a new filename - the file type *(Document Template)* and location should be set automatically.

When you want to use this template, you select it in the **New Document** dialog box as before.

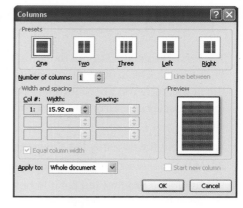

Figure 4.26 *The Columns dialog box*

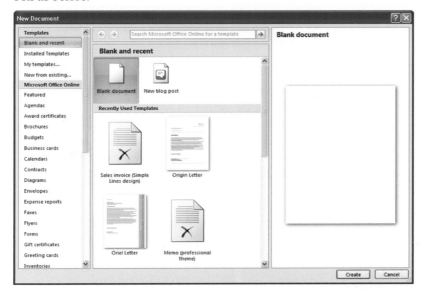

Figure 4.27 *The New Document dialog box*

Exercise 4.6

The First Trinidad National Bank has a newsletter called *Staff Agenda*. The articles shown below are to be placed in the newsletter. You are required to convert the document into an acceptable format by performing the following steps:

1. Type out the document as shown below.
2. At the top insert a heading: *Staff Agenda*.
3. Centre the heading and put it in bold. Ensure that it has a larger font than the rest of the document.
4. Use bold and capitals for the title of each article.
5. Put a blank line between each article and around headings where appropriate.
6. Change the left and right margins to 5 cm and the top and bottom margins to 4 cm.
7. Format the document using two newspaper-style columns. The heading should not be part of any column.
8. Insert the following header into every page of the document: *Staff Agenda, Volume 1, Number 10*
9. Insert the page number into the footer. Centre the page number.
10. Justify the text of each article so it has straight left and right edges.
11. Correct all spelling, grammatical and other errors in the document.
12. Save the document as *Staff Newsletter*.
13. Provide evidence that you have done this.

Here are the articles for the newsletter. When you have done Exercise 4.6, the articles should be much more presentable.

Staff Departures and arrivals

On behalf of the bank, I wish to express our sincere appreciation to and extend best wishes to the following employees:

Mr. John Cardinal, Accounting Supervisor, Fyzabad Branch has resigned with effect from September 25, I 2010. Mr. Cardinal served the bank for ten (10) years in the Accounting department.

Mrs. Leanna Achong, Clerk II, Head Office has resigned effective October 10, 2010. Mrs Achong served I the bank for eight (8) years in various departments.

New Staff

On behalf of the bank, I would like to welcome the following employees to our institution:

Mr. Larry Phillips has been employed as a Programmer I in the M.I.S. department. Mr. Phillips started on October 6,2010.

Mr. Glenn Singh, has been employed as an Professional Trainee in the Accounting department. Mr. Singh Started on October 6, 2010.

Staff Promotions

On behalf of the bank, I would like to congratulate Ms Teresa Black, Junior Accounting Supervisor, Fyzabad Branch. Ms. Black has been promoted to Accounting Supervisor, effective September 26, 2010.

Sports News

The Bank's annual Sports and Family Fun 2010 day will be held at the Centre of Excellence, Macoya, on January 14, 2011 at 9.00 am. All branches are asked to elect their team captains and to start making preparations for this grand day. There will be events for the entire family. Music will be provided and each employee and their family will receive chits for lunch and refreshments. We look forward to seeing each and every one of you with your family.

Fundraising Events

The Scrabble club will be having a Christmas breakfast on December 14, 2010 to raise funds to purchase hampers for the needy. For further information please contact Ms Gloria Simmons in the Personnel department at Head Office.

Training and Development

Seminar on Money Laundering

The Bank Inspection Department will be conducting a seminar for supervisors on January 17-20, 2010 at the Training centre in

Couva. This is the first in a series of seminars and workshops designed to empower our staff with the necessary skills to deal with the problem of money laundering.

Supervisors attending the seminar will conduct knowledge-sharing presentations within their banks upon their return.

Advance Excel Workshop

There will be a three-day Advance Excel workshop to be held on January 21-23, 2011 at the Training Centre in Couva. The workshop is designed for members of staff who have completed the Introductory Excel course. Notification will be sent to managers of respective branches, who would then make arrangements for individual employees to attend.

Examinations

The Bank would like to congratulate the following employees on obtaining their Institute of Bankers Diploma:

Mr. Kevin Khan

Mr. Daniel Ramjohn

Ms Roanna Gill

A Note on Customer Service

With the increasing competition from our competitors we must seek to differentiate ourselves, by standing out from the others. We believe this could be achieved by customer service. Customer service is the perception the public has of our institution. It is about delivering to our customers what we advertise, the personal touch that makes a customer feel special. Remember that poor customer service is an unpleasant experience and could lead to loss of business. Good customer service is a pleasant experience and leads to further business.

At this point in our bank's development, we would like all our employees to remember that good customer service is one of the main contributors to the growth of our organization.

Staff Christmas Diner

This years' annual Christmas diner will be held at the Main Ball Room of the Mohogany Hotel. All employees are invited along with a guest. Cocktails will be from 7.30 to 8.30 and Diner will be from 8.30 pm. Music will be provided by a DJ and a live band. Look forward to seeing all employees.

Extension activity

Set up a template for writing your letters. This could have in it your address and all the other text that doesn't change from one letter to the next. You could scan your signature and include it in the template as a graphic. Using this template, write letters to your friends and family.

Mail merge

Using the **mail merge** feature, you can produce personalised letters, mailing labels, memos and many other communications to send to a large number of people without having to type each one individually. For example, many companies send standard letters to customers in which the body of the letter is the same but the name, address and a few pieces of additional information may be different. This type of correspondence can be done easily using mail merge.

Mail merge uses two files: **a main document** (containing a **standard letter** or similar), and a **data source** containing the personal information. Data from the data source is inserted into the main document to produce personalised documents. Figure 4.28 shows the merging process. Figure 4.29 shows a standard letter in Word before merging with the data source shown in Figure 4.30. Figure 4.31 is one of the mail merge letters produced.

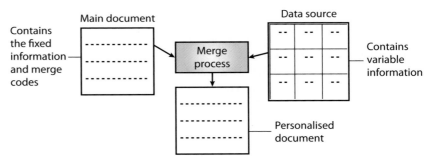

Figure 4.28 *How mail merge works*

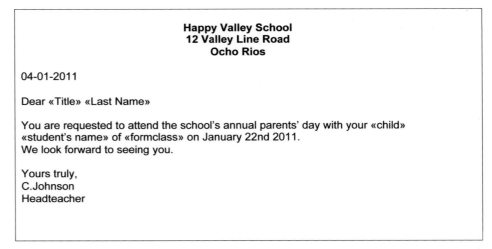

Happy Valley School
12 Valley Line Road
Ocho Rios

04-01-2011

Dear «Title» «Last Name»

You are requested to attend the school's annual parents' day with your «child» «student's name» of «formclass» on January 22nd 2011.
We look forward to seeing you.

Yours truly,
C.Johnson
Headteacher

Figure 4.29 *A standard letter before a mail merge*

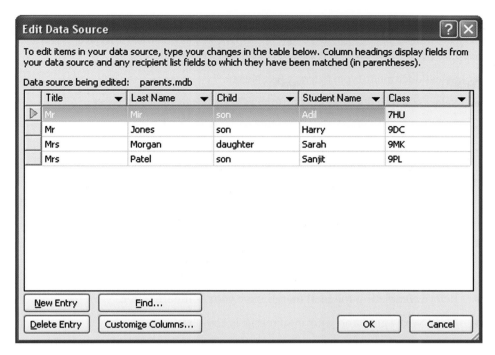

Figure 4.30 *The mail merge recipients list*

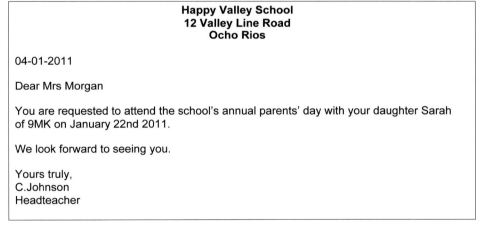

Figure 4.31 *One of the personalised letters after the mail merge*

In Word, one way to do a mail merge is to use the **Mail Merge Wizard.** Open a new document and in the **Mailings** tab, click on **Start Mail Merge** and select **Step by Step Mail Merge Wizard.** Follow the instructions:

● Select document type: *letters.* Click **Next.**

● Select starting document: *start from existing document.* Click **Next.**

● Select recipients: *type a new list.* Click **Create.**

● In the **New Address List** dialog box you will need to customise the field names. Change them to those needed in the standard letter (see Figure 4.29). Type in the new entries for your mail merge. When you have finished, close the dialog box and you will have the opportunity to save your data. Click **Next** to write your letter.

● As you write your letter you can insert the **merge fields.** To do this, select **More items** and the **Insert Merge Field** dialog box appears. Select the required field and click on **Insert.** Click **Next.**

● Before completing the mail merge, save your standard letter.

● Click **Next** again and your mail merge is complete.

Did you know?
If you select **Use an existing list**, this allows you to select a list produced using a database or other software.

Exercise 4.7

1. The Happy Valley High School is having its annual parents' day and wishes to invite parents. The principal wants each parent to receive a personal invitation. The school secretary has been asked to send personalised invitations to parents and is going to do this using mail merge.

> Happy Valley High School
>
> 12 Valley Line Road
>
> Ocho Rios
>
> 04-01-2011
>
>
> Dear «Title» «LastName»
>
> You are requested to attend the school's annual parents' day with your «child», «student_name» of «formclass» on January 22nd, 2011.
>
> We look forward to seeing you.
>
>
> Yours truly,
>
> C.Johnson
>
> Headteacher

When you type in this letter, centre the name and address of the school, and insert blank lines where these are necessary; for example, between the line beginning with 'Dear' and the following line.

When you save this document, give it the filename 'Open Day'.

The data source is to contain this information:

Title	Mr
Last Name	Jaffar
child	son
student_name	Ronald
formclass	8MX

Title	Mrs
Last Name	Morgan
child	daughter
student_name	Sarah
Form class	9MK

When you enter this data, add at least eight records of your own.

When you save this data, give it the filename 'Parents'.

Mail merge the standard letter with the data source and print all the letters.

2. Customers who do not pay their monthly instalment by the fifteenth day of the following month are sent the following reminder letter by Makhan Furniture Shop:

Makhan Furniture Shop

Broad Street Bridgetown

Barbados

«Title» «First Name» «Surname»

«First line of address»

«Second line of address»

Dear «Title» «Surname»

Please be informed that our accounts are showing that you have not paid your monthly instalment of «amount» towards your purchase on «date». Kindly pay this amount to your account, number «account number», to avoid any inconvenience.

Yours truly,

Lenore Brown

Manager

These defaulters were found in the current month:

Title:	Mr
First Name:	Kelvin
Surname:	Harry
First line of address:	3 Hisbiscus Lane
Second line of address:	Christ Church
Amount:	$450
Date:	08 08 2010
Account Number:	Aug134

Title:	Mr
First Name:	Conrad
Surname:	Lewis
First line of address:	10 Wilson Avenue
Second line of address:	St Lawerence Gap
Amount:	$650
Date:	12 10 2010
Account Number:	Oct256

Title:	Ms
First Name:	Sherry
Surname:	Roach
First line of address:	8 Railroad Street
Second line of address:	Blackrock
Amount:	$875
Date:	15 08 2010
Account Number:	Aug150

a) Add seven records of your own.

b) Using mail merge, print personalised letters to the customers who have defaulted on their payments.

c) Add a new field called *Item* and fill in possible names for the items for each customer.

d) Change the amount owing for Mr Lewis to $785.

e) Save all changes, produce personalised letters to the customers who have defaulted on their payments using mail merge, and provide evidence you have done this.

Graphics

Including graphics in a word processed document

Depending on the nature of your document, you may be able to enhance its appearance by including graphics. There are many ways to do this:

- Insert clip art from a clip art library.
- Insert a shape or chart.
- Insert a photograph from a digital camera.
- Insert a scanned image of a drawing or picture.
- Download graphics from the Web.
- Cut or copy a graphic from another application.
- Copy the whole or part of the screen and paste it into the document.
- Create a graphic using drawing tools.

Inserting a graphic

In Word, insert a graphic in a document as follows:

- Place the insertion point where you want the graphic displayed.
- On the **Insert** tab, select **Clip Art** (or **Picture** if the graphic is stored in a file).
- Next, select a picture and click on it.

Including the whole or a part of the screen in a document

On an IBM compatible personal computer, pressing the **Print Screen** key on the keyboard will copy an image of the screen display into the clipboard. Pressing the **Alt** key and the **Print Screen** key at the same time will copy the active window (or dialog box) into the clipboard. In Word, the contents of the clipboard can be included in a document by selecting **Paste.** Figure 4.30 is an example of a dialog box which has been pasted into a word processed document.

When you have inserted a graphic, you may find that you want to change its size, move it to a new position, allow text to flow round it or put a border on it. These tasks can be done in word processing software.

Changing the size of a graphic

When a graphic has been inserted, you may wish to change its size. This can be done by resizing and cropping. When a graphic is **resized,** the whole graphic is enlarged or reduced, but when a graphic is **cropped,** part of the graphic is removed.

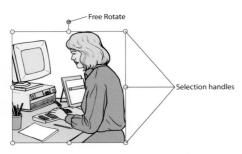

Figure 4.32 *Selection handles surrounding a graphic*

The Crop button

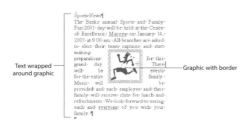

Text wrapped around graphic

Graphic with border

Figure 4.33 *Text wrapped around a graphic*

Resizing a graphic

A graphic is resized when it is enlarged or reduced but the whole graphic is retained. In Word, click once on the graphic and it is displayed with eight selection handles around it (see Figure 4.32).

You can change the height of the graphic using the selection handles at the top or bottom to stretch the graphic vertically.

You can change the width of the graphic using the handles at the sides to stretch the graphic horizontally.

To reduce or enlarge the graphic proportionately, drag the corner handles away from the centre of the graphic to enlarge its size or towards the centre of the graphic to reduce its size. This preserves the **aspect ratio,** which means that any changes to the graphic keep the same shape.

Cropping a graphic

When a graphic is cropped, it is reframed and the part of it outside the new rectangular frame is deleted. In Word, in the **Picture Tools | Format** tab, click on the **Crop** button and reframe the graphic. When you are satisfied this is as you want it, click on the crop button again and the part of the graphic outside the new frame is deleted. If you wish, you can now resize the cropped graphic.

Changing the position of the graphic

When a graphic has been inserted, you may wish to move it to another position in the document. You could highlight the graphic then drag it to the desired position. Alternatively, you could cut or copy and paste the graphic.

Rotating or reflecting a graphic

Graphics can be rotated and reflected (flipped). In Word, select the graphic and select **Rotate.** You can use the **Free Rotate** selection handle at the middle top to achieve any degree of rotation.

Wrapping text around a graphic

When a graphic is placed in a document, the text around the graphic is placed at the top and bottom of the graphic but not at the sides. However, for newsletters, newspapers and magazines, you may want the text to flow or wrap around the graphic. This can save space and enhance presentation. Figure 4.33 shows a graphic within a border with text wrapped around it.

In Word, you can wrap text around a graphic by selecting it and using the **Text Wrapping** options on the **Picture Tools | Format** tab.

Inserting a border around a graphic

You can put a border on a graphic to emphasise it rather like a picture frame. In Word, select the graphic and in use the **Picture Border** options on the **Picture Tools | Format** tab to select the border you want.

Inserting symbols and special characters

Some documents may need symbols that do not appear as keys on the keyboard. For example, α, ∏ and Σ are all symbols that might be part of a document. In Word, these symbols can be found listed in the **Symbol** drop-down list on the **Home** tab.

Drawing tools

Most word processing software now has a range of drawing tools so that you can add commentary to illustrations and graphics.

Drawing tools that can be found in word processing software include the following:

- Ready-made shapes – a variety of lines, arrows, connectors, flowchart symbols, callouts and other shapes. These will be available in different styles.

- SmartArt preformatted diagrams; for example, organisational charts.

- Text boxes.

- Colour which can be used to fill shapes.

- Shadow and 3-D effects.

To access these tools in Word, click on the **Insert** tab.

Order

If you insert several objects into a Word document, they may cover each other up. You can alter the order in which they cover each other by selecting the object you want to move and right-clicking on it. Next select **Order** and select the option you want. For example, **Bring to Front** places the selected object in front of all other overlapping objects.

Grouping

You might create a complex shape in Word by inserting several objects which together make up the whole shape. If you wanted to copy or move this whole shape, you might find it difficult because all the objects could separate. It might be time consuming to move all the objects individually to another location in your document or to another file. To keep the shapes together: hold down **Shift** and click on each; right-click and select **Grouping**, then select **Group**. The objects will now behave as if they were one object and the whole shape can be copied and moved easily.

A grouped shape can be difficult to edit and you may need to **ungroup** it. Select the grouped shape, right-click, select **Grouping** then **Ungroup**. You can quickly return to the grouped shape by selecting **Regroup**.

Activity

Type these expressions into word processing software:
✓ Well done
€ 500 Five hundred Euros
Circumference = 2 π × radius
m α A

Activity

Write a story about your holidays. Put pictures of your holidays in the story, and wrap the text round the pictures. Use **callouts** to point out particular features in the pictures.

Desktop publishing (DTP)

DTP software is used to produce leaflets, brochures, newspapers, magazines, etc. Popular examples are PageMaker and Microsoft Publisher. DTP software has many features in common with word processing software – for example, you can open, save and print documents, enter and edit text, change the font type and size, and insert new pages in a very similar way to when you use word processing software. However, DTP has much better controls for handling page layout. For example, Microsoft Publisher has templates for letterheads, flyers and brochures.

Very early word processing software did not allow you to format text using columns and tables and you could not import graphics. The DTP software available at the time provided these facilities but would not allow you to enter and edit text. Text had to be entered using word processing software then imported to the DTP software. This is sometimes still the case. However, as word processor software and DTP software have been improved over the years, a considerable overlap has developed and these now have many features in common. Even so, professional typographers would tend to use DTP software rather than word processing software to produce published materials such as magazines.

Figure 4.34 *The Microsoft Publisher opening screen*

At present, the main difference between DTP and word processing software is that DTP software emphasises page layout. When you are setting up a new DTP document you have to decide on the page layout before you can enter text or import clip art and other graphics.

As an illustration of the emphasis placed on page layout in DTP software, consider the options presented to the user when Microsoft Publisher is opened. First, you are presented with a screen that asks you to select from a variety of page layouts (see

Figure 4.34). Having selected a page layout you are guided through a range of layout and design options before entering text or inserting your own graphics.

If you immediately exit the opening screen, the software still persists in encouraging you to select a page layout. It does this using the **Format Publication** task pane (see Figure 4.35). Working through the various options you would take the following steps:

- Add suggested objects.
- Choose a colour scheme for your background.
- Choose a font scheme.
- Choose a template.
- Change the page size.

If you avoid both the opening screen and the **Format Publication** task pane and click on the page and start typing, a text frame is created for you. A text frame is a layout feature, as explained below.

Frames

Frames are a layout feature, and all text and graphics or any other object inserted into Publisher must be entered into a frame. In Publisher, you can insert frames using the toolbar shown in Figure 4.36. To do this, you click on the appropriate button and insert the required object.

Inserting a text frame

To insert a text frame you click on the **Text Box.** Dragging the mouse pointer across the page creates a text frame. When you type, the text appears in the text box.

Inserting a picture frame

To insert a picture frame you click on **Picture Frame Tool.** Dragging the mouse pointer across the page creates a picture frame. Double-click on the picture frame and a dialog box appears. Using this dialog box you can choose a picture file and this will be imported into the picture frame.

Importing objects from other applications

You will also need to use an appropriate frame if you import an object from another application. For example, in Publisher, when importing part of a spreadsheet by copying it from Excel and pasting into Publisher, the software will create a table frame for you.

Manipulating frames

Page layout is controlled by resizing and moving frames. Having inserted a frame you can resize it using the selection handles in a way similar to that described for resizing a graphic earlier in this chapter.

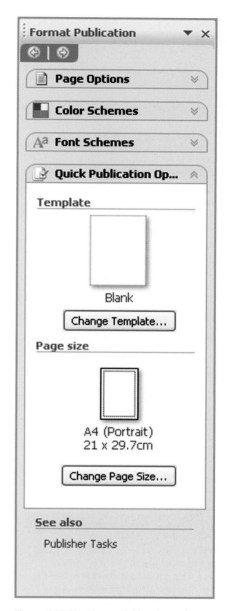

Figure 4.35 *The Format Publication task pane*

Figure 4.36 *The buttons on this toolbar allow you to insert frames*

Manipulating graphics

The crop feature works in much the same way as it does in Word. You can also move a graphic, rotate or reflect it, wrap text around it and put a border on the frame in much the same way as you would in Word.

Text flow

An important feature of DTP is the ability to make text **flow** between different text frames that are separate and in different positions on the page or on different pages. You will want text flow to work when you resize frames so that they can contain more or less text, and when you delete or insert text.

Let us suppose you want to type a story in two or more frames. In Publisher, you would create a text box and begin to type in the text. When the text box is full, the **Text in Overflow indicator** (see Figure 4.37) appears on the lower right-hand corner of the text frame. Create another text frame then click on the original text frame. Next, click on the **Create Text Box Link** button (see Figure 4.38) then click on the second text frame. The two frames are now linked and the story pours into the second text frame. These frames can now be manipulated so that the second text frame appears elsewhere on the page or on another page.

Figure 4.37 *The Text in Overflow indicator*

Figure 4.38 *The Create Text Box Link button*

Letterheads, flyers and brochures

Microsoft Publisher has **templates** that allow you to create business cards, letterheads, flyers, brochures and many other common forms of printed communication.

For example, here is how to create a flyer in Publisher:

- From the opening screen, click on the **Flyers** publication type.

- The templates for flyers with different layouts are displayed. Select one of these then press **Create.**

- To customise your design, you choose from a range of colour schemes and fonts.

- To complete the flyer, you replace the details shown, such as the name of the organisation, information about the product or service being advertised, and contact details.

- In the **Flyer Options** tab you can change the page size and orientation.

- To print or save your flyer, in the **File** menu, select the appropriate option.

Activity

Write a booklet about the place where you live. This could have several different articles describing how different people live, work and enjoy themselves. This should include photographs of local people, houses and industrial buildings. The booklet should be up to four pages long.

1. **Word processing software** allows you to prepare letters, reports, memos, books and other correspondence. These can be saved to be worked on later or printed. You can preview what your work will look like when it has been printed.

2. When entering text, the word wrap feature moves you to a new line automatically. You press the **Enter** key only if the line is a short line or to move to a new paragraph. You can also insert graphics and symbols into documents.

3. Word processing software contains many editing and proofing features that enable users to make changes to a document quickly and easily. Some of the editing features include the following:

   ✓ **Delete** (characters, words and blocks of text can easily be deleted).

   ✓ **Insert** (characters, words and blocks of text can easily be inserted).

   ✓ **Drag and Drop** (this is the easiest way to move text within a document).

   ✓ **Cut, Copy and Paste** (characters, words and blocks of text can be removed or copied from one part of a document and placed in another part of the same document, in another document or in another application).

4. You can check a document for accuracy using tools such as spelling and grammar checkers. You should also proofread your work carefully.

5. If you make a mistake in a document and immediately want to reverse the change, you can use the **Undo** function. If you then decide you preferred the changed document you can use **Redo** to reapply the change.

6. **Find** is used to search for a word or phrase in a document. **Replace** is used to replace a specific word or phrase with another word or phrase.

7. **Formatting** determines the final appearance of a document. Formatting can be carried out at three levels: character, paragraph and page.

   ✓ Characters can be formatted using **font** type (Arial, Times New Roman, etc.), font size (height of a character), font style (regular, bold, underline, italic), font colour and special effects (superscript, subscript, strikethrough, shadow, outline, emboss, engrave, caps).

   ✓ Paragraph formatting includes line spacing, alignment (centre, left, right and justified), indenting, bullets, numbering and sub numbering.

   ✓ The **Tab** key on the keyboard is a simple way to put text in columns.

   ✓ Page layout can be adjusted by changing the margins, changing the page orientation to landscape or portrait, altering the paper size, and by including headers and footers.

8. **Headers** can be used to display text or graphics across the top of the page (for example, the title of a document). **Footers** can be used to display text or graphics across the bottom of the page (for example, the page number).

9. **Page and section breaks** are used to control the start of new pages and sections of a document.

10. **Tables** can be inserted into a document to display statistical and numerical data. Rows, columns and cells can have borders and can be shaded for emphasis. The text in a cell can be left- and right-aligned or centred, and it can have different vertical orientation and alignment. Text outside a table can be wrapped round the table in different ways.

11. **Columns** are a useful feature for producing newsletters and newspaper-style documents.

12. **Templates** can be used to create new documents with the same format. This is useful for businesses wanting a consistent house style.

End of Chapter 4 Checklist

13. The **mail merge** feature allows you to produce personalised letters, mailing labels and memos without having to type each one individually. Mail merging requires two files: the main document or *standard letter,* and the *data source.* The standard letter contains the letter and the merge fields, which are positioned where the personalised information from the data source will be placed. The data source contains the personalised information needed to complete the standard letter.

14. **Graphics** can be included from many sources: images from a clip art library, photographs from a digital camera, scanned images and graphics downloaded from the Web. **Symbols** and special characters can be inserted.

15. Word processing software has have many tools for manipulating graphics. Graphics can be resized preserving the **aspect ratio** or stretched. They can be cropped, moved, rotated and reflected. Borders can be put on them and text can be wrapped round them.

16. **Drawing tools** are used to create graphics in word processing software. These might include auto shapes including callouts, preformatted diagrams, colours, shadows and 3-D effects.

17. A complex illustration can be put together using several smaller clip art or shape objects. You can change the **order** of these; for example, you can send them to the back or front. You can **group** them so they are easy to move and copy, and **ungroup** and **regroup** them for editing.

18. **Desktop publishing (DTP)** software is used to produce leaflets, newspapers and magazines.

19. DTP software has many features in common with word processing; for example, open, save, print, enter and edit text, change font type and size.

20. DTP software emphasises the importance of **page layout.** You cannot enter any information into DTP software until you have used some page layout features.

21. Information is inserted into DTP software in **frames.** There are different types of frame for text, pictures and other objects.

22. An important feature of DTP is the flow of text between different frames. These may be on the same page or on different pages.

Chapter 5: Spreadsheets and modelling

Spreadsheet software

Spreadsheets enable you to store numerical data and **formulae,** which can be used to carry out operations on the numerical data. These formulae are applied to the data whenever you make a change to it. If you change any data values, the entire spreadsheet can be **automatically recalculated.** This is one of the most important features of a spreadsheet. The ability to represent the numerical data quickly and easily as a chart is another important advantage.

A spreadsheet can also be used to set up numerical and financial models that can be used to help novices learn how these work and to forecast future events.

In this chapter you will learn about software and tools used to create different types of spreadsheet, and modelling techniques.

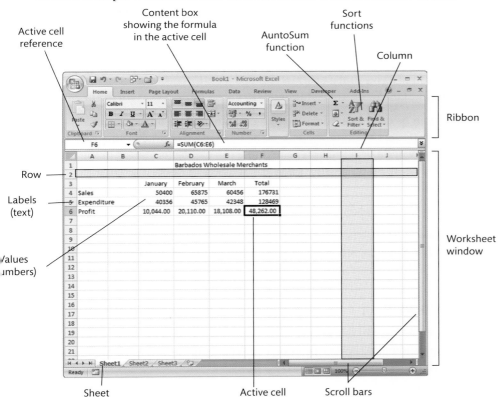

Figure 5.1 *A typical spreadsheet*

Here are some examples of the uses of spreadsheets:

- Loan calculations
- Financial plans – e.g. budgeting
- Keeping accounts in a club or for a business
- Statistics – e.g. finding averages or calculating the standard deviation.

Spreadsheets are made up of several worksheets. It is the active worksheet that you see on the screen. Multiple worksheets can be used to hide complex data and calculations so that the user is presented with a simplified summary. This feature is very useful for storing graphs and charts and in modelling.

Various spreadsheet software is available, such as the *Calc* spreadsheet (part of OpenOffice), *Lotus 1-2-3* (part of Lotus SmartSuite) and *Excel* (part of Microsoft Office). The examples in this chapter are illustrated using Microsoft Office Excel 2007 running on the Windows XP operating system.

Basic concepts

Spreadsheet software initially displays on the screen a large grid divided into rows and columns. This is the **active worksheet.** A typical screen display has horizontal rows from left to right which are numbered, and columns up and down the screen which are named using letters. What is displayed on the screen is only a small part of the available worksheet. An example of the screen displayed by Excel is shown in Figure 5.1. The grid in a spreadsheet can be given borders like a table in word processing software.

Cell contents

The intersection of a row and a column is called a **cell.** A cell can contain different types of information, for example: **label** (text), **value** (number) or **formula.**

- A **label** can be used as a title or heading. It can contain any string of characters (letters or numbers) but must start with a character that does not indicate a formula or number. The text in a cell can be formatted in the same way as text in word processing software. A label cannot be used in a calculation.

- A **value** is numerical data that can be used in a calculation.

- A **formula** is an instruction to perform operations on values. A formula must start with a special symbol (e.g. +, −, @, =) to identify it as a formula. For example, in Excel formulae start with =.

Cell references

Each cell in the active worksheet can be identified by its **cell reference**, which is the column position and the row position combined. For example, the address **F6** means that the cell is in column **F** and row **6**.

The **active cell** is the cell which is currently selected. For example, in Figure 5.1, the cell **F6** is the active cell. The cell reference **F6** only refers to a single cell, but you can use **a cell range reference** to refer to a range of cells. For example, in Figure 5.1, the data for January is contained in cells **C4:C6** in column C, and the sales figures are in cells **C4:F4** on row 4.

To refer to a rectangular block of cells, you would give the cell reference of the top left-hand corner and the bottom right-hand corner; for example, in Figure 5.2, the rectangular block that has been selected has the cell range reference **B2:D4**.

Hint!
If you are using a spreadsheet other than Excel, you must remember that formula may not start with =.
You should change any = you find used in this chapter to your special symbol that indicates a formula.

◢	A	B	C	D	E
1		Trinidad Wholesalers Ltd.			
2		January	February	March	
3	Sales	50400	65875	60456	
4	Expenditure	40356	45765	42348	
5					

Figure 5.2 *Sample spreadsheet with the range B2:D4 selected*

Moving around a worksheet and entering data

You can move around a worksheet using the mouse and the cursor control keys (or arrow keys). Before data can be placed in a cell, the cell must be selected. You can do this by moving the cursor to it and clicking the left mouse button or by using the cursor control keys. Notice that when you type data, it is displayed in the selected cell and in the content box at the top of the window. The data enters the cell only when the **Enter** key or an arrow key is pressed.

Alignment

After entering data, notice that numbers move to the right of the cell (they are right-aligned) and labels (text) move to the left (they are left-aligned). These alignments occur automatically, but can be changed.

In Excel, you can align the contents of a cell or range of cells by highlighting them and clicking one of the **Align** buttons in the Ribbon.

The Align buttons in Excel

Changing or deleting the contents of a cell

When you have entered data into a cell, you can edit or delete it. In Excel, follow these steps to edit data:

● Select the cell.

● Edit the data in the content box at the top of the screen (see Figure 5.1). You do this in a way similar to editing text in word processing software..

Hint!
To delete the data, select the cell and press the **Delete** key. The cell will be cleared.

Cut, copy and paste

In a spreadsheet, cut, copy and paste are used in the same way that you use them in word processing software, except that you highlight a cell or a block of cells. You can take the cells which have been cut or copied and paste them elsewhere in the active worksheet, in another worksheet in the same spreadsheet, in another spreadsheet or in another application. In this way, you can include part of a spreadsheet in a word-processed document.

In Excel, you can copy a cell or block of cells by selecting the cell or block and clicking the **Copy** button in the Ribbon. You then click the cell where you want to place the data, and click the **Paste** button.

The Copy button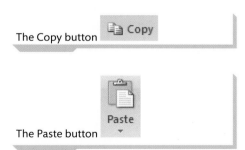

The Paste button

Exercise 5.1

1. **a)** Write down the name of the spreadsheet software you use.

   b) Write down the special character you would enter to show that you are entering a formula.

2. Look at the spreadsheet in Figure 5.3.

   Put a cross in one box to show the number of rows and the number of columns shown.

	A	7 rows and 5 columns
	B	4 rows and 5 columns
	C	6 rows and 5 columns
	D	5 rows and 4 columns

3. Describe what is meant by the following and give examples to illustrate your answer:

   a) Cell

   b) Cell reference

   c) Range reference

   d) Formula

   e) Worksheet

4. Give two situations where a spreadsheet may be used. Give reasons for your answers.

5. Create the worksheet shown in Figure 5.3. Save the spreadsheet giving it the file name **Sales.**

D4		f_x	42348
	A	B	C	D
1		Trinidad Wholesalers Ltd.		
2		January	February	March
3	Sales	50400	65875	60456
4	Expenditure	40356	45765	42348
5				

Figure 5.3 Sample spreadsheet for Exercise 5.1

Inserting and deleting rows and columns

A row or column can be inserted between existing rows or columns. You can also delete rows and columns.

In Excel, follow these steps to **insert a row**:

- Highlight the row below the place where you want the new row to go by clicking on the row number to the left of column A.
- Right-click and select **Insert.**

To **insert a column,** follow these steps:

- Highlight the column to the right of where you want the new column to go by clicking on the column letter above row 1.
- Right-click and select **Insert.**

To **delete a row,** follow these steps:

- Highlight the row to be deleted by clicking on the row number.
- Right-click and select **Delete.**

To **delete a column,** follow these steps:

- Highlight the column to be deleted by clicking on the column letter.
- Right-click and select **Delete.**

Did you know?
Highlighting and pressing the Delete key clears the contents but does not delete the row.

Changing column width and row height

You can change the width of columns to show all their contents, and you can change the height of rows.

In Excel, to change the width of, for example, column B, move the cursor between the column letters B and C until it changes to a vertical bar with horizontal arrows, then drag left or right.

In Excel, to change the height of, for example, row 4, move the cursor between the row numbers 4 and 5 until it changes to this shape ✛, then drag up or down.

Changing column width

Changing row height

Hint!
Changing the width of a column might be necessary if a number is too big to fit into a cell. If a number is too big to fit into a cell, a string of characters (usually #########) is displayed in the cell instead of the number. When the cell width is increased, the numbers will be displayed.

Borders

You can put **borders** of varying width around a cell or group of cells. Select the cells and in the **Home** tab in the **Font** group select from the **Borders** drop-down menu.

Merge

You can **merge** groups of cells, for example, for headings or comments. To merge cells, select the cells and in the **Home** tab in the **Alignment** group select from the **Merge** drop-down menu. To **unmerge**, select the cells and in the **Home** tab in the **Alignment** group select from the **Merge** drop-down menu.

Did you know?
Cell shading
You can add shading to cells by filling them with a colour or a pattern. To add a fill colour, select the cells and in the **Home** tab in the **Font** group select from the **Fill Color** drop-down menu. To change the fill pattern, select the cells and in the **Home** tab in the **Font** group activate the **Format Cells** dialog box. Under the **Fill** tab choose a **Pattern Style**.

Saving and opening spreadsheets

You save a spreadsheet on backing storage in the same way that you save a word processing document. All the worksheets you have used will be saved when you save the spreadsheet.

In Excel, click the Office Button and select **Save** or **Save As.** You can also retrieve a spreadsheet by opening it in the same way as you would in word processing software. In Excel, click on the Office Button and select **Open.**

Printing a spreadsheet

After saving a spreadsheet you may want to print it. You do this in the same ways that you would print a word processing document. In Excel, you can click on the Office Button and use the options in the **Print** menu.

In Excel, you can print the active worksheet, which is the default option, or you can choose to print the entire workbook, which prints all the worksheets.

Exercise 5.2

1. Retrieve the spreadsheet 'Sales', which was created in Exercise 5.1. Then, in the active worksheet:

   a) Change the value in cell C4 from 45765 to 40543.

   b) Change the alignment of the range B2 to D4 to right-aligned.

   c) Insert an empty row between row 1 and row 2.

   d) Insert an empty column between columns A and B.

   e) Adjust column widths and row heights so that the data in all the cells can be seen.

   f) Re-save the spreadsheet as 'Sales'.

   g) Print the spreadsheet.

Adding formulae to a spreadsheet

Formulae are used to do calculations based on values in other cells.

Operators

Formulae are made up from operators, cell references and functions. For example, in Excel, to create a formula to multiply the contents of cells B3 and C3, you enter the formula = **B3** * **C3** in a blank cell. Notice that you use cell references in the formula and not the values that are currently in cells B3 and C3. If you used values instead of cell references, the automatic recalculation feature of the spreadsheet package would not work. **Automatic recalculation** means that when a value in a cell is changed, all the values in cells with formulae that refer to the cell will be automatically updated.

Did you know?
To tell the spreadsheet that you will be entering a formula, you must start the formula with a particular symbol when you are entering data into a cell. For example, in Excel use =.

Operator	Description	Example in Excel	Comment
+	Addition	= B3 + B6	adds the contents of cells B3 and B6
-	Subtraction	= C4-C5	subtracts the contents of cell C5 from the contents of cell C4
*	Multiplication	= D6*E6	multiplies the contents of cells D6 and E6
/	Division	= D3/D4	divides the contents of cell D3 by the contents of cell D4
^	Exponentiation (raising to a power)	= B7^2	squares the contents of cell B7

Did you know?
An expression in a formula in a spreadsheet follows the same order of precedence as for normal arithmetic. This means that whatever is within brackets is performed first, then multiplication and/ or division, and then addition and/or subtraction.

Exercise 5.3

1. The manager of Trinidad Wholesalers Ltd wants to find the total sales for the months January to March. He also wants to calculate the profit made for January. Follow these instructions to do this:

   a) Look at Figure 5.4. This will be similar to the spreadsheet you have saved as 'Sales'. Open this spreadsheet and make sure it looks like Figure 5.4 but leave column F and row 6 blank.

   b) In cell F3, insert the label **Total.** To calculate the total sales for the three months we need to add the values in cells C4, D4 and E4. The formula to find the total sales is = **C4** + **D4** + **E4**. Enter this in cell F4.

   c) Insert the label **Profit** in cell A6.

   d) To calculate the profit made for January we need to subtract the contents of cell C5 from C4. Enter the formula to find the profit for the month of January in cell C6. This is = **C4** - **C5.**

	C6	▼		fx	=C4-C5	
	A	B	C	D	E	F
1			Trinidad Wholesalers Ltd.			
2						
3			January	February	March	Total
4	Sales		50400	65875	60456	176731
5	Expenditure		40356	45765	42348	
6	Profit		10044			
7						

Figure 5.4 *Calculating sales and profit*

2. Change the value in cell C5 to *39365*. Notice that the value in C6 changes. Explain what is meant by the term *recalculation* in this context.

3. Calculate the total expenditure for the months January to March.

4. Calculate the profit for the months February and March.

5. Calculate the total profit made.

6. Adjust column widths and row heights so that the data in all the cells can be seen.

7. Save the spreadsheet.

8. Print the spreadsheet.

The SUM function

A function is a predefined formula that can automatically calculate results, perform actions or assist with decision-making based on the information provided in your spreadsheet. For example, the **SUM** function is used to find the total of a group of cells. Whenever we want to add up the values of a column or row of continuous cells, we can use the **SUM** function. The general form of the sum function is **SUM(*cell range reference*)**.

> **Did you know?**
> The **SUM** function is used to add the values in cells.
> You should NOT enter = **SUM(C4+B4)**
> You should enter = **C4+B4**
> You should NOT enter
> = **SUM(B3+B4+B5+B6)**
> You should enter = **SUM (B3:B6)**

For example, the worksheet shown in Figure 5.5 shows the first quarter sales figures for the four branches of the Premium Furniture Store in the North, South, East and West. To find the total sales for the North branch for the period January to March, we need to find the total of cells B6, C6 and D6. Using the **SUM** function in Excel, the formula to put into cell E6 will be = **SUM(B6:D6).**

D6 | fx 23456

	A	B	C	D	E
1		Premium Furniture Store			
2					
3		First Quarter Sales			
4					
5		January	February	March	Total
6	North	20000	22442	23456	
7	South	45600	23246	67543	
8	East	78540	98755	65981	
9	West	53543	90453	43872	
10	Corporate				
11					

Figure 5.5 *Sample spreadsheet using sales figures*

Similarly, the total for the South branch in cell E7 will be = **SUM(B7:D7)**; for the East branch, = **SUM(B8:D8)**; and for the West branch, = **SUM(B9:D9)**.

The advantage of using the SUM function

Suppose that the Premium Furniture Store has reorganised and introduced an additional sales area called Home. This is to be inserted in the spreadsheet of Figure 5.5 above the sales data for the East area. The sales data for the Home area will become row 8, and current rows 8 and 9 will become new rows 9 and 10. If the formula in cell B10 was = **B6 + B7 + B8 + B9** instead of = **SUM(B6:B9),** this formula would become incorrect and would need editing. The spreadsheet will adjust the formula = **SUM(B6:B9)** to = **SUM(B6:B10)** as the new row is inserted. This is also true for the formula in cells C10 and D10. This is a major advantage of using the **SUM** function.

Relative cell addressing

Notice that in the spreadsheet shown in Figure 5.5, the formulae that would be entered in cells E6, E7, E8 and E9 are very similar except that the row numbers are different. You could enter the different formula into each of the four cells separately but there is a faster way of doing this. Instead of entering the four different formulae, a spreadsheet will let us enter one formula and copy this to the other cells and it will adjust the copied formula. The structure of the formula remains the same, but the addresses of the cells used in the formula will change relative to the position of the formula. This feature is called **relative cell addressing.** For example, if the formula **B3*C3** was in cell D3 and you copied this to cell D4 then the formula in D4 would be **B4*C4.**

Absolute cell references

You can copy a formula to other cells in a row or column and a spreadsheet will change the formula relative to the position of the cells (this is **relative cell referencing**). However, there are situations where you do not want the spreadsheet to adjust the cell references when a formula is copied from one location to another. To prevent this adjustment we use **absolute cell references.** In Excel, these are constructed by placing two dollar ($) signs in the cell reference. For example, in Figure 5.7, we would want formulae that refer to the percentage mark-up and the percentage VAT always to refer to cells B1 and B2 where their values are stored. To achieve this when we write formulae that refer to cells B1 and B2 we would enter $B$1 and $B$2 instead. These absolute cell references remain unchanged no matter where they are copied or moved to in the spreadsheet.

> **Did you know?**
> You can use just one dollar sign if you want to lock just the row (e.g. **B$1**) or just the column (e.g. **$B1**). However, usually you wish to lock both.

Exercise 5.4

1. Create the worksheet 'Premium Quarterly Sales' as shown in Figure 5.5.
2. In column E, calculate the total sales for the four branches using the **SUM** function.
3. In row 10, use the **SUM** function to calculate the total sales for all the branches for the months January to March.
4. In cell E10 calculate the grand total.
5. You are going to change the value in cell B6. Write down the cell references of the cells you think will change automatically. Print the worksheet.
6. Change the value in cell B6 to 20050. Write down the cell references of all the cells that are automatically recalculated.
7. Adjust column widths and row heights so that the data in all the cells can be seen.
8. Right-align the headings in row 5.
9. Save the spreadsheet with the name **Premium**.
10. Print the worksheet.

Copying and replication

You can cut or copy and paste a formula in the same way that you cut or copy and paste other cells. However, in Excel there is a particular method of copying cells that is useful when you copy formulae. You can copy a formula in the active cell to the cells in the same column immediately above or below it by dragging the fill handle. You can also copy to the left and right on the same row using this method, which is called **replication**.

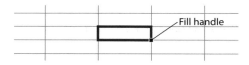
Figure 5.6 *The fill handle on the active cell*

Exercise 5.5

A store owner would like to build a spreadsheet to calculate the final selling price of each item in his store. The store owner first adds a mark-up of 20% to the cost price, to produce the marked-up price, and then adds 15% VAT to the marked-up price to get the final selling price.

	A	B	C	D	E
1	MARK-UP	20%			
2	VAT	15%			
3					
4	Item	Cost price	Marked-up price	Vat	Final selling price
5	Hat	$20.00			
6	Shirt	$75.00			
7	Pants	$235.00			
8	Jersey	$145.00			
9	Shoes	$225.00			

Figure 5.7 *Data for calculating a final selling price*

1. Enter the data as shown in Figure 5.7.
2. Move to cell C5. Type the formula = **B5 + (B5 * $B$1)**.
3. Copy the formula to cells C6, C7, C8 and C9.
4. Move to cell D5. Type the formula = **C5 * $B$2**.
5. Copy the formula to cells D6, D7, D8 and D9.

6. Move to cell E5. Type the formula = **C5 + D5.**
7. Copy the formula to cells E6, E7, E8 and E9.
8. Check that the screen display of your work now looks like that in Figure 5.8.

C5			f_x	=B5+(B5*$B$1)	
	A	B	C	D	E
1	MARK-UP	20%			
2	VAT	15%			
3					
4	Item	Cost price	Marked-up price	Vat	Final selling price
5	Hat	$20.00	$24.00	$3.60	$27.60
6	Shirt	$75.00	$90.00	$13.50	$103.50
7	Pants	$235.00	$282.00	$42.30	$324.30
8	Jersey	$145.00	$174.00	$26.10	$200.10
9	Shoes	$225.00	$270.00	$40.50	$310.50
10					

Figure 5.8 *Calculation of the final selling price*

9. Adjust column widths and row heights so that the data in all the cells can be seen.
10. Save the spreadsheet with the name 'Selling Price'.
11. Print the spreadsheet.

Other functions

There are many other functions in addition to the SUM function. Here are some examples:

- **The AVERAGE** function is used to find the mean of a set of values. The general form of the function is **=AVERAGE(*first cell:last cell*).** To find the mean price of an item in the spreadsheet in Figure 5.8, use the formula = **AVERAGE(E5:E9)**.

- The **IF** function is discussed later in this chapter.

Extension material: other useful funcions include **MAX** and **MIN** :

- The **MAX** (maximum) function is used to find the largest value of a set of values in a row or column. The general form of the maximum function is **=MAX(*first cell:last cell*)**. For example, if you want to find the item with the highest price in the spreadsheet in Figure 5.8, use the formula = **MAX(E5:E9)**.

- The **MIN** (minimum) function is used to find the smallest value in a set of values in a row or column. The general form of the minimum function is **=MIN(*first cell:last cell*)**. For example, if you want to find the item with the lowest price in the spreadsheet in Figure 5.8, use the formula = **MIN(E5:E9)**.

Formatting

Using formatting, you can control the appearance of cells and of the spreadsheet in general. We have already looked at one aspect of formatting – the alignment of the contents of cells. Changing the column width, row height, font size and style, and adding borders are also aspects of cell formatting. In Excel, you can alter the column width by dragging the edge of the column header next to the column letter to the left or to the right. You alter the row height by dragging the edge of the row header below the row number up or down. Font size and style and borders are adjusted in a way similar to using these features in word processing software.

Formatting numbers

Here are some formats for numbers:

- **General** – if you want no specific number format.

- **Number** – used for general display of numbers with decimal places and a negative sign.

- **Currency** – used to represent monetary values, e.g. $589.54.

- **Percentage** – used to represent percentage values, e.g. 15%.

- **Date** – you can choose to display dates as, for example, 24 March 2011 or 24/3/11.

- **Time** – you can choose to display times as, for example, 8:30:00 PM or 20:30:00.

Changing the formatting

You can change the formatting of a cell.

For example, in Excel to change the format to **Currency** you would do the following:

- Highlight the cells to be changed.
- On the **Home** tab, click on the little box in the bottom right of the **Number** area. The **Format Cells** dialog box appears.
- Select the **Number** tab, then select **Currency.**
- Choose the number of decimal places and the currency symbol you want to use.

Text wrap

When you enter too much text in a cell, if it is left-aligned it will overflow to the right on a single row (see figure 5.9). You can include blocks of text by merging cells and formatting them so that the text does not overflow to the right but wraps around the cell. Select the cell and on the **Home** tab in the **Alignment** group select **Wrap text**.

Hint!
The instructions for Exercise 5.6 below are given for Excel. Some functions may be named differently in other spreadsheets.

Figure 5.9 *Text wrap*

Exercise 5.6

The manager of the Premium Furniture Store Company would like the following information:

a) The profits before tax if the expenditure for the branches is as follows:

Branch	Expediture
North	5000
South	6754
East	3476
West	9043

b) The amount of tax paid if the profit is taxed at 15%.

c) The after-tax profit.

d) The average after-tax profit across all the stores.

Help with this Exercise

1. Retrieve the spreadsheet 'Premium' set up in Exercise 5.4.

2. Select cell B3. Change **First Quarter Sales** to **First Quarter Report**.

3. Select F5. Enter the label **Expenditure**.

4. Enter the expenditure data into the appropriate cells (see Figure 5.10).

5. Select cell G5. Enter the label **Profit before Tax**.

6. Change the width of the cell to accommodate the label.

7. Select cell G6. Enter the formula **= E6 - F6**. Copy the formula down to G9.

8. Select cell H5. Enter the label **Tax on Profit** and change the column width.

9. Select cell H6. Enter the formula **=G6 * .15**. Copy the formula down to H9.

10. Select cell I5. Enter the label **Profit after Tax** and change the column width.

11. Select cell I6. Enter the formula **= G6 - H6.** Copy the formula down to I9.

12. Highlight or mark off the range B6 to I10. Change the number format to currency.

13. Select cell A12. Enter the label **Average Profit.**

14. Select Cell C12. Enter the formula = **AVERAGE(I6:I9).**

15. Copy cell B10 across to cells C10: I10.

16. Highlight C12. Change the number format to currency if necessary.

17. Adjust column widths and row heights so that the data in all the cells can be seen.

18. Save the spreadsheet as 'Premium Profits'.

19. Print the spreadsheet.

Sorting

To sort means to arrange in order. A spreadsheet enables you to sort data (text or numbers) into ascending or descending order. **Ascending order** means the lowest is at the top of the sheet and the highest is at the bottom. **Descending order** is the opposite: the highest value comes first.

It may be useful to sort data in a number of ways. For example, a teacher who enters the names of students and their marks for five subjects could sort the column of names into alphabetical (ascending) order, with the students' marks being moved correspondingly. The teacher could also rank the students according to their marks in a particular subject by sorting the rows into descending order on the column with the marks in it, again with a corresponding movement of all the other data.

When sorting a list of data, most spreadsheet packages use the following guidelines:

- Rows with blank cells are placed at the bottom of the sorted list.
- Numbers used as text are sorted before text alone. An example of a number used as text is the numbers in this address: '67 High St'. In this case, a spreadsheet will treat the number 67 as if it was text and calculations cannot be done on it. If only the number 67 was in a cell then this could be treated as a number and used in calculations.

Sorting on a single column

The Sort A to Z button

All the data selected can be sorted according to the content of a single column. You might want to do this if you had a list of students and all their marks for the term in a worksheet and you wanted to display the list in alphabetic order. To do this in Excel, highlight all the data you wish to sort and click the **Sort A to Z** button in the toolbar.

Sorting on several columns

You may need to sort data by more than one field. For example, a book store may want to sort all their books by their author's name. The store may then want to sort each author's books alphabetically by title. To do this in Excel, highlight all the data to be sorted and in the **Data** tab select **Sort**. The **Sort** dialog box appears (see Figure 5.11). Set this up so that you first sort the data by the column with the author's name in it, then by the column with the book titles in it.

Figure 5.10 *The Sort dialog box*

Exercise 5.7

The spreadsheet in Figure 5.11 shows a list of books from a supplier to the Small Book Store. Do the following:

1. Create the worksheet.

2. Make the title and the labels in row 3 bold.

3. Sort the data into ascending order by author and then by title. Save the spreadsheet as 'Small Books'.

4. Add a column to calculate the total cost for each title. *(Total cost = No. of copies * Unit cost)*

5. Adjust column widths and row heights so that the data in all the cells can be seen.

6. Save the spreadsheet.

7. Print the spreadsheet.

	A	B	C	D	E
1		The Small Book Store			
2					
3	Author	Title	Classification	No. of Copies	Unit Cost
4	Mars Richard	Star Chase	Science Fiction	6	$ 39.00
5	Lucas Gary	Dracula	Horror	4	$ 40.00
6	Brown James	Faith Healers	Religious	10	$ 45.00
7	Brown James	Back to God Head	Religious	5	$ 50.00
8	Lucas Gary	Bad Omens	Horror	6	$ 54.00
9	Richards Jenifer	Outer Planet Experience	Science Fiction	5	$ 65.00
10	Jaira Kadine	Eagle and the Falcon	Thriller	3	$ 75.00
11	Lucas Gary	The Dark Side	Horror	6	$ 76.00
12	Jaira Kadine	Apocalypse	Thriller	3	$ 78.00
13	Mohammed Afzal	In Touch with God	Religious	3	$ 80.00
14					

Figure 5.11 *Book list sales*

Creating graphs and charts

Graphs and charts are important because they can simplify numerical data and make it easier to interpret. They get your attention almost instantly and allow information to be interpreted quickly. Therefore charts can be important tools for data analysis and the presentation of data.

The first step in creating a chart is to select the data values you want to place in it. A spreadsheet package enables you to plot any row or column of data against any other row or column of data. For example, if we want to represent the first quarter sales for the months of January to March for the four branches of the Premium Furniture Store for the spreadsheet created in Exercise 5.6, we need to select the range A5:D9.

After selecting the data values, you need to select an appropriate type of chart. The type of chart you choose depends on the type of data you have and how you want to represent it. Some charts are best for representing certain types of data. For example, the sales data may best be displayed using a column chart.

If any values in the data selected are changed after the chart has been created, they are immediately reflected in the chart. Also, more data can be inserted between the first and last rows or columns. These changes will also be automatically included in the chart. Before creating a chart, make yourself familiar with the elements of a chart. Figure 5.12 shows a completed chart for the first quarter sales of the Premium Furniture Store.

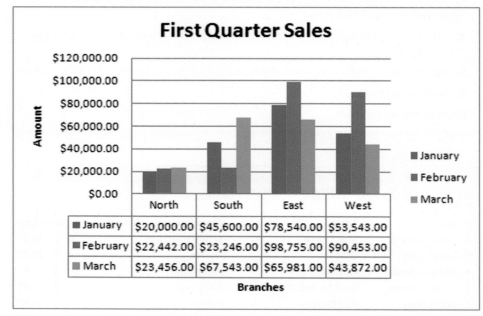

Figure 5.12 *A vertical bar chart or column chart showing the first quarter sales*

Chart elements

A chart has several elements:

- **Axes** – The vertical and horizontal lines against which data is plotted. The horizontal X-axis is referred to as the **category axis** and the vertical Y-axis is known as the **value axis.**

- **Titles** – There are three titles: for the chart, the category axis and the value axis.

- **Data range** – The range of cells selected to create the chart.

- **Data labels** – The actual value, percentage or name of a bar or segment of a chart.

- **Data table** – The range of values, included at the bottom of the chart that is used to draw the chart.

- **Series** – The data in a row or column that makes up the range of values that is used to create the chart.

- **Legend** – A cross-reference showing how each series is represented in the chart.

- **Gridlines** – Lines parallel to each axis that help you read values from the chart more easily.

Choosing a chart

The chart you choose should depend on the type of data you are displaying.

Data that represents portions of a whole could be represented using a **pie chart** (see Figure 5.13).

If the horizontal axis consists of discrete values or categories (e.g. North, South, East, West) and the vertical axis is a number line, then a **vertical bar chart** or **column chart** could be used (see Figure 5.12).

A **line chart** should be used if both axes are number lines.

A **scatter chart** should be used if you are comparing two data sets of discrete values or categories to see if they correlate, that is, to see whether a change in one set is related to a change in the other set.

Figure 5.13 *Line chart and scatter chart types from Excel*

Creating a chart

In Excel, you can use the **Insert** tab to create graphs and charts, as follows:

- Select the data to be displayed and click the **Insert** tab.
- Choose a type of chart from the **Charts** area.
- You can fine-tune the chart using the options in the **Chart Tools** tabs.

Enhancing a chart

Charts can be customised or enhanced for variety and emphasis.

A slice of a pie chart can be offset from the main body of the pie, perhaps for emphasis. In Figure 5.14, the slice representing the number of Ford vehicles in a car park has been offset slightly from the main body of the pie chart so it stands out.

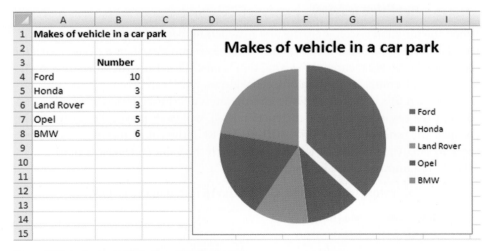

Figure 5.14 *A pie chart with a slice offset for emphasis*

To offset a slice of a pie, create a pie chart, select the pie, then click on the slice to be offset. Drag the slice out of the pie.

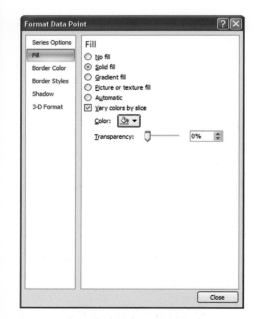

Figure 5.15 *The Format Data Point dialog box*

Several features of the slice of a pie can be changed, including its colour. Select the slice you wish to change, right-click it and select **Format Data Point.** The **Format Data Point** dialog box appears (see Figure 5.15). Click on the **Fill** tab then click on **Solid fill** and select a colour.

You can use the **Chart Tools** tabs in the Ribbon to enhance the whole chart or a single data point.

Exercise 5.8

Using the spreadsheet Premium Profits, created in Exercise 5.6, create a chart to show the first quarter sales for the Premium Furniture Store.

1. Select the range A5 to D9.

2. Choose a column chart from the **Insert** tab.

3. Overtype the 'Chart title' field with 'First Quarter Sales'.

4. Use the **Chart Tools | Layout** tab to set the 'Category (X) axis' field title to 'Branches' and the 'Value (Y) axis' field title to 'Amount'.

5. On the **Chart Tools | Layout** tab, select **Data Table** then choose **Select Data Table.**

6. Move the chart and adjust column widths and row heights so that the data in all the cells can be seen.

7. Save the spreadsheet.

The IF function

The **IF** function tests a condition to see if it is true or false.

The general form of the **IF** function is as follows:

> *= IF(condition, what to do if the condition is true, what to do if the condition is false)*

When the function is executed, the first instruction *(what to do if the condition is true)* is executed if the condition is true, and the second instruction *(what to do if the condition is false)* is executed if the condition is false. Either instruction can be text, a number, a formula, a function or a cell address. If an instruction is text or a number then this is displayed. If the instruction is a formula, function or cell address, the result, and not the instruction itself, will be displayed. For example, consider the function **=IF (F5 >= 50000, 10, 8)**. If the value in cell F5 is greater than 50 000, the number 10 will be displayed. If the value in F5 is less than 50 000, the number 8 will be displayed.

The logical operators which can be used in the **IF** function are as follows:

Operator	Meaning
>	Greater than
=	Equal to
>=	Greater than or equal to
<	Less than
<=	Less than or equal to
<>	Not equal to

Extension questions

Cell E4 contains this formula: **IF(D4<50, "reorder", "stock levels adequate").**
Write down what will be displayed in cell E4 if the value in cell D4 is 55.
Write down what will be displayed in cell E4 if the value in cell D4 is 23.

Look-up tables

The idea behind a look-up table is that if you know something about a person or object, you can look up other information. Look-up tables are widely used. If you know someone's name, you can look up his or her telephone number in a telephone directory or your address book.

In Excel, the general form of the function used to look for information in spreadsheet tables is as follows:

> **= LOOKUP(*what you are looking for, where you want to look, where the information you want is*)**

For example,

> **= LOOKUP("beef", A3:A11, B3:B11)**

means look for the word *beef* in cells A3 to A11. When you find it, display the contents of the corresponding cell from the range B3:B11. Looking at Figure 5.16, we would expect this **LOOKUP** function to return the value £5.60. Note that **LOOKUP** will not work unless the lookup data is sorted into ascending order.

Look-up tables are particularly useful when used with multiple worksheets within a spreadsheet.

Multiple worksheets

Spreadsheets can have multiple worksheets within them (see Figure 5.17). So far in this chapter, it has been assumed that only one worksheet is being used in the spreadsheet and that this is the active worksheet which is displayed on the screen. However, it is likely that a spreadsheet will have multiple worksheets within it, which may be hidden behind the active worksheet. A worksheet can be displayed by clicking on its name tab, and doing this makes the worksheet the active worksheet.

Multiple worksheets can be used to hide complex data and calculations so that the user is presented with a simplified summary. This feature is very useful in modelling.

Renaming worksheets

The default worksheets can be renamed so they reflect the purposes of the individual worksheet (see Figure 5.18). In Excel, to rename a worksheet, right-click on the worksheet tab, in the menu select **Rename** and type in the new name.

Look-up tables are particularly useful when used with multiple worksheets within a spreadsheet. You can store information on one worksheet and refer to it in another; and you can use the results calculated in one worksheet as part of a calculation in another worksheet. For example, you could put your budget for each month on a separate worksheet and use another worksheet to summarise your earnings and savings for the year.

	A	B	C
1			
2	Ingredients	Price	
3	bacon	£ 4.50	
4	beans	£ 1.30	
5	beef	£ 5.60	
6	cheese	£ 2.30	
7	chicken	£ 4.45	
8	egg	£ 1.20	
9	potatoes	£ 1.00	
10	spices	£ 0.50	
11	vegetables	£ 2.30	
12			

Figure 5.16 *List of ingredients in the Ingredients worksheet*

Quick question
- Write down the value returned by **= LOOKUP("potatoes", A3:A11, B3:B11)**.
- Write down the value returned by **= LOOKUP("chicken", A3:A11, B3:B11)**.
- Write down the value returned by **= LOOKUP("egg", A3:A11, B3:B11)**.

Figure 5.17 *The default multiple worksheets in Excel*

Figure 5.18 *The worksheets renamed*

Exercise 5.9

The First Trinidad National Bank pays a yearly interest of 8% on fixed-deposit balances less than or equal to $50 000, and 10% on fixed-deposit balances greater than $50 000. The interest earned is then added to the customer's balance at the beginning of the year to give the final balance.

	C4	▼		f_x	=IF(B4<50000,8%,10%)	
	A		B	C	D	E
1				First Trinidad Bank		
2						
3	Customer Name		Starting Balance	Interest Rate	Interest Earned	Final Balance
4	Larry Adams	$	45,000.00	8%	$ 3,600.00	$ 48,600.00
5	Marie Balfour	$	69,000.00	10%	$ 6,900.00	$ 75,900.00
6	James Chin-Fat	$	84,000.00	10%	$ 8,400.00	$ 92,400.00
7	Harry Doonath	$	35,000.00	8%	$ 2,800.00	$ 37,800.00
8	Krishna Harrylal	$	50,000.00	10%	$ 5,000.00	$ 55,000.00
9						

Figure 5.19 *A Banking spreadsheet*

The spreadsheet in Figure 5.19 shows some customers and their balances. The function = **IF(B4 <= 50000, 8%, 10%)** in cell C4 compares the value in cell B4 to see if it is less than or equal to 50 000. Since the value is 45 000, the condition is true, so the value 8% is returned. However, if the value in cell B4 had been greater than 50 000, the value 10% would have been returned, as is the case for C5 and C6.

1. Create the worksheet shown in Figure 5.17.

2. Insert five additional customers and their starting balances.

3. A 15% tax is charged on interest earned if this is more than $5 000. Insert a column with the heading 'Tax', and calculate the tax paid by each customer.

4. Calculate the interest after tax.

5. Calculate the final balance *(starting balance - interest after tax)*.

6. Adjust column widths and row heights so that the data in all the cells can be seen.

7. Save the spreadsheet with the file name 'Banking'.

8. Print the spreadsheet.

Quick question
- If you are working in Sheet1, write down the cell reference you would use for cell E4 in Sheet2.
- If you are working in Sheet3, write down the cell reference you would use for cell B2 in Sheet1.
- If you are working in the worksheet Cost of dish (see Figure 5.20), write down the cell reference you would use for cells B3 to B11 in the worksheet Ingredients.

Cell references between multiple worksheets

Cell references in one worksheet can refer to another worksheet. This is necessary if the data in one worksheet is to be copied to another. In Excel, to refer to cell A3 in Sheet1 when you are working in Sheet 2, you would write the cell reference like this: **Sheet1!A3.** If you wanted to refer to the cell range A3:A11 in Sheet1, you would use **Sheet1!A3:A11.**

Macros

Macros are useful if you wish to automate tasks that you do repeatedly. A macro is a series of instructions and commands to the software that you can group together so that they become a single command. You create a macro in three steps:

- turn on the macro recorder
- carry out the actions you want the macro to do
- turn off the macro recorder.

To do these steps in Excel, the **Developer** tab needs to be showing. If it is not showing, Click the Microsoft Office button and click on **Excel Options**. Select the **Popular** category and under **Top Options for working with Excel**, select **Show Developer tab in the Ribbon** and click on **OK**.

To turn on the macro recorder in Excel:

- In the **Developer** tab in the **Code** group, click on **Record Macro**.

- Give the macro a name, and a shortcut key (say **Ctrl+Q**) and a description, and click on **OK**.

Every action you do between turning on the macro recorder and turning it off is recorded and becomes a part of the macro.

To turn off the macro recorder in Excel:

- In the **Developer** tab in the **Code** group, click on **Stop Recording**.

To use the macro you have created use the short cut key (**Ctrl+Q**).

Macros can also be written in Visual Basic. In Excel, you can see the Visual Basic code generated by a macro: in the **Developer** tab, in the **Code** group, select **Macros**, select the macro and click on **Edit**. The Visual Basic code is displayed. You can edit this code if you wish.

Hint!
If the **Developer** tab is not available, click on the **Office Button**, select **Excel Options** and tick the box for **Show Developer Toolbar in the Ribbon**.

Exercise 5.10

A chef uses a spreadsheet to work out the cost of each dish on the menu. The ingredients are listed in a worksheet called 'Ingredients' (see Figure 5.16) and the costs are worked out in a worksheet called 'Cost of dish' (see Figure 5.18).

The Cost of dish worksheet has been set up so that the cost of an individual ingredient is looked up in the Ingredients worksheet. The total cost of the dish is then worked out by adding up the cost of the ingredients. You are to set up these worksheets and work out the cost of beef, potato and vegetable stew.

	B5			f_x	=LOOKUP(A5,Ingredients!$A$3:$A$11,Ingredients!$B$3:$B$11)				
	A	B	C	D	E	F	G	H	I
1	Dish: beef, potato and vegetable stew								
2									
3	beef	£ 5.60							
4	potatoes	£ 1.00							
5	vegetables	£ 2.30							
6									
7	Cost of dish	£ 8.90							
8									
9									

Figure 5.20 *The cost of dish worksheet*

Help with this exercise

a) Open a new spreadsheet and rename one worksheet to **Ingredients.**

b) Set up the Ingredients worksheet.

c) Make sure that the ingredients are in ascending order (alphabetic order).

d) Rename another worksheet to **Cost of dish.**

e) Enter all the text into the Cost of dish worksheet.

f) Working in the Cost of dish worksheet:

- To look up the cost of beef in the Ingredients worksheet, in cell B3, enter the formula **=LOOKUP(A3, Ingredients!A3:A11, Ingredients!B3:B11)**.

- Enter an appropriate formula in cell B4. This should use the **LOOKUP** function to find the cost of potatoes.

- Enter an appropriate formula in cell B5. This should use the **LOOKUP** function to find the cost of vegetables.

- Enter an appropriate formula in cell B7 to find the total cost of the dish. You should use the **SUM** function.

g) The worksheets should now look like those in Figures 5.16 and 5.20.

h) Save the spreadsheet (call it 'Chef').

i) Print all the worksheets.

The chef wants to make spicy chicken and egg with noodles. Noodles will cost £1.75. Use the Cost of dish worksheet to work out the cost of this dish.

Exercise 5.11

Jean is having problems with budgeting. Jean's budget for January is overdrawn (see Figure 5.21). In an attempt to control the budget, two buttons must be created and macros assigned to them. These are as follows:

- **RedCell,** which changes the font of a cell to Arial size 14 and colour red.

- **BlackCell,** which changes the font of a cell back to Arial size 10 and colour black.

Jean is going to use the **RedCell** button to emphasis the items of expenditure which can be reduced. **BlackCell** has been created to reverse the effects of **RedCell**.

Help with this exercise

1. Set up columns A and B in the worksheet in Figure 5.21. Make sure that the numbers and text are formatted as Arial size 10, colour black.

	A	B	C	D	E
1	My budget for January				
2					
3	Expenditure				
4	Mortgage	£ 300.00			
5	Council rates	£ 99.50		RedCell	
6	Electricity	£ 27.00			
7	Gas	£ 51.00			
8	Water rate	£ 39.59			
9	Telephone	£ 29.99		BlackCell	
10	Food	£ 200.00			
11	Clothes	£ 40.00			
12	Entertainment	£ 160.00			
13	Total Expenditure	£ 947.08			
14					
15	Income				
16	Wages after tax, etc.	£ 900.00			
17					
18	Balance	-£ 47.08			
19					

Figure 521 *Jean's budget*

2. In Excel, record the macro **RedCell** as follows:
   - Click on the **Record Macro** button in the status bar.
   - In the **Record Macro** dialog box, give the new macro the name **RedCell,** and click the **OK** button to begin recording.
   - Perform the actions necessary to format a cell to Arial size 14, colour red. This can all be done using the options in the **Home** tab.
   - To stop recording the macro, click on the **Stop Recording** button in the status bar.

3. A convenient way to run a macro is to use a command button on the worksheet itself. Buttons labelled *RedCell and BlackCell* are shown in Figure 5.21. In Excel, to create a button to run the macro **RedCell:**

   - In the **Developer** tab select **Insert** and select **Button** (not *Command Button*).
   - Drag the mouse across the worksheet to create a button. When you release the mouse button, the button will appear along with the **Assign Macro** dialog box.
   - In the **Assign Macro** dialog box, select the macro **RedCell** and click **OK**.
   - Type the name **RedCell** on the button itself.
   - Click in the worksheet, but not on the button, to deselect the button.
   - The macro will now execute immediately whenever the button is clicked.

4. Test the macro by clicking on cell B13 then clicking on the **RedCell** button. When you do this the number in B13 should be changed to Arial size 14, colour red.

5. Create a button to run the macro **BlackCell.** This should change the format of the cell to Arial size 10, colour black.

6. Test **BlackCell** by changing the number in B13 back to Arial size 10, colour black.

7. Use **RedCell** to emphasise the items of expenditure which Jean might be able to reduce.

Form Controls

Figure 5.22 *The Form Controls*

Modelling

Models are representations of the real world. We are all familiar with some form of model. Our earliest introduction to modelling is likely to be moulding modelling clay to make representations of people or animals. You can buy toy soldiers and model cars, dolls and dolls' houses. They are all models; that is, representations of the real world. Models in some form are used throughout commerce and industry. You can build a physical model of a shopping centre or other building project to demonstrate the architectural style and layout of the planned development. Models of such developments can also be built using computer software.

It is essential to remember that a model is a representation of the real world. It is not the real world. You cannot expect reality to be exactly like a model of it. The better the model, the more exactly it copies reality. The advantage of using models is that they allow us to experiment with reality. We can try out strategies and forecast what will happen. However, a forecast is based on experience of the past. The future may not mimic the past. Consequently, we must recognise that the accuracy of models is limited and we should treat forecasts based on models with care.

This ability to try out strategies is an important use of models. Models are safe. Managers do not have to bankrupt their employers when trying out new commercial strategies; farmers have no need to devastate their crops by blindly trying new methods of pest control. While exploring a model is unlikely to lead us to the perfect solution to our problems, we may well improve our understanding of them and discover a range of useful strategies to tackle them. Even so, a model can be such a good representation of reality that we can use it for training. For example, car drivers and pilots can be trained using simulators before trying out the real thing.

Spreadsheet models

Spreadsheets can be used for a variety of tasks. We can use spreadsheets to record information from day to day and to do simple calculations. However, when a model is constructed using a spreadsheet, there is usually an intention to use it to improve our understanding of a real system, for problem solving or for prediction.

Typically, a spreadsheet-based model will have a limited number of input variables. These variables will be processed using the rules defined by the structure of the spreadsheet and the underlying formulae. These rules will reflect the assumptions made by the author about the relationships evident in the real world. These relationships will be built into the model. However, the author may simplify these relationships or otherwise modify them. The rules built into a model when it is constructed do not always exactly reflect the complexities of the real world.

Supermarket queue model

A supermarket queue model is shown in Figure 5.23. The model can be used to regulate the average time customers spend in the queue at a checkout.

The input variables are the number of customers waiting, the number of checkouts in use and the average time taken to serve a customer at a checkout. These are changed when the model is used.

The rules are the formulae in cells A10 and C10.

The formula in A10 is = **A6/C6,** which represents the relationship:

$$the\ average\ number\ of\ customers\ = \frac{number\ of\ customers\ waiting}{number\ of\ checkouts\ in\ use}$$

The formula in C10 is =**A10*E6**, which represents the relationship:

$$\begin{matrix} the\ time\ the\ last\ customer\ in \\ the\ queue\ will\ have\ to\ wait \end{matrix} = \begin{matrix} average\ number\ of\ customers \\ queuing\ per\ checkout \end{matrix} \times average\ time\ at\ checkout$$

The information output from the model is the average number of customers queuing per checkout and the length of time the last customer in the queue will have to wait.

A supermarket manager could use the model to quickly see the effects of adjusting the number of checkouts and the time taken to get a person through a checkout. For example, Figure 5.23 shows that the length of time the last customer in the queue will have to wait is 10 minutes.

If the manager considers this unacceptable, the model can be used to explore alternatives. Suppose the manager wished to reduce the last customer wait time to 5 minutes. The input variables could be adjusted to show how this can be done. A 5 minute waiting time could be achieved by increasing the number of checkouts to 20. However, this would double the costs involved, such as the wages paid to checkout operators.

A 5 minute waiting time could also be achieved by reducing the time to get a customer through a checkout to 1 minute. However, this might involve training staff, introducing a productivity scheme or buying more up-to-date checkout technology. Other solutions could be found by both increasing the number of checkouts and reducing the time to get a customer through a checkout.

This model has some serious limitations. It is assumed that there will be a steady flow of customers to the checkouts, that customers will distribute themselves equally across all the checkouts, that every checkout operator works at the same speed, and that people will not get tired of waiting and simply leave. These assumptions are needed so that a simple, understandable model can be constructed. In reality, it is unlikely that any of these assumptions will hold true. Clearly, the rate at which customers arrive at the checkouts will vary considerably and different checkout operators will work at different speeds. However, making these assumptions helps us construct a model that will be useful, providing its limitations are taken into account.

	A	B	C	D	E	F	G
1	**Supermarket queue model**						
2							
3	**Inputs:**						
4							
5	Number of customers waiting		Number of checkouts in use		Average time at checkout (minutes)		
6	50		10		2		
7	**Outputs:**						
8							
9	Average number of customers queuing per checkout		Time before last customer through checkout (minutes)				
10	5		10				
11							

Figure 5.23 *Supermarket queue model*

Exercise 5.12

1. a) A supermarket has five checkouts and the checkout operators take an average of 3 minutes to get a customer through the checkout.

- If there are 20 customers and 5 checkouts open, calculate how long the last customer will have to wait.

- If there are 15 customers and an acceptable waiting time is 10 minutes, calculate how many checkouts need to be open.

b) A retail company is building a new supermarket. Describe how the supermarket queue model could be used to help with the design of the supermarket.

Testing a model

Because a model is intended to mimic a real-world situation, it should be tested against this situation to see if it does make accurate predictions. For example, in the supermarket queue model, the average waiting time for customers should be manually measured using stopwatches and the results compared to the predictions of the model. This comparison is likely to show whether the rules built into the model are reasonable. A likely finding is that the measured average waiting time is longer than that predicted by the model. This is because the model assumes that customers distribute themselves evenly between the open checkouts but in the real world customers do not do this.

The supermarket manager could respond to this information in various ways:

- accepting the model, as the difference in average waiting time results from customers' choices and could be minimal

- introducing ways of managing the queues of customers so that they distribute themselves evenly between checkouts

- changing the rules built into the model to make it more accurate.

Other types of modelling

More complex models can be built based on specific application software. This include games, simulations, science experiments, economic models and weather forecasting. These can be virtual reality models. These types of models are far more complex than those based on spreadsheets.

Exercise 5.13

1. A student receives an allowance of $50.00 a week. This is how the student spends the money each day.

	Monday	Tuesday	Wednesday	Thursday	Friday
Travelling	4	4	4	4	4
Lunch	2	3	2	4	6
Snacks	3	2	1	2	2
Games World	10	9	5	6	10

Using a spreadsheet, complete the following tasks:

a) Calculate the total money spent each day of the week.

b) Calculate the total money spent on each item for the week.

c) Calculate the total expenses for the week.

d) Calculate the amount left from the student's allowance.

e) Add currency symbols.

f) Centre all headings.

g) Save the spreadsheet as 'Allowance' and print it.

h) The student is spending more than the weekly allowance. Propose ways to reduce spending to an acceptable level.

2. The owner of a small contracting firm has six employees, divided into two categories: skilled and unskilled. The set rate for an unskilled worker is $20 per hour and a skilled worker gets $30 per hour. The rates of pay are subject to change over time. Overtime is paid at the set rate.

		Hours worked			
		Week 1	Week 2	Week 3	Week 4
Agard, Jason	skilled	45	56	45	40
Brown, Sarah	skilled	56	45	50	68
Patel, Rani	unskilled	35	40	67	40
Maraj, Rudy	unskilled	40	55	43	55
Parker, Anne	unskilled	56	45	76	45
Bobart, Richard	unskilled	65	45	45	57

a) Create a spreadsheet that will show information about each employee: the employee's name and category, the total number of hours worked each month and total monthly salary.

b) Calculate and display the average monthly salary.

c) Format the spreadsheet so that all column labels are centred, and the currency is shown.

d) Sort the spreadsheet in ascending order on employees' names.

e) Save the spreadsheet as 'July wages 1' and print it.

f) Delete all information for Richard Bobart.

g) Add the following data to the spreadsheet:

- Employee – Wesley Taylor
- Category – unskilled
- Hours worked – week 1: 50, week 2: 60, week 3: 45, week 4: 40.

h) Change the rate of pay for unskilled workers from $20 to $25 and for skilled workers from $30 to $40

i) Save the spreadsheet as 'July wages 2'.

j) The employees want more pay. The owner can afford to pay $40 000 in wages each month. Use the model to find what rate of pay the owner should offer employees.

1. A spreadsheet has several worksheets. Each **worksheet** is a large grid divided into **rows** and **columns**.

2. The intersection of a row and a column is called a **cell**.

3. A cell can hold different kinds of information: **labels** (text), **values** (numbers) or **formulae**.

4. **Formulae** are used to perform operations on numbers. A formula must start with a character that identifies it as a formula (in Excel, this is =), and this is followed by numbers, operators or cell references that are part of the calculation.

5. A single cell is referred to using its **cell reference**; for example, B3.

6. A group of continuous cells that forms part of a column or row or a rectangular block is called a **range** of cells and is identified by the addresses of the top left-hand and bottom right-hand cells. For example, B3:E6.

7. You can use a single command to affect a range of cells. For example, a range of cells can be formatted for currency, or the contents of the cells can all be centred, by selecting the range and using the command.

8. Formulae usually contain cell addresses so that if a value in a cell is changed, all the values in the dependent cells will be automatically updated. This is referred to as **automatic recalculation**.

9. Formula can include functions for performing calculations. For example, in Excel:

   ✓ = **SUM(*cell range reference*)** – finds the sum of a row or column of numbers.

   ✓ = **AVERAGE(*cell range reference*)** – finds the mean of a row or column of numbers.

   ✓ = **IF(*condition, what to do if the condition is true, what to do if the condition is false*)** – tests a condition and responds depending on whether the condition is true or false.

10. A formula can be copied or moved from one cell to another cell or range of cells. When the formula is moved, all cell references in the formula change with respect to the formula's location. This is referred to as **relative cell referencing.** However, it may be necessary to move or copy a formula but keep the cell reference in the formula fixed. This is done using **absolute cell referencing.** In Excel for example, F6 is a relative cell reference but $F$6 is an absolute cell reference.

11. Most of the editing features available in word processing software are also available in a spreadsheet. For example, in Excel you can use these commands: **Delete**, **Cut**, **Copy**, **Paste**, **Save**, **Print** and **Open**.

12. **Formatting** enables you to control the appearance of cells and the spreadsheet in general. Formatting includes the following:

   ✓ Alignment of cells (left, centre or right).

   ✓ Representation of numbers (general, number, currency, percentage).

   ✓ Changing the column width and row height, and adding borders and patterns.

   ✓ Merging groups of cells, and unmerging them.

   ✓ Text wrap to make the text wrap round the cell rather than overflow.

   ✓ Using borders to emphasise cells.

13. You can **sort** data into ascending or descending order according to the content of one or more fields.

14. Data can be represented using a wide range of different types of **charts**; for example, pie, bar, line and scatter charts. In Excel, select the data range that you want to use to create the chart and then use the **Charts** options on the **Insert** tab of the Ribbon.

15. You can cut or copy and paste charts or part of a worksheet to word processing software for including in a report.

16. Spreadsheets can have multiple **worksheets** within them. The active worksheet is displayed on the screen; however, other worksheets may be hidden behind it. A worksheet can be displayed by clicking on its name tab, and doing this makes the worksheet the active worksheet.

17. Multiple worksheets can be used to hide complex data and calculations so that the user is presented with a simplified summary. This feature is very useful in modelling.

✓ You can rename a worksheet: right-click on the worksheet tab, select **Rename**, and type in the new name.

✓ **Look-up** tables are particularly useful when used with multiple worksheets within a spreadsheet. You can store information on one worksheet and refer to it in another; and you can use the results calculated in one worksheet as part of a calculation in another worksheet.

✓ Cell references in one worksheet can refer to another worksheet so that the data in one worksheet can be used in another. In Excel, to refer to cell A3 in Sheet1 when you are working in Sheet 2, you would write the cell reference like this: **Sheet1!A3**.

18. A **model** is a representation of the real world. Models are used to improve understanding of a real system, to solve a problem, or to predict what will happen. It is important to remember that a model is only a representation of the real world; it is not the real world. Models are used so that you can learn about an unfamiliar situation and experiment without danger or expense.

19. Models can be constructed using a spreadsheet. This involves deciding on the **input** variables, how the **rules** will be expressed as formulae, and the information that will be **output**. Spreadsheet models can help us understand a situation, but they are often very restricted in scope and it is important to take this into account when making decisions based on the results.

Chapter 6: Databases

Database software

A **database** is an organised collection of structured data. Database software enables you to organise and store data so that specific items of information can be retrieved easily and quickly in a structured fashion.

Databases can be used for many different applications. They may be used to keep track of students' progress in schools, or to organise and store information about vehicle registrations, stock in a supermarket, employees at a company, books in a library and many other areas.

Many businesses use databases to produce mail shots to customers. Lists of customers' names and addresses are generated from a more extensive database, and are then input by the mail merge feature in word processing software to produce personalised letters and envelopes.

Different database software is available, for example:

- OpenOffice has a collection of Database User Tools that gives you all the tools you need for day-to-day database work. They also make it simple to drag and drop data into other OpenOffice programs like Calc and Writer.

- The Microsoft Access database is a part of Microsoft Office. The examples in this chapter are based on Access.

> In this chapter you will look at databases and the software used to organise and store data.

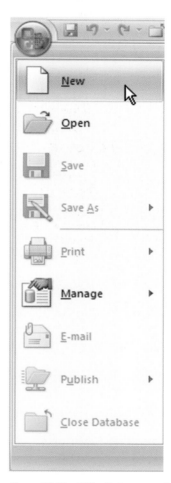

Figure 6.1 *The Office Button menu in Access*

Figure 6.2 *The Getting Started screen*

Creating a database

Unlike a word processing or spreadsheet document, which you can name after you have started or completed it, a database may have to be named before work is started on it. For example, to create a database in Access, run the software and select **New** from the Office Button menu (see Figure 6.1). The **Getting Started** screen appears (see Figure 6.2).

Using the **Blank Database** area, select a location to store the database, give your database a meaningful filename and click on **Create**. The window shown in Figure 6.3 is displayed.

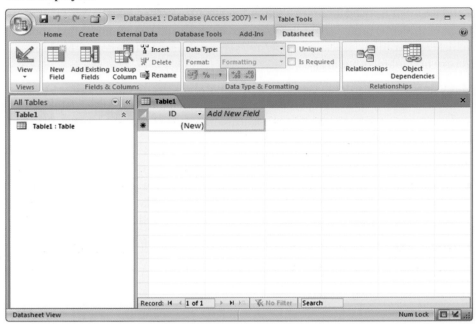

Figure 6.3 *The window shown before entering data into a database table*

The database objects used in this chapter are listed below with their meanings.

Object	Description
Table	A collection of related data about a subject (person, place or thing). One or more tables make up a database **file**. A **flat file database** will have only one table in the database file, whereas a **relational database** will have more than one table in the database file.
Query	You use a query to **search** a database.
Report	A customised printout of the information in a table or from a query.
Form	Forms make it easy to input data. You can easily find, edit and enter new data into a table by using a form.

Designing a database

Designing a database is the first and most important step towards providing easy and fast access to information. If you plan your database carefully you will save time and inconvenience when you are creating queries and reports. The steps involved in designing a database are as follows:

- **Determine the purposes of the database**. By determining your purposes, you will be able to define what data should be stored on your database. For example, one purpose might be to keep track of the stock in a supermarket.

- **Analyse each purpose**. Break down what you need to know into a series of well-defined needs and wants.

- **Determine the data you need**. Write down all the data items that you will need in order to meet these purposes.

- **Design your tables**. Separate the data items into groups, depending on how each is related to the others. This will allow you to decide what data will be in each table.

- **State the field names and define each field**. Give each data item a unique field name and describe its properties. For example, a person's first name could be given the field name 'firstname'; its data type would be alphabetic; and it would probably be sufficient to give it a length of 15 characters.

- **Determine how the tables will be related**. Two tables are related if the records in both share some common fields. Creating relationships between tables allows the tables to be linked so that information can be cross-referenced. You may need to add further fields to tables to create the necessary relationships.

Hint!
Here are some example purposes:
- I need to know which items are selling well.
- I want a list of the best-selling items and their selling prices.
- I need to know who supplies a particular item and at what cost.

Tables

A **table** is an organised collection of related records about a specific subject (for example, customers). A table is divided into rows and columns. Each row holds a record and each column represents a unique field.

A **record** is a group of related fields (for example, about one customer).

A **field** is a data item within a record (for example, the customer's name).

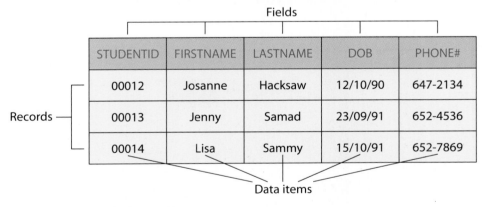

Figure 6.4 *Part of a table about students*

Figure 6.4 shows part of a table about students. All the information about one student is contained in a single row or record. The first row of the table consists of the field names.

Creating tables

In Access, you can create a table using any one of the following methods:

- **Design View** – This method enables you to create a table by naming the fields and selecting their data types and properties. You can precisely determine all the characteristics of the table.

- **Table Wizard** – This is the easiest and fastest method of creating a table. The table wizard guides you through a process that is very easy to follow, although the resulting table may not meet your exact requirements.

- **Datasheet View** – You enter data into the datasheet grid, which consists of rows and columns labelled *Field 1, Field 2, Field 3* and so on. The database software determines the data type based on the data you enter.

This chapter describes how to create a table in Design View, because this will show you more about how data is organised in a database.

Creating a table in Design View

Click on the **Create** tab then on **Table Design**. The **Table Design View** window appears, as shown in Figure 6.5.

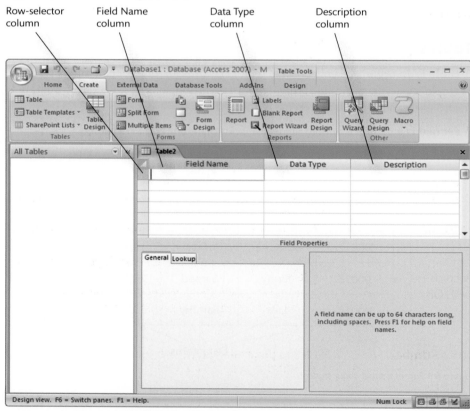

Figure 6.5 *The Table Design View window*

Defining and adding fields

The **Table Design View** window (Figure 6.5) shows four columns:

- The **Row Selector** enables you to select the field in which you wish to enter, change or delete information, by using the mouse or the up and down arrow keys. The selected row has an arrow in the row selector column.

- The **Field Name** column is where you type in a field name.

- The **Data Type** column enables you to select an appropriate data type from a drop-down list. Various data types and their descriptions are listed in the table below. Some of these data types are used in Access but others are included which are used elsewhere. In Access, when you have selected a data type, the **Field Properties** pane appears at the bottom of the window. Access provides default field properties that are suitable for many applications, but you can change these.

- The **Description** column is for your use in typing out a short description of the field as a form of documentation.

Data type	Description
Number	Contains a number. Use this type for data to be used in calculations, except calculations involving money.
Real number	Stores any number expressed as a decimal number, e.g. *54.371*
Integer	Stores a whole number, which can be positive, negative or zero, e.g. *15*.
Text or Alphanumeric	Can store any alphanumeric character (alphabetic or numeric) and special characters, such as punctuation marks, e.g. *'27 Parkland Avenue, Bolton BL7 4RT'.*
Memo	Used to hold notes about a record.
Date/Time	Stores the date and time in one of several different formats.
Currency	Holds a monetary value and is used in calculations involving money.
Logical or Boolean	Holds one of two values, e.g. 1 or 0; yes or no; true or false.
OLE Object	Contains an object created by another application. If the object is edited or updated in the other application, the change will also be made in the database.
AutoNumber	Used to generate unique numbers in a specific field each time a record is added.
Hyperlink	Stores a web address (a URL).

Did you know?
In the UK, post codes can help you find a house or tourist attraction. Type them into Google Earth and you can see where they are. They are used to deliver mail and Internet shopping (*Note*: BL7 4RT is not a real postcode).

Adding fields to a table in Design View

The process for adding fields to a table in Design View is as follows:

1. Type in a field name in the **Field Name** column.

2. Press the **Tab** key or use the mouse to move to the **Data Type** column.

3. Select a data type from the drop-down list (the default field properties are displayed at the bottom of the window).

4. Move to the **Description** column and type a short description of the information that will be held in the field.

5. Once you have done this for all the fields, click on the **Office** button.

6. Select **Save** or **Save As** to save the table within the current database. (The **Save As Table** dialog box appears, as shown in Figure 6.6.)

7. Type in a name for the table and click **OK**. A default table name, 'Table2', is shown in Figure 6.6. You should give the table your own meaningful table name.

Figure 6.6 *The Save As Table dialog box*

Adding a field between two rows

Open the table in Design View. Place the record selector in the row below where you want the new field to be inserted. Right-click and select **Insert Rows**. A blank row appears. Type in the new field name, data type and description.

Deleting a field

Open the table in Design View and select the row to be deleted. Right-click and select **Delete**.

Primary keys

A **primary key** (often referred to as a **key field**) is a field such that the contents of the field uniquely identify each record. Using a primary key field has the following benefits:

● It can speed up data retrieval and the running of queries.

● It enables you to establish relationships between tables.

To define a primary key in Access, display the table in Design View, then select the field, right-click in the row containing it and select **Primary Key**.

If you do not select a primary key while building the structure of a table, the message box shown in Figure 6.7 will appear when you try to close the table. If you click on **Yes**, Access adds an **AutoNumber** field to the table and defines it as the primary key. If you click on **No**, the table is saved without a primary key being defined.

Figure 6.7 *'There is no primary key defined' message*

Did you know?
Primary keys must have unique values. This is why **AutoNumber** is a good choice of data type.

Deselecting a primary key

In Access, display the table in Design View and select the **Primary Key** field. On the **Table Tools | Design** tab, the primary key should show as being selected. Select the **Primary Key** option to deselect the primary key.

Foreign keys

A record can have only one primary key, but there is no restriction on the number of foreign keys it can have. A **foreign key** is a primary key from another table. It shows the relationship between the current table and the other table.

For example, an autoparts database, where each record stores details about a part used in manufacturing a car, might have a foreign key which identifies the warehouse where the part is kept. If the part is available from several different warehouses, there could be several different foreign key fields in the record.

Exercise 6.1

1. Write down the name of the database software you use.

2. Put a cross in one box to show a feature of a primary key (also known as a key field).

A	A primary key has a value that can only occur once in a column
B	A primary key has the same value throughout a row
C	A primary key cannot be used more than 5 times
D	Each row must have two primary keys

☐ A ☐ B ☐ C ☐ D

3. Explain what is meant by the following, giving examples of each:

   a) Table
   b) File
   c) Record
   d) Field
   e) Key Field.

4. The manager of Betterprices Hardware wants to move away from the manual method of stock keeping to a computerised method. He decides to place the information about his stock into a database. Complete the following tasks:

   a) Create a database called **Betterprices Hardware Stock List.**

   b) Create a table called **Stock** within the database, with the structure shown below.

Field Name	Data Type	Description
Itemno	Text	The code used to identify each item (this is a mix of numeric and alphabetic characters)
Itemdesc	Text	Name of each item
Quantity	Number	Amount in stock
Sectstored	Text	The hardware section in which the item is stored
Price	Currency	The selling price of the item

   c) Define **Itemno** as the primary key field.

Help with this question

To create a table called **Stock**:

✓ Create a new database named **Betterprices Hardware Stock List**.

✓ A default table is created. Click on **View, Design View** and save the table as **Stock** when prompted. The **Table Design View** window appears, as shown in Figure 6.5.

✓ Place the cursor in the **Field Name** column in the first row.

✓ Type **Itemno** into the column.

✓ Move to the **Data Type** column. The default data type, **Text**, will be displayed.

✓ Move to the **Description** column. Type *The number used to identify each product*.

✓ Move to the second row and enter the field name, data type and description for the second field.

✓ Do likewise for all the remaining fields.

To define **Itemno** as the primary key field (if this doesn't happen automatically):

✓ Click anywhere in the **Itemno** row.

✓ Right-click and select **Primary Key**.

To save the table structure:

✓ Pull down the **Office Button** menu.

✓ Select **Save**.

✓ Type the table name, **Stock,** into the **Save As** dialog box.

The complete structure for the **Stock** table is displayed in Figure 6.8.

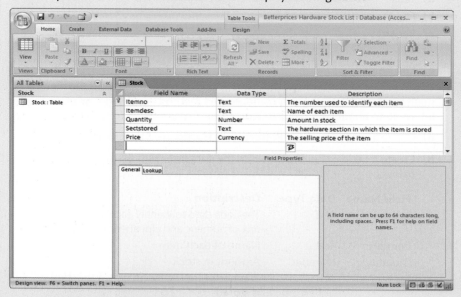

Figure 6.8 *Structure of the Stock table*

5. Create a database named **Employees**. Create a table in the database with the following structure (include field names, data types and descriptions). Make **EmpID** the primary key and give the table the filename **Salary**.

Field name	Data type	Description
EmpID	Number	Number assigned to each employee when hired
Surname	Text	
Firstname	Text	
Age	Number	Age of employee
Phone	Text	Employee home phone number or contact number
Department	Text	Department in which employee is currently working
Salary	Currency	Gross salary

Software note
If the database package you are using is **not** Microsoft Access, investigate and write down how you would perform the following operations:
a) Creating a database
b) Creating a table
c) Defining, adding, editing and deleting fields
d) Creating a primary key field.

Field properties

A field's properties determine how it is stored, what can be done with it and how it is displayed. Default field properties will be assigned to each field, depending on the data type. The default field properties are appropriate for many databases but you can change them if you wish.

Validation checks help ensure that the data stored in each field is reasonable and accurate. Some of the different field properties that can be used to validate data in Access are listed below.

Field property	Description of field property and validation check
Field size	The field size specifies the maximum number of characters that can be stored in a field, so that a **fieldlength** check can be carried out. For instance, the field size for a student's first name could be 15. If a name longer than 15 characters were to be entered, the computer would reject it.
Input mask	Enables you to define a character string to act as a template so that a **format** check can be carried out on the data. For example, a date may have to be entered in dd/mm/yyyy form for the UK. Dates not entered in this form would be rejected.
Validation rule	Despite its name, this field property is a generally considered to be a type of validation check called a **range** check. This ensures that the values entered into the field are within a specific range. For example, a domestic gas bill might be checked to see if it lies between $0 and $500. Bills outside this range would be considered exceptional and checked for errors.
Validation text	The message you would like displayed if the validation rule is not satisfied. In our example, the message could be 'Value must not exceed $500'.
Required	This is a **presence** check. If a record is selected but no value is inserted in this field, the record will be rejected and an error message displayed, such as 'Employee name is required for an Employee table'.
Default value	A value that is automatically entered in a field in each record of the table.
Allow zero length	Allows a text or memo field to be left blank.
Indexed	Builds an index on a field. Tables are searched or sorted faster when a field is indexed. A primary key field is always indexed.
Format	Determines the way a field is displayed or printed. For instance, a date could be displayed as short (15/01/10) or medium (15 Jan 2010).
Caption	A label other than the field name that you can use for forms and reports.

Field sizes

If you select **Number** as the data type in Access, you can choose different field sizes. Some of these are listed below.

Numeric field size	Description
Byte	A number in the range 0 to 255
Decimal	A decimal number with up to 28 digits of accuracy
Double	A double-precision floating-point value with about 15 digits of accuracy
Integer	A number in the range -32 768 to 32 767
Long Integer	A number in the range -2 147 483 648 to 2 147 483 647
Single	A single-precision floating-point value with about seven digits of accuracy

Exercise 6.2

1. In the Betterprices Hardware Stock List database (created in Exercise 6.1) open the table named **Stock** and perform the following tasks:

a) Change the field sizes of the following fields to their new field size:

Field name	New field size
Itemno	6
Itemdesc	30

b) Delete the **Sectstored** field.

c) Insert the following new field:

Field name:	SupplierID
Data type:	Text
Description:	The number used to identify each supplier
Field size:	5

d) The **Quantity** field must not hold a value greater than 1000. Include a validation rule that would ensure the condition is met, and validation text to display an appropriate message if the entered value falls outside the limit.

e) Save the table.

Help with Question 1

To change the field sizes for **Itemno** and **Itemdesc:**

- ✓ Display the **Stock** table in Design View.
- ✓ Click anywhere in the **Itemno** row (the **Field Properties** pane will be displayed).
- ✓ Click on the **Field Size** box; delete 50 and type in 6.
- ✓ Do similarly for the **Itemdesc** field.

To delete the **Sectstored** field:

- ✓ Click the row selector column for the **Sectstored** field (the row becomes highlighted).
- ✓ Right-click and select **Delete Rows.**

To insert the **SupplierID** field:

    ✓ Click in the next empty row in the **Betterprices Hardware Stock List** table in Design View.

    ✓ Type **SupplierID** in the **Field Name** column (Text will be displayed in the **Data Type** column).

    ✓ Move to the **Description** column and type *The number used to identify each supplier.*

To add a validation rule and validation text for the **Quantity** field:

    ✓ Click on the **Quantity** field row.

    ✓ Move to the **Field Properties** pane and click on the **Validation Rule** box.

    ✓ Type in = **1000 or <1000.**

    ✓ Click on the **Validation Text** box and type *Quantity is greater than 1000. Please re-enter.*

Figure 6.9 shows the new field properties for the **Quantity** field.

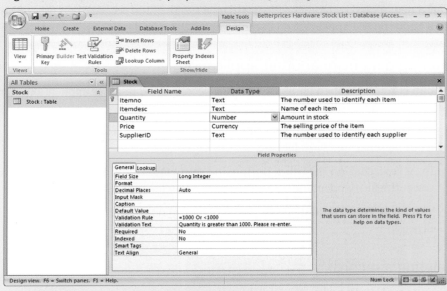

Figure 6.9 *Field properties for the Quantity field*

2. Using the **Salary** table from the **Employees** database created in Exercise 6.1:

   a) Change the field sizes of the **Surname** and **Firstname** fields to 25.

   b) Include the following validation rule and validation text for the Salary field:

       ✓ Validation rule: "<10000"

       ✓ Validation text: "Salary cannot be more than $10 000"

   c) Explain why it is better to store the date of birth of an employee than their age.

   d) Delete the **Age** field, and insert the **DOB** (Date of Birth) field between the **Firstname** and **Phone** fields.

Entering data

Entering data into a table

You can insert data into each field of each record in Datasheet View. For example, to do this from the database window shown in Figure 6.9, select the Stock table and click on the **View** button. Click on the field and edit it. To enter a new record, edit the fields in the blank record at the bottom of the table.

Entering data using an input form

Select the table you wish to enter data into, select the **Create** tab and click on the **Form** button. An input form is created.

The Form button

Use the search feature to find the field you want to edit by typing in the current contents of the field. You can then edit the field.

Enter a new record by using fast forward to get to the final record, then press **Play** and a blank record appears. You can now enter the new data.

Entering data from another application

You can enter data into a database that has been created in other applications, for example, in a spreadsheet. To do this:

● Save the spreadsheet file. Typically, this would be saved as a .txt (text) or .csv (comma separated variable) file.

● In Access, click on the Office Button and select **Open**. In the **Open** dialog box, select the file to open and select the appropriate file type. Click on **Open**.

● The **Link Text Wizard** opens. This will guide you through the conversion process.

Deleting a record

Open the table in Datasheet View. Select the record to be deleted, right-click and select **Delete Record**.

Editing a record

Open the table in Datasheet View. Select the required field of the appropriate record and edit the information as you would in word processing software.

Sorting data

It is often useful to sort a table into order on a particular field. This can be particularly helpful when editing a large table. To do this in Access, open the table in Datasheet View and select the field (column) on which you wish to sort the table. Next click the **Sort Ascending** or **Sort Descending** button in the Ribbon.

The Sort Ascending button

The Sort Descending button

Sorting data on multiple fields

It may be necessary to sort a table on more than one field. For example, you may wish to sort a list of students by their last name and then by their first name. You use an **advanced filter sort.**

- In the **Home** tab, locate the **Sort & Filter** area and select **Advanced** (a submenu appears), and select **Advanced Filter/Sort**. The **Filter** window appears. The top part of the window contains the table to be sorted and the bottom part contains the grid to select the fields you would like sorted.

- Click in the first box in the **Field** row and select from the drop-down list the field you would like sorted. Click on the corresponding sort field to select the sort order. Do this for as many fields as you wish to sort on.

- To sort the table, in the **Advanced** drop-down list, select **Apply Filter/Sort.**

Exercise 6.3

1. a) Enter the records shown below into the **Stock** table created in the previous exercises:

Itemno	ItemDesc	Quantity	Price	SupplierID
FK0025	Fork	20	$250.00	SP030
FK0035	Fork	40	$200.00	SP015
FK0040	Fork	50	$150.00	SP020
H0005	Hammer	20	$45.00	SP010
H0006	Hammer	35	$50.00	SP015
H0007	Hammer	50	$25.00	SP020
PD2000	Power drill	10	$850.00	SP075
PG0100	Pigfoot	25	$90.00	SP050
SH0010	Shovel	50	$125.00	SP030
SH0011	Shovel	60	$75.00	SP020
SH0110	Sledge hammer	10	$125.00	SP050
SP0015	Spade	40	$65.00	SP020
SP0061	Spirit level	25	$60.00	SP010
TR0090	Trowel	15	$65.00	SP010

b) Delete the record for item PG0100.

c) Change the price of item FK0025 from $250 to $225.

d) Add the following field to the table immediately after **Itemno**:

Field Name:	Brand
Data Type:	Text
Description:	The brand name of each item
Field Size:	20

e) Add the following data to the **Brand** field for each corresponding **SupplierID**:

SupplierID	Brand
SP010	Superior Brand
SP015	Nicholson
SP020	Star
SP030	Bulldog
SP050	OX
SP075	Alligator

f) Sort the table on brand name and then on item description, in ascending order.

Help with Question 1

Figure 6.10 *Datasheet view of the Betterprices Hardware Stock List database*

a) To enter the records:
- ✓ Open the **Betterprices Hardware Stock List** database window.
- ✓ Select the **Stock** table.
- ✓ Click on **Open**. The Datasheet view window appears with the field names as shown in Figure 6.10.
- ✓ Type *FK0025* under **Itemno.**
- ✓ Press the **Tab** key to move to the next column.
- ✓ Type in *Fork* in the **Itemdesc** column.
- ✓ Continue to type in the data for the first record in the appropriate columns.
- ✓ Press **Enter** or use the mouse to move to the next row.
- ✓ Enter all the records one by one.

b) To delete the record for item PG0100:
- ✓ Display the **Stock** table in Datasheet View.
- ✓ Find the record for PG0100.
- ✓ Select it by clicking on the record selector column (the row becomes highlighted).
- ✓ Right-click and select **Delete**.

c) To change the price of item FK0025 from $250 to $225.
- ✓ Display the **Stock** table in Datasheet View.
- ✓ Find the record for FK0025.
- ✓ Click on the **250** and change it to **225**.

d) To add the field **Brand** to the table:
- ✓ Open the **Stock** table in Design view.
- ✓ Select the **Itemdesc** field.
- ✓ Right-click and select **Insert** from the menu.
- ✓ Select **Rows** (a blank row will be inserted between the **Itemno** and **Itemdesc** fields).
- ✓ Type in the new field name, data type, description and field size.

e) To input the given data into the **Brand** field:
- ✓ Open the table in Datasheet View.
- ✓ Type in the data in the appropriate column.
- ✓ The completed table is shown in Figure 6.11.

Itemno ▾	Brand ▾	Itemdesc ▾	Quantity ▾	Price ▾	SupplierID ▾	Add New Field
FK0025	Bulldog	Fork	20	$225.00	SP030	
FK0035	Nicholson	Fork	40	$200.00	SP015	
FK0040	Star	Fork	50	$150.00	SP020	
H0005	Superior Brand	Hammer	20	$45.00	SP010	
H0006	Nicholson	Hammer	35	$50.00	SP015	
H0007	Nicholson	Hammer	50	$25.00	SP020	
PD2000	Alligator	Power drill	10	$850.00	SP075	
SH0010	Bulldog	Shovel	50	$125.00	SP030	
SH0011	Star	Shovel	60	$75.00	SP020	
SH0110	OX	Sledge hammer	10	$125.00	SP050	
SP0015	Star	Spade	40	$65.00	SP020	
SP0061	Superior Brand	Spirit level	25	$60.00	SP010	
TR0090	Superior Brand	Trowel	15	$65.00	SP010	
*						

Figure 6.11 *The Stock table with brand information added*

f) To sort the table on brand name and then on item description:

✓ Display the **Stock** table in Datasheet View.

✓ Select **Advanced** then **Advanced Filter/Sort** on the **Home** tab. The **Advanced Filter/Sort** grid for the **Stock** table appears.

✓ Select the **Brand** and **Itemdesc** fields as shown in Figure 6.12.

✓ On the **Home** tab, select **Advanced** then click on **Apply Filter/Sort**.

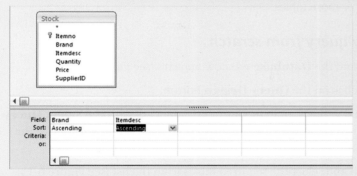

Figure 6.12 *Preparing to sort on two fields*

2. Using the **Salary** table created within the **Employees** database in Exercises 6.1 and 6.2:

a) Make any changes needed to the fields.

b) Change the validation rule to allow a salary of $12,000.

c) Enter the records shown below:

EMPID	SURNAME	FIRST NAME	DOB	PHONE	JOB	SALARY ($)
10	Viera	Edison	19/03/79	648-5432	Manager	12,000.00
25	Moore	Ian	04/11/78	677-5865	Janitor	2,500.00
46	St. Louis	Allan	17/07/80	634-7806	Engineer	8,000.00
56	Moore	Sean	15/10/62	648-2343	Accountant	8,000.00
63	Neptune	Kent	23/09/68	658-4533	Programmer	6,000.00
75	Achong	Lisa	26/06/80	656-7687	Secretary	4,000.00
81	Sakawat	Amit	14/03/75	678-9651	Systems Analyst	9,000.00
125	Baptiste	Lisa	11/08/76	634-5478	Clerk	3,500.00
131	Griffith	Viola	25/10/73	697-2532	Engineer	9,500.00
143	Alexander	Anthony	02/03/83	622-5667	Janitor	3,000.00
187	Rattiram	Nalini	21/04/72	687-3213	Secretary	3,800.00
245	Moore	Gillian	15/10/65	615-1234	Clerk	4,000.00

d) Delete the record for employee 75.

e) Change the name of employee 187 from **Nalini Rattiram** to **Nalini Ramrattan**.

f) Sort the table on surname and then on first name, in ascending order.

Queries

Queries are used to **search** a database and extract information. A **query** enables you to find and view data stored in one or more tables. You can also do calculations and other operations on the data and view the results. Queries can be saved and used again.

After you run a query, the answer is displayed in a **dynaset** – a group of records that answers a query. It looks and behaves like a table but is really a dynamic subset of data from one or more tables that has been selected and sorted as specified in the query. Information in a dynaset can be modified like information in a table, and the changes are automatically reflected in the relevant tables.

Types of query

There are several types of query but we will consider only the following:

- **Select query**: This is the most common type. It is used to search tables to retrieve data that satisfies the query, and to display the data as a dynaset.
- **Update query**: This makes specified changes to a group of records, or to all records, in one or more tables.

Creating a new query from scratch

Open the database and the **Database** window appears (see Figure 6.3).

On the **Create** tab click on the **Query Design** button.

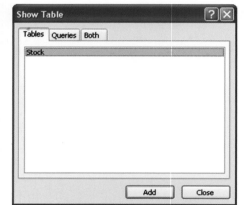

Figure 6.13 *The Show Table dialog box*

The **Show Table** dialog box shown in Figure 6.13 appears with the **Select Query** design grid behind it. The **Show Table** dialog box enables you to select (add) the tables that contain the data you wish to be included in the new query.

Click the **Tables** tab and select the required tables from the list (see Figure 6.13). Click **Add** to add them to the upper part of the query design window (see Figure 6.14), and then click **Close**.

Removing a table from a query

Select the table in the **Select Query** design window and right-click the mouse. Select **Remove Table**.

Creating joins or relationships with tables

A query can operate on a single table but if you want to extract data from more than one table, you have to create a join or relationship between the tables.

The relationship between tables can be of these types:

- A **one-to-one** relationship exists when each record in a table corresponds to exactly one record in the other table.
- A **one-to-many** relationship exists when each record in one table corresponds to many records in the other table.
- A **many-to-many** relationship exists when multiple records in one table correspond to multiple records in the other table.

You can create a join or relationship as follows (you will try this in Exercise 6.4):

1. Open the database. The **Database** window appears (see Figure 6.3).

2. In the **Database** tab, select **Relationships** (the **Relationships** and **Show Table** dialog boxes appear). If the **Show Table** dialog box does not appear, in the **Relationships Tools | Design** tab select **Show Table.**

3. In the **Show Table** dialog box, select the tables between which you want to create joins or relationships, then click **Close.**

4. In the **Relationships** dialog box, click the field name you would like to join in one table and drag this onto the field name in the other table. The **Edit Relationships** dialog box appears, showing the names of the two tables and the fields you would like to join.

5. Click on **OK.** A line connecting the two fields is displayed in the **Relationships** dialog box, as shown in the upper part of Figure 6.14.

6. Save the relationships.

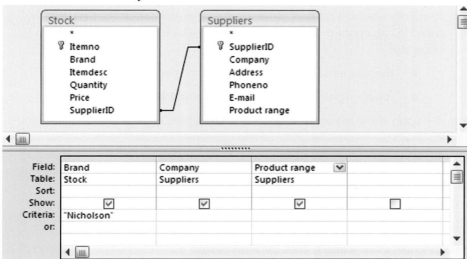

Figure 6.14 *A Select Query design window, showing a relationship between tables*

When you have created relationships between the tables, you can proceed to create queries.

Working with a Select query

Figure 6.14 shows a **Select Query** design window. The top part of the pane holds the tables and shows the relationship between them. The bottom part of the pane is the **query by example grid** or **design grid,** consisting of rows and columns. The row labels and a description of what they are used for is shown below:

Row label	Explanation
Field	Select the field to be searched.
Table	Select the table that the selected field is taken from.
Sort	Select any fields you would like sorted in ascending or descending order in the query.
Show	Specify whether you want the field to be displayed.
Criteria	Specify the criteria used to select a record during the search.
Or	Specify any additional criteria.

Setting up a Select query

In a Select query, you define what data values you want to find in what fields, and what fields you want to display. You can use a Select query to view specific data, reorganise data and calculate data.

1. Click in the leftmost column, which is blank. Click on the row labelled **Table** and select the table from which the field is to be chosen.

2. Click in the same column on the row labelled **Field** and select a field.

3. Click in the same column on the row labelled **Sort** and select **Ascending** or **Descending.**

4. The **Show** row contains a check box in each column. If you would like the value in a field to be displayed, tick the box. You do not have to show all the fields used to select the data, and the fields shown do not have to be part of the selection criteria.

5. To specify selection criteria, enter a value or expression in the **Criteria** row. A criterion can contain values or expressions, which can be combined with the following:

   - the relational operators $>,<,> = ,< = ,=$ and $<>$

   - functions such as **ADD**, **OR**, **NOT** and **BETWEEN**.

   You can apply these to date or number fields to return records within a designated range.

6. Repeat steps 1 to 5 for each field involved in the selection.

7. Select **Save** to save the query.

Running a query

The Run button

To carry out or run a query, click the **Run** button.

Using logical AND and OR and NOT in a query

Logical AND and OR are used to connect the criteria used in setting up a query.

AND tests two or more criteria, and if they are **all** individually true, then AND is true.

OR tests two or more criteria, and if **at least one of them** is individually true, then the OR is true.

In Access, when setting up a query in the **Select Query** design window (see Figure 6.16):

- if the criteria are on the same row then **AND** is implied

- if the criteria are in the same column then **OR** is implied.

NOT is true if the criteria are not true.

AND example

Looking at the **Salary** table in Exercise 6.2, suppose we wanted to find out which employees were engineers and earned more than $8,500.00 salary. We would need an **AND** condition which can be paraphrased as follows:

JOB is Engineer AND SALARY is more than $8,500.00.

To set up this condition in Access, in the **Select Query** design window, for the fields **JOB** and **SALARY,** the criteria =*"Engineer"* and >*8,500.00* would be set up **on the same row.**

OR example

Looking at the **Salary** table in Exercise 6.2, suppose we wanted to find out which employees were engineers or programmers. We would need an **OR** condition which can be paraphrased as follows:

JOB is Engineer OR JOB is Programmer.

To set up this condition in Access, in the **Select Query** design window, for the field **JOB** the criterion = *"Engineer"* is set up, and **in the same column** on the row underneath, the criterion = *"Programmer"* would be set up.

NOT example

Looking at the **Salary** table in Exercise 6.2, suppose we wanted to find out which employees were not engineers. We would need a **NOT** condition which can be paraphrased as follows:

JOB is NOT Engineer.

To set up this condition in Access, in the **Select Query** design window, for the field **JOB** the criteria = *not "Engineer"* is set up.

Working with an Update query (extension material)

An update query makes changes to a group of records, or to all of the records, in one or more tables.

Creating an update query

1. Create a new query as you did for a Select query, just completing the **Field, Table,** and **Criteria** rows as appropriate.

2. In the **Query Tools | Design** tab, click on **Update.**

3. Notice that the **Sort** and **Show** rows have been replaced by an **Update To** row. This is where you will be able to enter a formula, value or expression to make changes to records in the tables.

Building a formula and running an update query

1. Click on the **Update To** cell where the formula will be placed.

2. Right-click the mouse and select **Build.** The **Expression Builder** dialog box appears, as shown in Figure 6.15. The top pane of the window is a clear area used to display the formula. Buttons for the relational and arithmetic operators

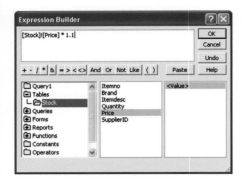

Figure 6.15 *The Expression Builder dialog box*

are displayed under the typing area. The bottom pane is divided into three columns. The first column is a list that includes folders called **Tables, Queries, Forms, Reports** and **Functions.**

3. Double-click on the **Tables** folder (a list of all the tables in the database is displayed).

4. To select fields from a particular table, click once on its name (its fields are displayed in the second column).

5. Double-click on a field that will be part of your formula (the field together with the table it comes from is displayed in the top pane).

6. Click on any of the operators (for example, * **or +**) to begin to build a formula, which is displayed in the top pane.

7. Click on other fields and operators, or type values directly into the top pane, to complete the formula.

8. Click on **OK** (the formula will be displayed in the **Update To** cell of your query grid).

9. Click on the **Run** button (a message box appears to ask you to confirm that you want to update the database).

10. Click **Yes** to make the changes to the database.

Creating a calculated field (Extension material)

A **calculated field** contains an expression that calculates a value by referencing one or more fields from one or more tables. The value derived is placed in a new field, which is displayed in the query. Calculations can only be performed on numeric, date and text fields.

1. Display the query in Design View.

2. Select an empty field in the design grid.

3. Type in the new field name, followed by a colon (:), followed by the field names that form part of the expression, each in square brackets and with the relevant operator in between each pair. For example:

    Totalrentalcost: [Daysrented][Dailycost].*

Including totals in a query (Extension material)

You can adapt your query to produce a list of statistical information from the numeric fields you retrieve. Some of the functions that you can use are shown below:

Function	Description
Sum	Calculates the total of all the values in a field
Avg	Calculates the average of all the values in a field
Min	Returns the lowest value in a field
Max	Returns the highest value in a field
Count	Returns the number of values in a field, ignoring null (empty) values
StDev	Calculates the standard deviation of all the values in a field
Var	Calculates the variance of all the values in a field
First	Returns the first value in a field
Last	Returns the last value in a field

1. With the query design grid displayed, in the **Query Tools | Design** tab, select **Totals** (a *Total* row is added to the query design grid).

2. To find the total for a particular field across all the records:

    a) Click on the arrow in the **Total** cell of the appropriate field (a drop-down menu appears, listing the functions shown above).
    b) Select **Sum.**
    c) Run the query.

Exercise 6.4

1. Within the database called the Betterprices Hardware Stock List create a table called **Orders** with the structure shown below:

Field name	Data type	Description	Field size	Format
Date	Date/Time	Date order was placed		Short Date
Orderno	Text	Order number	5	
Itemno	Text	Item number of product	6	
Quantity	Number	Quantity ordered		
SupplierID	Text	Supplier identification number	5	

2. Enter these records into the **Orders** table (note that the dates are listed here in mm/dd/yy format so you may have to swap the months and days).

Date	Orderno	Itemno	Quantity	SupplierID
06/04/00	A0100	H0005	8	SP010
06/06/00	D0800	TR0090	10	SP010
05/12/00	B0079	FK0035	45	SP015
06/08/00	E0450	H0006	5	SP015
05/07/00	B0067	H0007	25	SP020
05/10/00	D0432	SH0011	15	SP020
06/12/00	E0500	SP0015	15	SP020
06/15/00	F0120	SP0040	20	SP020
05/04/00	A0051	FK0025	20	SP030
05/06/00	A0051	SH0010	12	SP030
05/15/00	C0056	SH0110	14	SP050
05/20/00	D0567	TR0078	10	SP060
05/25/00	B0089	PD2000	5	SP075

3. Create another table called **Suppliers** within the **Betterprices Hardware Stock List** database with the structure shown below:

Field name	Data type	Description	Field size
SupplierID	Text	Supplier identification number	5
Company	Text	Name of company	30
Address	Text	Address of supplier	50
Phoneno	Text	Phone number of supplier	8
Email	Text	Supplier's email address	20
Product Range	Memo	Name of products sold by supplier	

4. Enter these records into the **Suppliers** table.

SupplierID	Company	Address	Phoneno	Email	ProductRange
SP010	S and S Distributors	18 West Cost Drive, Arima	632-6778	sdist@ hotmail .com	Superior Brand Tools: Hammers, Shovels, Spades, Forks, Trowels, Hatchets, Spirit levels
SP015	Tools Specialist	25 Royal Road, Pt. Lisas	654-4435	tools@ tstools .net. tt	Nicholson Tools: Files, Hammers, Shovels, Forks, Spades, Pigfoot, Hacksaw blades, Saws
SP020	Star Wholesalers	12 Hammond Drive, Pt. Fortin	648-2356	star@ hotmail .com	Star Tools and merchandise
SP030	BD Suppliers	3 Main Road, Cova	636-7894	bdog@ hotmail.com	Bulldog Tools
SP050	Construction Helpers	Addams Building, California	678-9712	cons@ yahoo.com	Suppliers of OX brand tools
SP060	The Tool Master	78 Fitter Street, San Fernando	692-3398	tools@ yahoo.com	Suppliers of Mason tools
SP075	Alligator	Regent Street, San Fernando	632-7846	gator@ carib-link. net	Alligator

5. Using the **Stock** table:

   a) List all the products with brand name 'Superior Brand'.

   b) List all the items whose quantity is less than or equal to 20.

   c) Display a list of all brands and their suppliers. Sort the list in descending order.

Help with Question 5

a) To list all the products with brand name 'Superior Brand':

- ✓ On the **Create** tab click on **Query Design.**
- ✓ Select **Stock** from the **Show Table** dialog box.
- ✓ Click on **Add** (the table becomes visible in the upper pane of the **Select Query** window).
- ✓ Click on **Close.** (The query design grid is displayed.)
- ✓ Click on the arrow in the first column of the **Field** row and select **Itemno.**
- ✓ Move to the next column and select **Brand.**
- ✓ Move to the next column and select **Itemdesc.**
- ✓ Move to the **Criteria** row in the **Brand** column and type "Superior Brand".
- ✓ Click on the **Run** button on the Ribbon.

Figure 6.16 shows the Design View and the results.

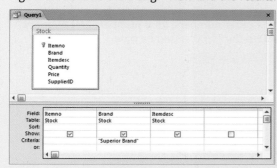
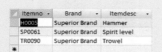

Figure 6.16 *Design View and results for Exercise 6.4, Question 5(a)*

b) To list all items whose quantity is less than or equal to 20:

- ✓ The procedure will be the same as in 5(a) except that the field names and criteria will be different.

Figure 6.16 shows the Design View and the results.

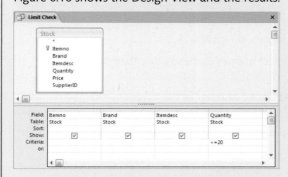

Figure 6.17 *Design View and results for Exercise 6.4, Question 5(b)*

c) To list the brands and their suppliers, sorted in ascending order:

- ✓ The procedure is essentially the same as above.
- ✓ In the **Sort** row, click the arrow and select **Ascending.**

Figure 6.18 shows the Design View and the results.

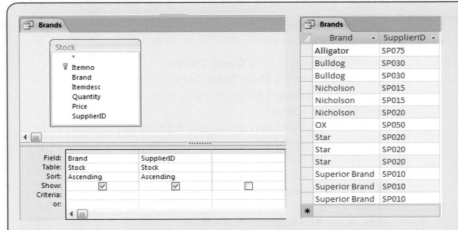

Figure 6.18 *Design View and results for Exercise 6.4, Question 5(c)*

6. Using the **Orders** table, list all the order numbers, item numbers and quantity ordered from the period 5/04/00 to 05/25/00 sorted by date.

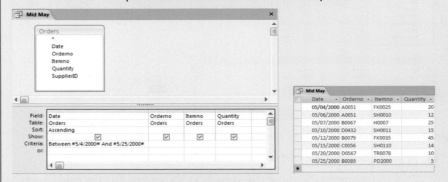

Figure 6.19 *Design View and results for Exercise 6.4, Question 6*

Help with Question 6

The Design View and results are shown in Figure 6.19.

7. **Extension exercise:** Create Select queries that use more than one table, as follows:

   a) List the name, address and phone number of the company that distributes the OX brand.

   b) List the item description, brand, date, order number, quantity and companies that sell forks.

Help with Question 7

   a) Since the data required to do this is in two different tables, you need to join the tables to carry out the query. Here is one way to do this in Access:

   ✓ Select the **Stock** and **Suppliers** tables using the **Show Table** dialog box.

   ✓ Click on **SupplierID** in the **Stock** table and drag across to **SupplierID** in the **Suppliers** table. A line connecting the two fields is displayed, as shown in Figure 6.20 (this may happen automatically).

   ✓ Fill out the query design grid as shown in Figure 6.20.

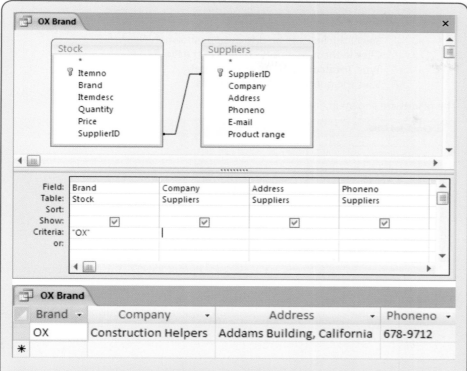

Figure 6.20 *Joining the Stock and Suppliers tables to answer a query*

b) In this case, the data required is in three different tables: **Stock, Suppliers** and **Orders List.** Proceed as in (a), but this time also joining the **Stock** and **Orders** tables on their **Itemno** fields. The Design View and results are shown in Figure 6.21.

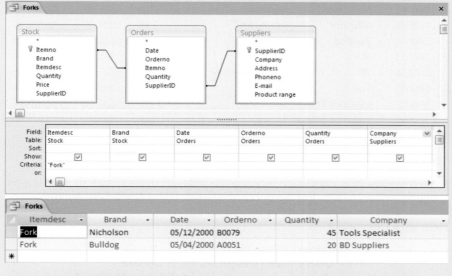

Figure 6.21 *Joining three tables to answer a query*

8. Calculate the total cost of all the items listed in the **Stock** table.

Help with Question 8

✓ Select the fields to be displayed as shown in Figure 6.22.
✓ Click in the next empty column in the **Field** row.
✓ Type **Totalcost: [Quantity] * [Price].**
✓ Save the query as **Calculated Field.**

The results are shown in Figure 6.22.

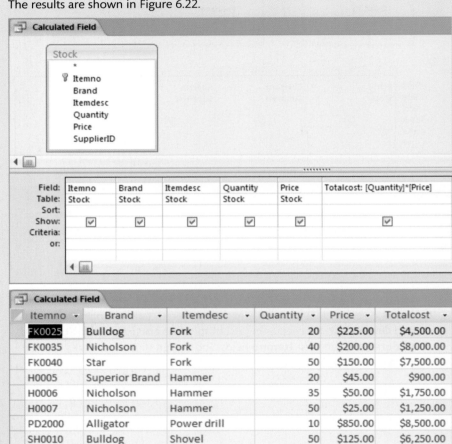

Figure 6.22 *Including a calculated field in a query*

9. Betterprices have decided to increase the prices of all their stock by 10%. Use an update query to increase the prices of all items in the **Stock** table by **10%.**

Help with Question 9

✓ Add the **Stock** table to the query grid.
✓ On the **Query Tools | Design** tab select **Update.**
✓ Add the **Price** field to the query and click in its **Update To** row.
✓ Right-click the mouse and select **Build** from the Ribbon (the **Expression Builder** dialog box appears as shown in Figure 6.15).

✓ Double-click on **Tables** (the names of the tables within the database are displayed).
✓ Click on **Stock** (the field names appear in the second column of the bottom pane of the window).
✓ Double-click on the **Price** field (the upper pane displays *'[Stock]![Price]'*).
✓ Click on the multiplication sign (*).
✓ Type in **1.1** (the formula displayed in the window is now *'[Stock]![Price]*1.1'*).
✓ Click on **OK** (the formula is added to the query design grid).
✓ Click on the **Run** button in the Ribbon (Access displays a message informing you how many rows will be updated).
✓ Click **Yes** to update the database.

The results are shown in Figure 6.23.

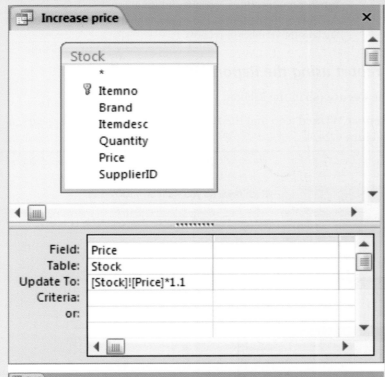

Figure 6.23 *Increasing stock prices by 10%*

Reports

A report is a display on the monitor or a printout of the information in a table or query. It displays details as well as summary information.

A report is divided into sections, which are listed below:

Report section	Description
Report header	Displayed at the beginning of the report. It usually contains the name of the report and describes the information listed in it.
Page header	Appears just after the report header and at the top of every page. It displays the column headings (field names) and page numbers.
Group header and footer	If records are sorted into groups based on a common value, a group header is placed at the start of each group, and a group footer after the last record in the group.
Details section	The primary information that the report is there to display.
Page footer	Last item on each page of the report. It could contain a page number or any other descriptive information.
Report footer	Appears at the bottom of the report. It holds summary values, such as the number of records.

Creating a report using the Report Wizard

1. Click on the **Create** tab in the Ribbon.

2. Click on **Report Wizard** icon and the **Report Wizard** dialog box appears, as shown in Figure 6.24.

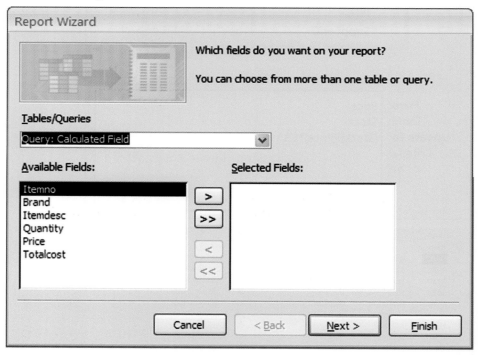

Figure 6.24 *The Report Wizard dialog box*

3. Select the tables or queries that contain the fields you want displayed in the report. When a table or query is selected, all the field names contained in it are displayed in the **Available Fields** pane.

4. Select the fields you would like displayed in the report by clicking on the single arrow to select one field and the double arrow to select all the fields displayed. The fields are placed in the **Selected Fields** pane.

5. Click **Next** after you have selected all the fields you want to display.

6. The selected fields are displayed as shown in Figure 6.25, and you now have the opportunity to add grouping levels. This means that you can group records according to date, code, colour or some other field that is common to a group of records. If you select a field, it is placed in a box above the remaining fields. If you then select another field, it is also placed in a box below the first selected field. When you have finished, click **Next.**

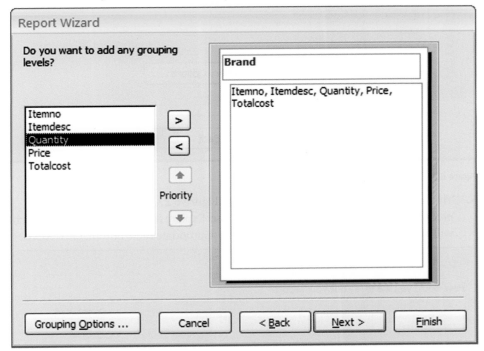

Figure 6.25 *The grouping levels dialog box*

7. The **Sort Options** dialog box appears, as shown in Figure 6.26. You can sort the report output using up to four fields in either ascending or descending order. Select the fields you would like sorted.

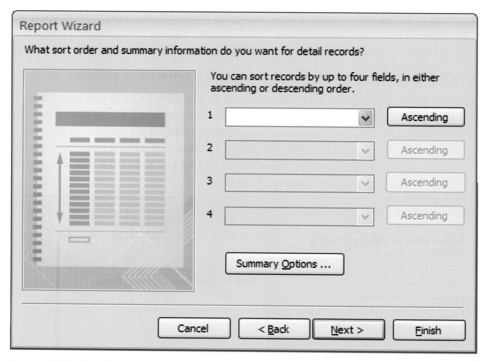

Figure 6.26 *The Sort Options dialog box*

8. The **Layout** dialog box appears, as shown in Figure 6.27. Access has a set of predefined layouts from which you can choose. Explore the options to find out which will best suit your report, and then check the appropriate radio button. Click **Next.**

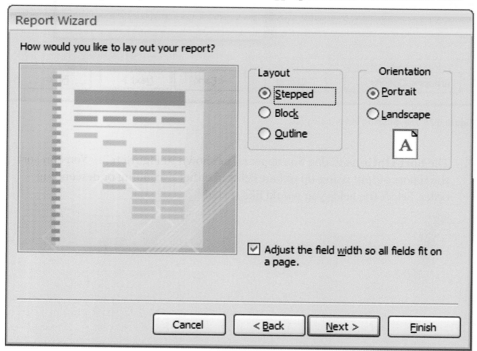

Figure 6.27 *The Layout dialog box*

9. The **Style** dialog box appears, as shown in Figure 6.28. From here you can choose the font style for your report. Then click **Next.**

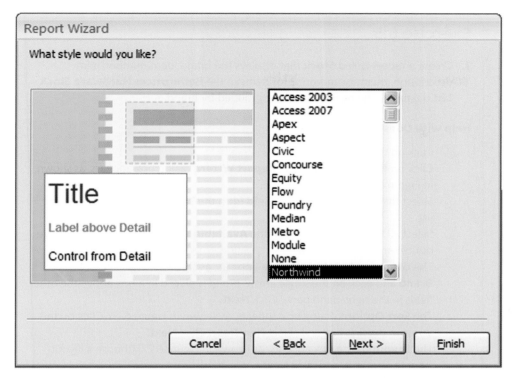

Figure 6.28 *The Style dialog box*

10. The **Title** dialog box appears, as shown in Figure 6.29. Type in a title for your report.

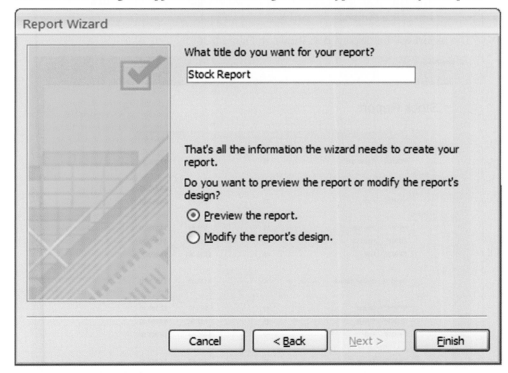

Figure 6.29 *The Title dialog box*

11. Click on **Finish** to see the report.

12. Print the report.

Exercise 6.5

1. Create a report called **Stock** that displays the brand, item number, item description, quantity and price for items in the **Betterprices Hardware Stock List** database. The report should be grouped by brand.

Help with Question 1

- ✓ Click on the **Create** tab.
- ✓ Click on **Report Wizard.** The **Report Wizard** dialog box appears, as shown in Figure 6.24.
- ✓ Select the **Query: Calculated Field** from the **Tables/Queries** drop-down list.
- ✓ Select all the fields displayed in the **Available Fields** box, by clicking on the double arrow. Click **Next.**
- ✓ The **Grouping Levels** dialog box appears, as shown in Figure 6.25. Select **Brand** and click on the single arrow. *Brand* is placed in a box above the other fields in the right-hand pane. Click **Next.**
- ✓ The **Sort Options** dialog box appears, as shown in Figure 6.26. Click on the arrow in the first box and select **ItemDesc.** Click **Next.**
- ✓ The **Layout** dialog box appears, as shown in Figure 6.27. Choose a layout from the options, and click **Next.**
- ✓ The **Style** dialog box appears, as shown in Figure 6.28. Choose a style and click **Next.**
- ✓ The **Title** dialog box appears, as shown in Figure 6.29. Type **Stock** in the title box. Click **Finish.**

The report will be displayed as shown in Figure 6.30.

Figure 6.30 *The Stock report created in Exercise 6.5, Question 1*

School student record system

2. Set up three tables called **Students, Test** and **Parents,** with names and structures as shown below. Include field sizes for the fields in the three tables and justify these choices.

Table: Students

Field name	Data type	Size	Justification for the field size
StudID	Number		
Surname	Text		
Firstname	Text		
DOB	Date/Time		
Address	Text		
Hphone	Text		
Religion	Text		
Sex	Text		

Table: Test

Field name	Data type	Size	Justification for the field size
StudID	Number		
Maths	Number		
Phys	Number		
Chem	Number		
Bio	Number		
Eng	Number		
Comp	Number		
Total	Number		
Average	Number		

Table: Parents

Field name	Data type	Size	Justification for the field size
StudID	Number		
Fatherfirstname	Text		
Fathersurname	Text		
Fatheroccup	Text		
Motherfirstname	Text		
Motheroccup	Text		

3. Enter the following records into the **Students** table.

StudID	Surname	Firstname	DOB	Address	HPhone	Religion	Sex
010056	Ali	Fyzool	5/10/91	Gonzales	6483216	M	M
010048	Barnes	David	6/8/91	Siparia	6492546	C	M
010123	Lara	Leanna	23/3/91	Phillipine	6525335	C	F
010105	King	Mary	12/12/90	Fyzabad	6779784	C	F
010065	Singh	Vishnu	28/9/90	Debe	6474226	H	M

4. Enter the following records into the **Test** table:

StudID	Maths	Phys	Chem	Bio	Eng	Comp
010056	70	85	80	65	75	65
010048	25	40	55	45	65	60
010123	80	70	60	41	75	86
010105	75	65	76	65	80	72
010065	60	65	75	65	88	55

5. Enter the following records into the **Parents** table:

StudID	Father firstname	Father surname	Father occup	Mother firstname	Mother occup
010056	Karim	Ali	Teacher	Razia	Housewife
010048	Anthony	Barnes	Engineer	Trudy	Clerk
010123	Mathew	Lara	Taxi Driver	Kerry	Housewife
010105	Jason	Walcott	Accountant	Elizabeth	Teacher
010065	Krishna	Singh	Supervisor	Leela	Banker

6. Add 10 records of your own to each table.

7. Change the DOB of Fyzool Ali from 5/10/91 to 15/10/91.

8. List the name and date of birth of each female student in the class.

9. List the name and date of birth of each student born before 1991.

10. Sort the **Students** table by surname and then by first name.

11. List the students who scored more than 70 in their Maths test.

12. List the students, their marks in each subject and their total mark.

13. List the students and their total mark, and their father's name and occupation. Display the list in alphabetic order on the surname.

Loading data from an existing file

Data in an existing file can be loaded into a table in a database. Imported files often have these file types: **.csv** (comma-separated variables), **.txt** (text) and **.rtf** (rich text format).

For example, consider the file **events.txt** with data in this format in it:

"105","Judo","Experienced","Fitness","Gymnasium","Saturday",10.00

"109","Tennis","Novice","Racquets","TennisCourts","Sunday",13.30

In Access, to create a table with this data in it:

● Click the Office Button and select **Open.**

● In the **Open** dialog box, browse to the file **events.txt** and open it.

● The **Link Text Wizard** dialog box appears.

● Choose the delimiter used. The delimiter separates one item of data from the next. In **events.txt,** this is a comma. Click on the **Next** button.

● Name each field. Click on **Next.**

● Click on the **Finish** button.

● The data in the file **events.txt** is imported into a table.

1. A **database** is an organised collection of structured data. Database software enables you to organise and store data so that specific items of information can be retrieved easily and quickly in a structured fashion.

2. A database file contains one or more tables. A **table** is a collection of related data about a subject (person, place or thing) and is divided into rows and columns. Each row is a record and each column is a field. A **record** is a group of related fields. A **field** is a data item within a record.

3. Each record has a **key field (primary field)** which uniquely identifies a record. Using a key field can speed up operations such as searching and sorting. A key field also allows tables to be linked. Linking tables enables a database to create queries that retrieve data from several tables.

4. A **flat-file database** has only one table, whereas a relational database has several linked tables.

5. Each field is automatically assigned default field properties depending on the data type. The field **properties**, which can be changed, determine how a field is stored, how it works and how it is displayed.

6. The **data type** determines the type of data that will be stored in a field and how it will be treated. The data types available in the Access are as follows: **Number, Text, Memo, Date/Time, Currency, Yes/No, OLE Object, AutoNumber** and **Hyperlink.**

7. Data can be **input** by entering it in a table in Datasheet View, using an input form or uploading it from an existing file, for example, a file created in a spreadsheet.

8. A **query** enables you to view data from one or more tables in a specified order. It is used for storing and answering questions about information in a database. When you run a query, the answer is displayed in a **dynaset** – an editable group of records that answers a query. There are several types of queries; for example, Select and Update queries.

9. A **Select query** is the most common type. It is used to search tables to retrieve data that satisfies the query.

10. An **Update query** makes changes to a group of records or to all of the records in one or more tables.

11. A **report** is an attractive display of the data or information in a table or query. It is a method used to display details as well as summary information about the contents of a database. Reports can be displayed in either a columnar or a tabular format. A **columnar** report displays each record in a single column. A **tabular** report displays all the data under the respective field names.

12. Data can be loaded from an existing file and a table created with the data in it.

Chapter 6: Databases

Chapter 7: Graphics, video and audio editing software

In this chapter, you will look at software that will enable you to do the following:
- create and edit simple graphics
- edit video
- edit audio (sounds and music)

Graphics software

Software that enables you to create and edit graphics can be very useful, especially when preparing a presentation or setting up a website. There is a wide range of such software; for example, Adobe Photoshop. A more straightforward example that is free on computers with Windows is Microsoft Paint. We will have a brief look at how to use this. In Windows, Paint can usually be found in the **Accessories** group in the Programs menu. Select this and the software will display the opening window shown in Figure 7.1.

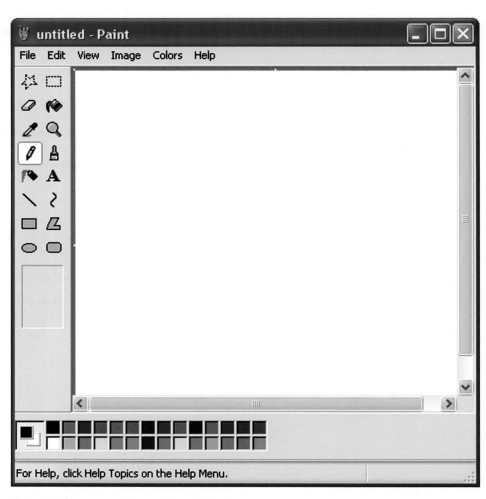

Figure 7.1 *The opening window of Microsoft Paint*

Tools

On the left-hand side of the window (see Figure 7.1) you can see the toolbox (see also Figure 7.2). The tools available allow you to create and edit graphics. These are the functions of some of the tools:

- **Pencil** and **Brush** both allow you to draw on the work area. Different nib and brush shapes can be chosen.

- **Airbrush** allows you to spray paint onto the work area.

- **Text** allows you to type in text. You drag the mouse to create a rectangular text box, and then type in the text.

- The **Eraser** is used to rub out parts of the graphic.

- **Fill** allows you to fill an enclosed space with colour. You create an enclosed space, select a colour (see Figure 7.3) by clicking on it, and click inside the enclosed space.

- **Pick** allows you to choose an existing colour already present on the graphic you are editing. This can then be used with other tools.

- **Magnifier** allows you to magnify your view of the graphic. This helps you to do more detailed editing.

- There are also tools for drawing a variety of shapes, such as lines, curved lines, ellipses (hold down the **Shift** key to draw a circle), rectangles (hold down the **Shift** key to draw a square), polygons and rounded rectangles.

- **Select** allows you to select a rectangular part of a graphic by dragging the mouse and then releasing the mouse button. **Freeform select** is similar but the shape of the selection does not have to be a rectangle.

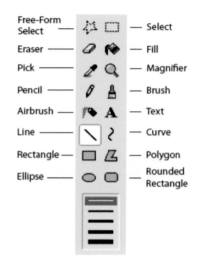

Figure 7.2 *The toolbox*

Figure 7.3 *The colour box*

The menus in Paint

File menu

In the **File** menu, you will find familiar options such as **Save**, **Save As** and **Print**. You can save graphics in several common file formats, such as **.bmp**, **.jpg** and **.gif**. There is also a useful option entitled **From scanner or camera**. This will input an image directly from a scanner or digital camera connected to the computer without need to cut or copy and paste the image.

Edit menu

The **Edit** menu options include **Copy**, **Cut** and **Paste**, and other options which are likely to be familiar.

To copy a part of a graphic, select the part to be copied and in the **Edit** menu select **Copy**. Next, again in the **Edit** menu, select **Paste**. The block copied appears on the work area and it is selected. Drag this across to the location you wish to place it in.

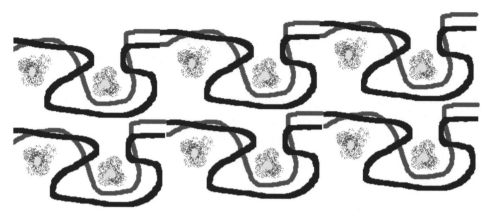

Figure 7.4 *A repeating pattern produced using graphics software*

View menu

The **View** menu allows you to turn on or off the display of the toolbox, colour box and status bar. It also allows you to choose to zoom in on the graphic so that you can edit it in detail.

Image menu

In the **Image** menu (see Figure 7.5) you can choose to flip, rotate, stretch or skew an image. For example to reflect in a vertical axis (or mirror line) select the part of the graphic to be reflected; in the **Image** menu select **Flip/Rotate**, in the **Flip and Rotate** dialog box (see Figure 7.6) select **Flip vertical** and click on **OK**.

Colors menu

In the **Colors** menu you can define custom colours. Select **Edit Colors** and the **Edit Colors** dialog box appears (see Figure 7.7). Click on **Define Custom Colors** and the colour spectrum appears. Click on the colour that you want in the spectrum and click on **OK**. This colour will now be available in the colour palette, and you can use it with the other tools.

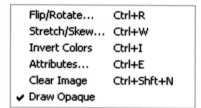

Figure 7.5 *The options in the Image menu*

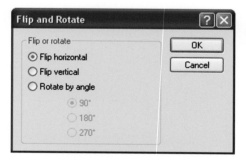

Figure 7.6 *The Flip and Rotate dialog box*

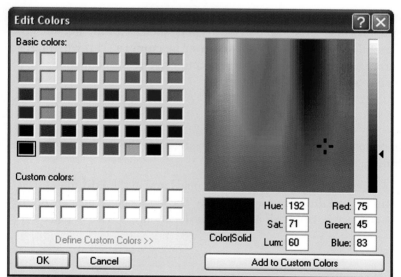

Figure 7.7 *The Edit Colors dialog box after Define Custom Colors has been selected*

Screen images

Paint has only a very restricted range of tools and options but it is readily available. It is very useful when you want to write help documentation and user guides because it is very easy to capture parts of the screen and edit them in Paint.

- To capture the whole screen, follow these steps. On the keyboard, press the **Print Screen** key. This copies an image of the screen into the paste buffer. In Paint, in the **Edit** menu select **Paste**. This places the screen image into the work area where it can be edited. If you just wanted an image of the whole screen, you could paste this directly into Word or other software.

- To capture part of the screen, the process is similar. Capture the whole screen, and then in Paint select the part of the screen you want. Copy this and paste it into Word or other software. You can use this method to capture images of icons and menus.

- To capture a dialog box, you can hold down the **Alt** key when you press **Print Screen**. The dialog box is copied to the paste buffer. This can now be pasted into Paint, Word or other software.

Bit mapped graphics

Bit mapped graphics or **raster** graphics are used in applications such as photography and scanning where an exact copy of the detail is needed. Bitmap software is used for retouching photographic images.

If a very high resolution is used then bit mapped graphics can provide very clear and detailed images. However, if a bit mapped image is enlarged, or zipped and unzipped, the detail of the image can become unclear. Bit mapped images can be created in, for example, Paint and Adobe Photoshop. Common file formats are **.gif**, **.jpg** and **.bmp**.

Low resolution bit mapped images need much less storage space than high resolution images. This is because of the number of pixels that must be represented and the information that must be stored about each pixel. The display on a monitor is made up of tiny dots or picture elements called **pixels** which are used to make a picture. A monitor can have a display that measures 1024 by 768 pixels, and each pixel can display a different colour.

A simple black and white bit mapped graphic could have each pixel controlled by one bit. 0 would be white and 1 would be black. The patterns of 0s and 1s would make up a black and white picture.

To use colours, each pixel could be mapped to a byte (8 bits). A byte can have up to 256 different bit patterns so 256 different colours could be used. If more colours are needed, the pixel could be mapped to several bytes which taken together could have many more different patterns and represent many more colours. Some computers map 24 bits (3 bytes) to a pixel which gives up to 16,777,216 different colours. This means that a display of 1024 by 768 pixels will need 2,359,296 bytes or 2.24 MB of memory for the monitor display. A small image will occupy much less memory than a large image if bit mapped graphic representation is used as the small image will use fewer pixels.

Bit patterns stored in memory

0	1	0	0	1	0	0	1
1	1	1	0	1	1	0	0

Pattern of pixels displayed on part of the monitor screen

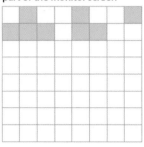

Figure 7.8 *The pattern produced by simple bit mapped graphics*

Vector graphics

Vector graphics are produced using mathematical codes rather than bit patterns. Vector graphics software is used to create cartoons, clip art, technical illustrations, diagrams and flowcharts. Almost all CAD/CAM systems and animation software use vector graphics. Vector images can be produced in software such as, Adobe Acrobat, Adobe Flash and Adobe Fireworks. Common file formats are **.pdf** and **.wmf**.

Vector graphics can take up less storage space when enlarged and image quality is not lost. For example, to represent a square on the screen the coordinates of its corners would be stored. One advantage of this method is that if the square was enlarged this could be done by changing the stored coordinates but no more storage space would be need. Information about the colours used in producing the image is also stored in a vector graphic file. Vector graphic images can be re-sized and still retain their original quality, and a large image will occupy the same memory as a small image.

Exercise 7.1

1. Write down the name of the graphics software you use.
2. Using drawing software, create a repeating textile or wallpaper pattern using copy and paste (see Figure 7.4).
3. Write a help sheet that shows someone how to create, save, print and close a document for the first time in word processing software. This should include images of the following items:
   - ✓ The **File** menu
   - ✓ The **Save As** dialog box
   - ✓ The **Save** button
   - ✓ The **Print and Close** buttons.
4. Write a help sheet that shows someone how to open an existing spreadsheet, edit it, save and print it. You should illustrate this with the menus, icons and buttons used.
5. Bitmapped and vector graphics have different characteristics.
   a) When a low-resolution bitmapped graphic is enlarged picture quality is degraded. Explain this.
   b) When a vector graphic is enlarged there is no loss of picture quality. Explain this.
   c) A large bitmapped graphic will have a larger file size than a smaller version of the same bitmapped graphic. However, a large vector graphic will have the same file size as a smaller version of the same vector graphic. Explain this.

Video editing software

Video editing software is used to edit video that has been captured using, for example, a video camera or camcorder. Many digital cameras are able to capture short video sequences. Using video editing software you can:

- Import video, pictures and sounds and combine these
- Edit the video and sound
- Insert titles
- Insert transitions between one video clip and the next
- Insert effects
- Save the edited video.

There is a variety of video editing software available. For example, Pinnacle Studio and Microsoft Windows Movie Maker. Movie Maker is used to illustrate what can be done as it is straight forward and easy to use and available as a free download from the Microsoft download centre: http://www.microsoft.com/downloads/

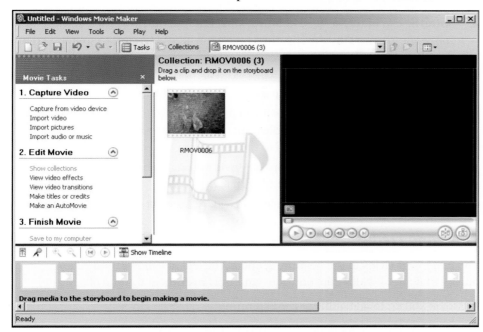

Figure 7.9 *The opening screen of Microsoft Windows Movie Maker*

Movies and Projects

A **movie** is a video file that can be played on media players, in a web browser, or on TV, etc. A **project** is the construction of a movie using a collection of resources, such as audio and video clips, transitions, effects and titles. While a movie is being constructed, it is saved as a project file; when the movie is complete, it is saved as a movie file.

A project is built up on the **timeline** or **storyboard.** A resource is placed on the timeline or storyboard by dragging and dropping it. In Movie Maker, you can toggle between the timeline and storyboard by clicking the button in the timeline or storyboard panel.

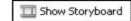

Figure 7.10 *The Show Storyboard button shown when the Timeline is displayed*

During the construction of a movie, the project is saved as a project file which can be opened and edited as required. Movie Maker project files are saved with the file extension .mswmm. When the movie is complete, the project can be saved as a movie file. Movie Maker saves movies in the .wmv (Windows Media Video) format and this can be converted to other formats, such as, .mp4.

Importing video

You can **import** video taken on a video camera or any other device that can be used to record video clips, such as a webcam, digital camera or smart phone. This could be recorded in a variety of file formats, for example, .avi. In Movie Maker, in the **Movie Tasks** pane, select **Import video**, browse to find the video you want to import, and click on the **Import** button.

Editing video clips

To edit a video clip you can:

- **Split** the clip into two clips. In Movie Maker, in the timeline, click on the clip you want to split. Play the clip, then pause it where you want to split it, and in the **Clip** menu select **Split**.

- **Combine** two clips into one. In Movie Maker, in the timeline, select contiguous clips, and in the **Clip** menu, select **Combine**.

- **Trim** a clip, that is, hide parts of it you do not want to use. In Movie Maker, in the timeline, drag the trim handle from the start to the right to trim the start of a video clip, and from the end to the left to trim the end.

- **Change the position** of the clip. In Movie Maker, in the timeline, select the clip, drag it to its new position and drop it.

- **Delete** a clip. In Movie Maker, select the video clip, right click and select **Delete**.

Titles and credits

You can insert **titles** at the beginning and at the end of a movie, and before, during and after a video clip, and you can insert **credits** at the end of a movie.

In Movie Maker, to add a title at the beginning:

- In the **Movie Tasks** pane, select **Make titles or credits**.

- Select **Add title at the beginning of the movie**.

- Type the main title into the top text box and the sub title into the lower text box.

- Change the title animation and the text font and colour.

- Click on **Done, add title to movie**.

Transitions

A **transition** controls the way that the clip being played merges into the next clip to be played. You insert transitions between video clips.

In Movie Maker, to add a transition:

- Display the storyboard.

- In the **Movie Tasks** pane, select **View video transitions**.
- Select a transition and click on the **play** button to try it out.
- Drag the transition and drop it in the transition box between two clips.

Effects

An **effect** controls the way that the clip being played is seen. You add effects to video clips.

In Movie Maker, to add an effect:

- Display the storyboard.
- In the **Movie Tasks** pane, select **View video effects**.
- Select an effect and click on the **play** button to try it out.
- Drag the effect and drop it on a clip.

Pictures

You can import pictures and include them in a movie. In Movie Maker, in the Movie Tasks pane, select **Import pictures**, browse to find the picture you want to import, and click on the **Import** button. Drag and drop the picture from the **Collection** pane onto the timeline.

Audio or music

You can import audio or music that will play at the same time as your video. You can edit the sounds recorded with a video clip or import and edit a music file.

The **sound recorded with a video clip** will be imported with the video clip and affected by your editing of the video clip. Additional audio editing can be done, for example: fade in, fade out, mute and volume adjustment. In Movie Maker, to adjust the volume, select the clip in the timeline. In the **Clip** menu, select **Audio**, then **Volume**. Adjust the volume level and click on **OK**.

You can import **music**. This could be recorded in a variety of file formats, for example, .mp3. In Movie Maker, in the **Movie Tasks Pane**, select **Import audio or music**, browse to find the music file you want to import, and click on the **Import** button.

To include the music in your video, from the **Collections** panel, drag the music file to the Audio/Music timeline and drop it.

In video editing software, you can edit a music file in the same ways you edit a video clip, that is, you can: **split** the clip into two clips; **combine** two clips into one; **trim** a clip; **change the position** of a clip; and **delete** a clip. You can also edit a music file in the same ways you can edit the sound recorded with a video clip, that is: fade in, fade out, mute and volume adjustment. More extensive sound editing facilities are available in audio editing software (see below). It may be that recorded sound or music is edited in audio editing software before importing into video editing software.

Saving your movie

When the movie is complete, the project can be saved as a movie file. In Movie Maker, in the **Movie Tasks** panel, select **Save to my computer**. Choose a file name and a place to save your movie. Next, choose the picture quality and the movie is saved as a .wmv (Windows Media Video) file.

Exercise 7.2

1. Write down the name of the video editing software you use.

2. Put a cross in one box to show which feature is not usually found in video editing software.

A	Titles and credits
B	Trim
C	Effects
D	Formula

 A

 B

☐ C

☐ D

3. You are going to make a short movie about your journey from home to school.

  a) Decide at which key points in the journey you will make video recordings.

  b) Record video clips at the key points in the journey.

  c) Import the video clips and place them on the storyboard.

  d) Save your project now and as you work through this exercise.

  e) If necessary, edit the video clips.

  f) Insert a picture of yourself at the beginning.

  g) Insert a title at the beginning.

  h) Change the title animation and the text font and colour.

  i) Insert credits at the end.

  j) If necessary, insert transitions, titles and effects between the video clips. Titles that describe what the next video clip is about can be very helpful.

  k) Import music to play in the background when your movie is played. This should relate to your journey.

  l) Save your movie.

  m) Play your movie on a media player.

  n) Evaluate your movie. Could it be improved? If so, open your project and edit it.

  o) Save your movie and play and evaluate it again.

4. Make a movie about your favourite pet. Sketch out a storyboard first then follow through the steps in Question 3.

5. Make a movie about a topic of your choice.

Audio editing software

Most sound or music that we listen to is pre-recorded and is of a sufficiently high quality; for example, music or video on CD/DVD, on TV or broadcast on the web. Why would we want to edit audio? Some uses of audio editing software are as follows:

- To record speech or live music and edit it. We may want to add speech to a video we are making or record our own sound track. Sometimes when recording ourselves speaking or playing we also record sounds we do not want, such as the wail of a police car siren, and it may be possible to edit this out. Similarly, we may want to edit out sections which are not needed.

- To improve recorded sound. For example, when transferring music from legacy media, such as cassette tape, to create music files that can be stored on hard disk or CD, it is not unusual for there to be background noise or extended silences at the start and end of tracks – these can be edited out.

There is a wide range of audio editing software, such as Goldwave and Audacity. Audacity (see Figure 7.11) is used to illustrate this section and it can be downloaded free from: www.audacity.sourceforge.net

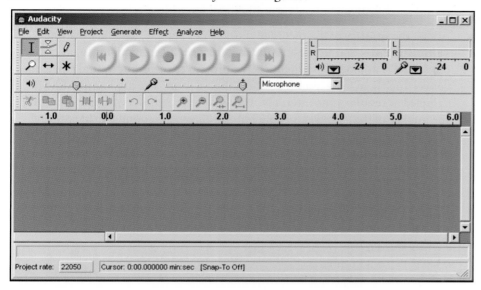

Figure 7.11 *The opening screen of Audacity*

Audio files and Projects

An **audio file** can be played on media players, in a web browser, or on a stereo, etc. or imported into audio or video editing software. A **project** is the construction of an audio file. While an audio file is being constructed, it is saved as a project file. When it is complete, it is saved as an audio file.

Audio editing software will usually have these features:

- **Import** an audio file. In Audacity, in the **Project** menu, select **Import Audio** and browse to the audio file you wish to import. Click on **Open** and the file is imported. For example, you could import an .mp3 file. If you intend to record speech to accompany an imported audio file, you should record this at the sampling rate of the imported audio file.

- **Record sound** from one or more **inputs**. For example, in Audacity, speech would be recorded using a **microphone**, and a cassette tape being played would be recorded on **line in**. These can be selected using the input drop-down menu in the tool bar (see Figure 7.12). To record speech, press the **record** button in the tool bar and speak into the microphone. To halt the recording, press the **stop** button.

Figure 7.12 *The drop-down menu used to select the input*

- Adjust the **volume** at which the input is recorded and the output played. In Audacity, this can be done by operating the sliders in the tool bar.

- Record input in **mono** (one channel) or **stereo** (two channels) or more channels. In Audacity, in the **Edit** menu, select **Preferences**, and in the **Audio I/O** tab, select the number of channels in the drop-down menu. Most sound cards will only allow recording in mono or stereo.

- Adjust the **quality** of the recorded sound. For example, by adjusting the **sampling rate**. Sound must be in a digital form for a computer to process it, but sound is analogue. Sampling is the process of recording sound waves and converting them from analogue into a digital form. The analogue sound is sampled at regular time intervals. The smaller these intervals are, the better the quality of the sound recording but the bigger the sound file. Ideally, the time between sampling should be so small that we hear a continuous sound without any gaps. In Audacity, in the **Edit** menu, select **Preferences**, and in the **Quality** tab, select the **Default Sample Rate** in the drop-down menu. This is applied to the whole project.

- Display a **visual illustration** of the recorded sound (see Figure 7.13). For example, in Audacity a sound clip can be displayed as a waveform.

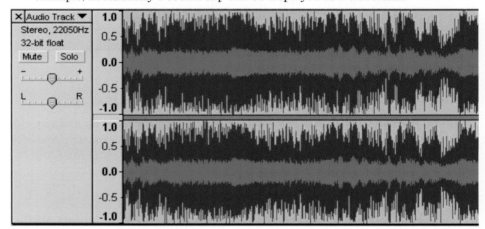

Figure 7.13 *A sound clip displayed as a waveform*

- **Play** one or more channels or sound clips. In Audacity:
  - To play all the channels, press the **Play** button in the tool bar.
  - To play one channel, click the solo button (see Figure 7.13), then press **Play**.
  - To play a sound clip, select the sound clip, then press **Play**.

- **Select a sound clip**. Drag the cursor over the section of the timeline to be selected.

- **Copy, cut** and **paste** a sound clip from one position to another on the timeline or between channels. In Audacity, use the **copy**, **cut** and **paste** buttons in the tool bar. Drag the cursor over the clip you want to copy or cut, click on the new location and click paste. You can use this feature to repeat sections of music or sound.

- **Generate silence**, white noise and other tones. In Audacity, to insert a period of silence, select the section of the timeline where you want silence, and in the **Generate** menu, select **Silence**.

- **Fade in or out** of a clip. For example, you might want to fade out a crowd laughing or clapping. In Audacity, in the **Effect** menu, select **Fade in** or **Fade out**. Various other effects are available.

- **Noise removal** to remove particular noises from a clip. For example, input from a cassette tape may include clicks due to the operation of the tape recorder. In Audacity, on the timeline select a few seconds of only the noise to be removed. In the **Effect** menu, select **Noise Removal**. The **Noise Removal** dialog box appears (see Figure 7.14). Under Step 1, click the **Get Noise Profile** button. The dialog box disappears. Select all of the audio you want filtered. Once again, in the **Effect** menu, select **Noise Removal** so that the **Noise Removal** dialog box reappears. Move the slider to choose how much noise you want filtered out. Click the **Preview** button and the selection is played. If this sounds satisfactory, click on the **Remove Noise** button.

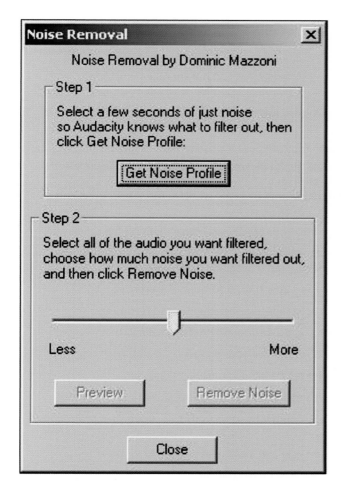

Figure 7.14: *The Noise Removal dialog box*

- **Save** an audio file. A **project** is the construction of an audio file. While an audio file is being constructed, it is saved as a project file. In Audacity, you save a project file as a .aup file. When it is complete, it is saved as an audio file. In Audacity, an audio file is saved by exporting it as a .wav or .mp3 file.

Exercise 7.3

1. Write down the name of the audio editing software you use.

2. Put a cross in one box to show which feature is not usually found in audio editing software.

A	Record sound
B	Change sampling rate
C	Insert table
D	Remove noise

    ☐ A

    ☐ B

    ☐ C

    ☐ D

3. You are going to create a radio programme about shopping at a local supermarket.

    a) Plan the programme. A storyboard might be helpful. Decide what you will record.

    b) Record the audio clips. You could use a cassette tape recorder.
    - ✓ Recordings could be significant background noises, for example, the beeping at the checkout.
    - ✓ You could interview someone who works at the supermarket and record this.

    c) Input your recordings into your project and place them on the timelines.

    d) Record your commentary. You could do this using a microphone. At the beginning, explain what the radio programme is about.

    e) Save your project now and as you work through this exercise.

    f) If necessary, edit the audio clips to remove unwanted recording.

    g) If necessary, move the audio clips around on the timelines.

    h) If necessary, use effects to improve your project.

    i) Save your project and produce the audio file.

    j) Play your audio file on a media player.

    k) Evaluate your audio file. Could it be improved? If so, open your project and edit it.

    l) Save your audio file and play and evaluate it again.

4. Produce a radio programme about farm animals.

5. Produce a commentary for the movie you made about your favourite pet.

1. **Graphics software**, such as Microsoft Paint, enables you to create and edit graphics.

2. In Paint you can:

✓ **Draw** your own graphic or input a graphic from a file or direct from a scanner.

✓ **Save** and **print** graphics.

✓ **Edit** a graphic using a variety of editing tools.

✓ **Cut**, **copy** and **paste** the whole graphic or part of it.

✓ **Zoom** in on a part of the graphic for more detailed editing.

3. Some of the editing tools you can use in Paint are:

✓ **Pencil**, **Brush** and **Airbrush.**

✓ **Text box.**

✓ **Eraser.**

✓ The **colour palette**, where you can pick a standard colour, define custom colours or pick a colour from one already used in the graphic.

✓ **Fill**, which you can use to fill an area of the screen with colour.

✓ Tools for drawing various **shapes**: lines, curved lines, circles and ellipses, squares and rectangles, polygons, and rounded rectangles.

✓ **Selection tools.**

✓ **Flip/Rotate** and **Stretch/Skew.**

4. You can copy the whole screen or the active window using **Print Screen**. These can be pasted into Paint and edited, or pasted into other application software, such as Word. This can be useful when you write help sheets and other documentation.

5. **Video editing** software, such as Microsoft Windows Movie Maker, is used to produce a movie. A **movie** is a video file that can be played on media players, in a web browser, or on TV, etc.

6. A **project** is the construction of a movie using, for example, audio and video clips, transitions, effects and titles. A project is built up by placing video clips and other resources on a **timeline** or **storyboard.** When a project is complete, it is saved as a movie. While the project is being developed, it is saved as a project.

7. You can **import** into a project video clips taken on video cameras, webcams, digital cameras or smart phones.

8. You can use video editing software to:

✓ **Import** video, pictures and audio files.

✓ **Edit** the video and sound.

✓ Insert **titles.**

✓ Insert **transitions** between one video clip and the next.

✓ Insert **effects.**

✓ **Split** a video clip into two clips.

✓ **Combine** two video clips into one.

End of Chapter 7 Checklist

✓ **Trim** a video clip, that is, hide parts of it you do not want to use.

✓ Change the position of a video clip in the storyboard or timeline.

✓ Delete a video clip.

✓ Insert **titles** at the beginning and at the end of a movie, and before, during and after video clips.

✓ Insert **credits** at the end of a movie.

✓ Insert **transitions** that control the way that the video clip being played merges into the next clip to be played.

✓ Insert **effects** that control the way that the video clip being played is seen. For example, fade in.

✓ **Save** the project as a movie.

9. **Audio editing software**, such as Goldwave and Audacity, is used to record speech, sound or live music and to edit it.

10. An **audio file** can be played on media players, in a web browser, or on a stereo, etc. or imported into audio or video editing software.

11. A **project** is the construction of an audio file. While an audio file is being constructed, it is saved as a project file. When it is complete, it is saved as an audio file.

12. Using **audio editing software** you can:

✓ **Import** an audio file.

✓ **Record sound** from one or more **inputs**. For example, using a **microphone**, or a cassette tape being played would be recorded on **line in**.

✓ Adjust the **volume** at which the input is recorded and the output played.

✓ Record input in **mono** (one channel) or **stereo** (two channels) or more channels.

✓ Adjust the **quality** of the recorded sound. For example, by adjusting the **sampling rate**.

✓ Display a **visual illustration** of the recorded sound, for example, a waveform.

✓ **Play** one or more channels or sound clips.

✓ **Select** a sound clip and **copy, cut and paste** it from one position to another on the timeline or between channels. You can use this feature to repeat sections of music or sound.

✓ **Generate silence**, white noise and other tones.

✓ **Fade in or out** a clip. For example, you might want to fade out a crowd laughing or clapping.

✓ **Noise removal** to remove particular noises from a clip; for example, to remove the clicks on input from a cassette tape.

✓ **Save** an audio file.

Chapter 8: Presentation software

Presentation software

Presentation software can be helpful when you are preparing to give a presentation to an audience. Such presentations are usually a series of slides projected onto a large screen using a multimedia projector connected to a computer. What appears on the computer's monitor is projected onto the screen. The slides may have links to, for example, pictures, documents or websites, so that these can be easily accessed during the presentation. One example of presentation software is Impress which is a part of OpenOffice. The presentation software used below is Microsoft PowerPoint.

In this chapter, you will look at software that will enable you to prepare a multimedia presentation.

Preparing slides

When you open Microsoft PowerPoint, the default opening screen has a template for an introductory slide, and you enter the title of the presentation. Next you add the slides that make up your presentation.

Adding a new slide

To add a new slide to your presentation, on the **Home** tab of the Ribbon select **New Slide.** The new slide is added after the current slide. The default layout and design of the slides following the introductory slide is shown in Figure 8.1.

If you click in the appropriate box, you can add a title and some text. Text is automatically bulleted.

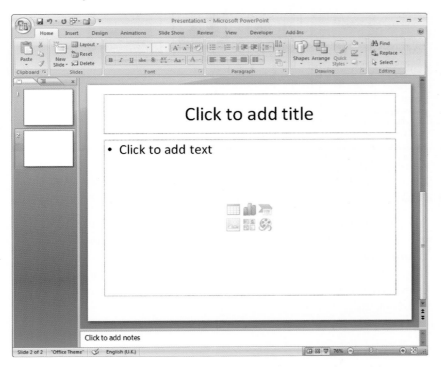

Figure 8.1 *The default for slides following the introductory slide in Microsoft PowerPoint*

Inserting images

Images, such as clip art and pictures can be inserted. To insert clip art, on the **Insert** tab, select **Clip Art.** A selection of clip art appears in the task pane on the right-hand side of the screen (see Figure 8.2). Click on the clip art you want to insert and it appears on the slide.

You can move, rotate and resize clip art. You select the clip art. You can move it by dragging and dropping. You can drag the rotation handle to turn the clip art. Dragging a resizing handle changes the size of the clip art. Dragging a handle on a corner changes the size but keeps the proportions (the **aspect ratio**) the same. Dragging a handle on a side stretches the clip art in the direction of movement.

Inserting a picture is a similar process. You are asked to use a dialog box to identify the picture file you want to insert. When you have done this, click on **OK.**

Figure 8.2 *Inserting clip art*

Animation

You can add animation to an image, which will play when it is first displayed. To do this, switch to the **Animations** tab and select **Custom Animation**. The **Custom Animation** task pane is displayed. Select **Add Effect**, then **Entrance** and you can choose from several animations, such as *Diamond*, *Fly In* and *Wheel*. Select each in turn and play them to see their effect. You can add several animations to one image which will be played in turn when the image is displayed.

Inserting charts

PowerPoint allows you to insert and modify charts. For example, in PowerPoint, on the **Insert** tab, select **Chart**. The **Insert Chart** dialog box appears, which you can use to change the type and settings of the graph to be generated.

To alter the data which is displayed in the chart you edit the data in Excel.

You can also insert charts by cutting and pasting from a spreadsheet.

Slide layout

PowerPoint has a range of slide layouts that you can use. These are available from the **Layout** drop-down menu in the **Home** tab. Select a slide layout by clicking on it. You can do this repeatedly until you find a suitable layout. Notice that some layouts already have bullets built into them so that when you type in text, bullets appear.

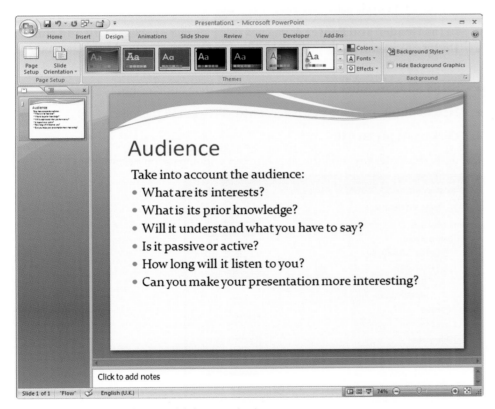

Figure 8.3 *A slide prepared using a slide layout and a theme*

Themes

PowerPoint also has a range of slide themes that you can use. In the **Design** tab, hover over a theme to preview its effect and then click on the one you wish to choose.

You can change the colours used in the theme you have chosen by selecting **Colors** from the **Design** tab and choosing a colour scheme.

Did you know?
You can use animation schemes to control how the title and lines of text are added when a slide is displayed. You have already seen how to do this for images.

Master slides

You can create your own layout and design, and use other features, such as a footer that includes the date, footer text and automatic page numbering, by editing the master slide. Whatever is shown on the master slide is visible on every slide in the presentation and cannot be changed when editing them.

The master slide is not normally visible. To display the master slide, on the **View** tab, select **Slide Master**. This can then be edited as you would edit any other slide. You can do the following:

- Set up the styles to be applied to the title and text.

- Insert an image that will appear on every slide. For example, the logo of your company.

- Insert the date, automatic slide numbering and a footer on every slide.

To insert the date, automatic slide numbering and a footer on every slide:

- On the **Insert** tab, select **Header and Footer**.

- In the **Header and Footer** dialog box (see Figure 8.4), select **Date and time**, **Update automatically** or **Fixed** and select from the available formats in the drop-down menu.

- Select **Slide number** to activate automatic slide numbering.

- Select **Footer** and type in whatever text you want in the footer.

- Click on **Apply to All**.

The date, the footer text and the slide number will appear on every slide.

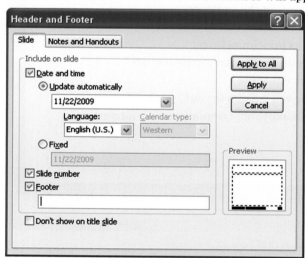

Figure 8.4 *The Header and Footer dialog box*

Saving

Your presentation can be saved in the usual manner: click on the **Save** button. You should save your work on disk before showing the whole presentation or printing it.

The Save button in PowerPoint: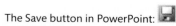

Showing a presentation

To show the whole presentation, click on the **View** tab and select **Slide Show**. When you do this the slide show is shown on the whole monitor screen as it will appear when projected. Left-click on the mouse to move through the presentation; to end the show, right-click and select **End Show**.

The Slide Show button – click this to show your presentation:

Slide transitions

A slide transition takes place as you move from one slide to another as you show a presentation. The default transition is to quickly move from one slide to the next; however, there are many transitions available. In the **Animations** tab the range of transitions available is displayed. For example, you can choose from *blinds horizontal, box out, checkerboard down, comb horizontal* and many more. You can vary the speed of the transition and add a sound (for example, a drum roll) which plays during the transition.

To use the same transition between all the slides in the presentation, click on **Apply To All**. If you want a different transition for different slides, highlight a slide or group of slides in the slide pane on the left-hand side of the screen and select a transition. This will be applied only to the slide or group of slides.

Did you know?
Animated images and text with sound can be used effectively to attract your audience's attention. However, if you use animation and slide transitions without restraint this can lead to a very messy and fragmented presentation.

Printing slides

To print your presentation, click the **Office Button** and select **Print** from the **Print** menu. The **Print** dialog box appears, and if you click on **OK** the default settings will print all your slides one to a page. If you want to give your audience copies of your slides, you can print several on one page. You can print six slides on a page by selecting the following:

The Office button:

- Print what: handouts
- Slides per page: 6

Exercise 8.1

1   Prepare a presentation about yourself:

   a) Choose a slide layout, design template, colour scheme and animation scheme.

   b) The first slide should introduce you to your audience.

   c) Next, include one slide on each of the following:
   - ✓ Your likes and dislikes
   - ✓ Your family
   - ✓ Your home
   - ✓ Your school
   - ✓ Your ambitions.

   d) Save your work.

   e) Print your work showing six slides on one page.

   f) Show your presentation.

2   You need a loan from your bank manager to buy a local business. Prepare a presentation to be given to the bank manager about the business.

   a) Choose a slide layout, theme, colour scheme and animation scheme.

   b) The first slide should describe the business.

   c) Next, include slides on each of the following:
   - ✓ The opening hours
   - ✓ How to find the business
   - ✓ The products sold
   - ✓ The staff
   - ✓ The monthly sales figures for the previous year displayed as a column graph.

   d) Put the date, your name and the slide number on every slide.

   e) Use slide transitions to stimulate your audience.

   f) Save your work.

   g) Print your work showing six slides on one page.

   h) Show your presentation.

Notes pages

When your presentation is shown to an audience by projecting it onto a large screen, if the font size is too small your audience will not be able to read it. As a result, when you enter text on a slide this is usually in a much larger font size than you would use in word processing software. Consequently, you cannot get much detail on one slide. However, you may want to write detailed notes that underpin the bullet points made on a slide. This can be done using the **Notes Page** attached to each slide.

To use the notes pages, in the **View** tab select **Notes Page** (see Figure 8.5). Click to add text, and you can type in notes for the slide as you would type text into word processing software.

To return to the normal view showing only one slide, in the **View** tab select **Normal**.

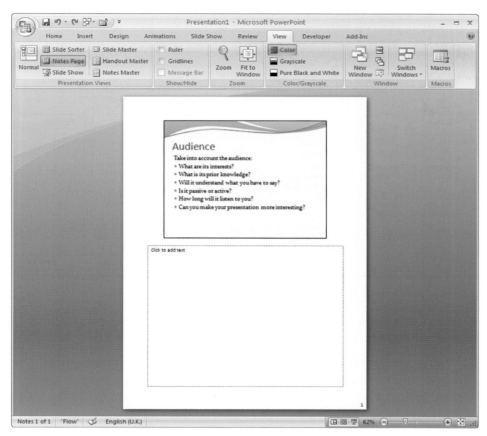

Figure 8.5 *A notes page*

Printing notes pages

To print your presentation and notes, click on the **Office Button** and select **Print** from the **Print** menu. The **Print** dialog box appears. If you want to print a copy of each slide with its associated notes on the same page, set **Print what** to **Notes Pages**, and click on **OK**.

Links

During a presentation you may want to refer to materials that are not a part of your presentation. For example, you might want to refer to a website or a document you have prepared in word processing software or a spreadsheet.

To insert a link to a website, in the **Insert** tab select **Hyperlink**, and the **Insert Hyperlink** dialog box appears (see Figure 8.6). In the dialog box, do the following:

- Set **Link to** to **Existing File or Web Page**.

- Set **Text to display** to 'Huddersfield University'.

- Set **Address** to 'http://www.hud.ac.uk'.

- Click on **OK**.

The Hyperlink button in PowerPoint:

A hyperlink is inserted into your PowerPoint slide. If you show your presentation on a computer that is connected to the Internet, you can click on this link and the display will change to the Huddersfield University web page. To return to your presentation, close the web browser.

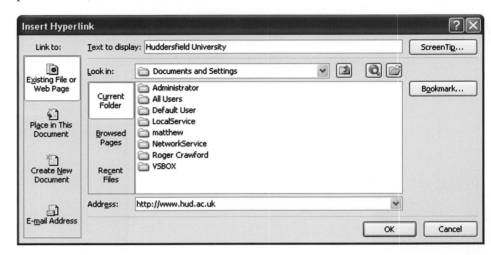

Figure 8.6 *The Insert Hyperlink dialog box*

To insert a link to a word processed document, the technique is the same but you select a file instead of typing in a URL.

If you show your presentation, you can click on this link and the display will change to the word processed document. To return to your presentation, close the word processing software. Using this method you can also link to spreadsheets and other files during a presentation.

Creating an information kiosk

You can also insert links to other slides in the same presentation. You can use this feature to create, for example, an information kiosk. This has a menu on the first slide; for example, a list of dishes available at a restaurant. Each item in the menu will have a link to another slide which has more information about the dish; for example, an illustration of the dish and a recipe for it. This slide will also have a link back to the menu slide.

Exercise 8.2

1 Prepare a presentation about search engines.

   a) Choose a slide layout, theme, colour scheme and animation scheme.

   b) The first slide should introduce the topic to your audience.

   c) Next, slides should prompt you to explain:
   - Why you would want to use a search engine.
   - What search engines do.
   - How you use a search engine.

   d) In order that you can demonstrate the why, what and how of search engines, include one slide that links to each of the following search engines:
   - Google
   - Yahoo!
   - Bing.

   e) The final slide should have a summary and conclusion.

   f) Put the date, your name and the slide number on every slide.

   g) Save your work.

   h) Print your work showing six slides on one page.

   i) Show your presentation.

2. Prepare a presentation about tourism in the Yorkshire Dales, UK.

   a) Choose a slide layout, theme, colour scheme and animation scheme.

   b) The first slide should describe the topic.

   c) Next, include slides on each of the following:
   - Where the Yorkshire Dales region is located.
   - Why tourists go on holiday to the Yorkshire Dales.
   - Where you could stay if you went on holiday to the Yorkshire Dales, including the accommodation available in self-catering cottages, hotels and campsites.
   - The cost of accommodation and how you could book.

   d) Put the date, your name and the slide number on every slide.

   e) The final slide should have a summary and conclusion.

   f) Save your work.

   g) Print your work showing six slides on one page.

   h) Show your presentation.

3. Create an information kiosk for a sports centre.

   a) The first slide should have a list of five different activities that are available.

   b) There should be a slide for each activity. This slide should have on it:
   - The name of the activity.
   - Who the activity is suitable for.
   - Information about what times the activity is available.
   - The cost of taking part.
   - A link back to the menu slide.

1. **Presentations** consist of a series of slides projected onto a large screen using a multimedia projector connected to a computer. What appears on the computer's monitor is projected onto the screen. The slides may have links to pictures, documents, websites and other slides in the presentation so that these can be easily accessed during the presentation. An example is when a teacher uses Microsoft PowerPoint when teaching a class.

2. Using PowerPoint you can:

   ✓ Design a presentation with slides and notes.

   ✓ Insert text, images and charts on a slide.

   ✓ Select from a range of different slide layouts, themes, colour schemes and slide animations.

   ✓ Create a **master slide** which includes the date and automatic slide numbering.

   ✓ Save your presentation.

   ✓ Print your presentation in a variety of ways; for example, one slide to a page, six slides to a page for handouts, and one slide with notes for presenters.

   ✓ Insert links to other resources you want to use during your presentation; for example, websites or word processed documents.

   ✓ Set up slide **transitions** that take place as you move from one slide to the next when you show the presentation.

   ✓ Show the presentation using a **multimedia projector** connected to a computer.

   ✓ Prepare an **information kiosk** that will be operated independently by someone seeking information.

Chapter 9: Communications, networks and the Internet

Communications

Countries, companies, organisations and individuals need fast communications and up-to-date information to improve competitiveness and for entertainment. They can achieve this using local, national and international computer network.

Networks

A network is a group of two or more computers linked together so that they can share resources (hardware, software and data) and can communicate with one another. A standalone computer is a computer not connected to a network.

Here are some types of computer network:

- Local area network (LAN)
- Wide area network (WAN)
- The Internet
- Intranet
- Extranet
- VPN (Virtual Private Network).

Local area networks (LANs)

A **LAN** consists of a collection of computers that can share peripherals, share information and communicate with each other over a network. These are likely to be in the same room, building, department, school or workplace. Each computer that forms part of the network can function both as an independent personal computer running its own software and as a workstation on the network accessing information from the network server. The **server** is a powerful computer that runs the network operating system and allows resources to be shared over the network by other devices connected to it, including other computers (called **clients**). The devices shared by a LAN may include printers, hard drives, disk drives, CD-ROM drives, modems and fax machines.

Advantages and disadvantages of LANs

A LAN's ability to share information and communicate with the devices and computers on the network has many advantages for its users:

- Software and data files can be shared by many users.
- Users can work together on a single shared document.
- Users can communicate; for example, using instant messaging or email.
- Users can stream media, so that they can view video and play audio on any computer or other device attached to the network.

- Users can access the network from any computer or other device that can be attached to the network. This might be via the LAN or the Internet.

- It is usually cheaper to buy one copy of a software application and pay the licence fee for several computers, than to buy individual licences for each computer.

- Users can share hardware devices. For example, an expensive, very good quality, high speed, A3 printer could be shared by network users at a lower cost per user than if each user had to be provided with a local printer that would be likely to be cheap, poor quality, slow and print on A4 paper.

- Users can share an Internet connection. A faster, higher bandwidth broadband Internet connection could be purchased for a LAN, and this could allow every user to be connected at the same time. If each user was connected individually, then the Internet connections would be more expensive and slower.

- Users' access rights can be controlled centrally. For example, a user can be given a username and password that will work on any connected computer. When the user logs on to the network, they may see their own customised screen and be given access to some resources but blocked from accessing other files. For example, teachers might be given access to records of pupils' progress in school. Pupils might be allowed to see only their own record of progress and blocked from seeing others.

- Computers attached to the network can be maintained either centrally or from any network station. For example, if some software has become corrupted on a network station, the network technician can log on at any other network station, and remove and reinstall the software. Similarly, users' passwords can be reset and the printer queue can be maintained.

There are disadvantages too:

- The initial set-up costs are higher than for the same number of individual computers because a server and network cabling have to be installed. However, this has to be set against the need to buy printers and scanners, etc, for the individual computers whereas fewer would be needed for a LAN.

- There is an increased risk of data corruption. Since many users will be using the system, there is a greater chance of data being corrupted or tampered with.

- There is a greater risk from viruses, because they are easily spread between the computers that are part of the LAN. If the server breaks down then the entire network will not function.

Types of LAN

LANs can be divided into two categories based on how the computers communicate with one another:

- client/server networks

- peer-to-peer networks.

On a **client/server** network, one or more computers are designated as the servers. Client computers (or network stations) are those computers available for you to use (most of the computers attached to the network). Clients communicate with each other and externally through the server. The **server** will have a faster processor, more RAM and a lot more backing storage space that the client computers. A large LAN may have several servers to perform different tasks. For instance, a **file server** may look after the organisation of the files on the network, while a **print server** coordinates printing on the network. Each server will also have software that manages the services it provides: email and Internet access, shared peripherals (such as hard disks) and the security of the system (for example, automatic backups and virus protection). Any computer that gives a user access to any type of network, including a connection to a mainframe computer, can be called a **terminal.**

A peer-to-peer network allows every computer to communicate directly with every other computer in the network. A user can access data from any computer on the network. Peer-to-peer LANs are limited to about ten machines, after which the performance drops and the system becomes cumbersome. They are used mainly in small businesses and departments.

Cabled LAN

In a cabled LAN, all the computers and other peripheral devices on the network are attached to cables that are used to transmit data between them. A computer must be connected to a cabled LAN using a network interface card (NIC). The network cable is plugged into the NIC.

Wireless LAN (WLAN)

A wireless LAN (WLAN) differs from a cabled LAN in that computers can use a wireless link to connect to the network instead of being attached using a cable. The wireless connection is made possible by three sets of components: **wireless access points;** wireless **network interface cards (NICs)** and **routers.**

A **wireless access point** contains a radio receiver, encryption and communications software so that it can broadcast and receive wireless communications. It translates computer signals into wireless signals (and back), so that it can broadcast to and receive signals from wireless network interface cards (NICs) on the network. NICs equipped for wireless communications have a fixed or detachable radio antenna instead of the usual coaxial cable. **Routers** enable several computers to communicate through a wireless access point at the same time.

A WLAN can be used where it may be difficult or impractical to use a cabled LAN (for example, in homes, large offices, warehouses and lecture halls). A device can be as far as 100 metres from an access point and it may still be able to access the Internet. In a building with many rooms or large halls, several access points may be needed. A user may take a laptop and walk from one room to the next or from one end of a building to the other and still have access. This is because the laptop will lock on to the strongest signal from an access point and will transfer its link to another access point if the signal there is stronger. Alternatively, the range of a wireless network can be extended using a **booster** which is a device that applifies a wireless signal so that it can be detected at greater distances from the wireless access point.

A WLAN has the same features that are available in a wired LAN. In addition, access to it can be more flexible. Users can be in any location in a building or outside, and still have access to Internet services. Wireless access points are now installed in public places, so that, for example, someone waiting for a train can connect to the Internet using a laptop. However, WLANs have relatively slow transmission speed, and other users or devices could interfere with the operation of the network. Illegal access is also a major concern, since anyone with a compatible NIC can access the network.

Bluetooth

Bluetooth is a form of wireless communication designed to enable PDAs, mobile phones, computers and similar devices to share information and to synchronise data. Bluetooth requires a transceiver chip in each device. The data transfer rate is 720 Kbps with a 10 metre range.

Bluetooth has a much slower data transfer rate than WiFi and a much shorter range, and is designed for communication between devices that are next to each other. For example, a mobile phone could communicate with a separate GPS antenna using Bluetooth, enabling it to run satellite navigation software for guiding cars and other vehicles to their destination.

Wide area networks (WANs)

A WAN can connect networks across a large geographical area, such as a city or a country or even internationally. Information can be transmitted in many ways; for example, using high-speed telephone lines, fibre optic cables, microwave links and satellite links, or a combination of these. WANs are used mainly by universities, large companies and banks with branches in different countries, to share information and processing loads. Figure 9.1 shows LANs in different countries connected together to form a WAN, using telecommunications links.

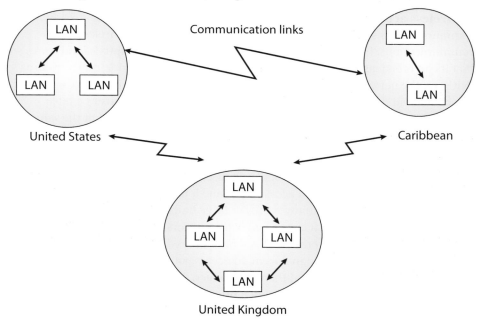

Figure 9.1 *A wide area network (WAN)*

Did you know?
Mbps is short for *megabits per second*. A megabit is just over a million bits.

Data transmission

Data communication can be broadly described as the transmission of data from one location to another for direct use or for further processing. A data communication system is made up of hardware, software and communications facilities. It may consist of computer terminals and other input/output devices linked together locally or it can consist of computers linked on a global scale. No matter what type of data communication system it is, data transmission channels are needed to carry the data from one location to another.

Data transmission channels carry the data from one location to another and can be classified according to bandwidth. The **bandwidth** determines the volume of data that can be transmitted in a given time. The wider (higher) the bandwidth, the more data it can transmit. The terms narrowband and broadband are used to describe the capacity of transmission channels, but these terms are not exact.

Narrowband is used to refer to data transmission over a telephone line using an analogue modem that can transmit data at speeds up to 56 Kbps (or 56 Kbaud). To access the Internet, narrowband users dial up a remote computer that provides Internet access.

A standard telephone line transmits analogue signals, whereas signals emitted from a computer are in digital form. A **modem** (short for 'modulator/demodulator') is a device used to convert the digital signals emitted by the computer into analogue signals that can be transmitted over a telephone line. When the signals get to the other end of the line, another modem converts the analogue signals back into digital signals for the other computer at that end of the line to process. The signal transmitted can be voice, pictures, video, audio or text. Figure 9.2 shows how **external** modems are used in data transmission over telephone lines. An **internal** modem performs the same function but is built into a PC when you buy it.

> **Did you know?**
> Transmission speed is measured in bits per second (bps) or baud. 1 **baud** is a speed of 1 bps.

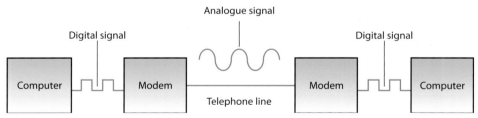

Figure 9.2 *Transmission of signals over a telephone line*

Broadband refers to data transmission using ADSL (Asymmetric Digital Subscriber Line) and cable. **ADSL** is a means of transmitting digital signals using telephone lines and can be many times faster than narrowband. Coaxial cables, fibre optic cables, microwave links and communication satellites are commonly used to provide broadband. Microwave signals are very high-frequency radio signals that can be transmitted through space. A communications satellite accepts signals beamed to it from a point on Earth and then reflects the signals to another point. Communication satellites can transmit data that includes text, voice, pictures and video.

Exercise 9.1

1. One of the following statements is not an advantage of using a LAN:

A	Data can be shared by many users
B	Users can communicate using email
C	Software licensing is likely to be less expensive
D	Viruses can be sent to many users

Put a cross in one box to show which statement is not an advantage of using a LAN.

☐ A

☐ B

☐ C

☐ D

2. a) Explain what is meant by a LAN.

   b) Explain what is meant by a WAN.

3. a) Describe a LAN you are familiar with.

   b) Draw a map of the LAN showing all the computers connected to it and show how they are connected.

   c) Discuss the advantages and disadvantages of LANs.

4. Wireless LANs are now used in many homes and offices.

   a) Name three essential components of a wireless LAN.

   b) Explain why you might choose to install a wireless LAN instead of a cabled LAN.

5. a) Explain what is meant by *bandwidth*.

   b) Discuss the advantages and disadvantages to a home user of replacing dial-up Internet access with broadband.

The Internet

What is the Internet?

The Internet is an international network of networks that connects computers worldwide. It connects universities, research facilities, governmental organisations, businesses, non-profit-making organisations and individuals, allowing them to access, share and exchange information.

Who owns the Internet?

No one owns the entire Internet. The Internet consists of many linked but independently maintained and administered networks. Each network on the Internet is responsible for formulating its own policies, procedures and rules.

Connecting to the Internet

To access the Internet you need to subscribe to an **Internet Service Provider (ISP).** This is a company that is directly connected to the Internet and gives you access to it, usually for a fee.

The most common ways for home users to connect to the Internet are as follows:

- **Dial up** is when your computer dials a phone number to connect you to your ISP using a telephone line. This is a legacy method used by individual home users to access the Internet. Dial up connections are very slow but inexpensive if you do not access the Internet very often.

- **Broadband** is usually available over telephone land lines or cable. In many countries, TV cable companies install a single cable to provide cable TV, telephone and Internet services to customers. Broadband is also available using a mobile telephone 3G network.

Hardware requirements are a personal computer and a modem or a similar device. You also need software to connect to and access information or other services on the Internet. Most users would have a web browser, email and other software that allows them to use the services and facilities available on the Web.

Did you know?
A computer attached to a network and making use of the network as required by the user, is said to be **online**. In contrast, a computer that is normally attached to a network but is being used as a standalone computer is said to be **offline**.

Transmission Control Protocol/Internet Protocol (TCP/IP)

TCP/IP is a set of protocols used to transfer data from one computer to another over the Internet. A **protocol** is a set of rules that defines how computers interact or communicate with each other. TCP/IP is a universal standard that enables hardware and operating systems software from different computers to communicate. Most modern operating systems implement the TCP/IP standard.

World Wide Web

The **World Wide Web** (or the Web) is a multimedia service that runs on the Internet. It was originally developed to help physicists at CERN in Geneva, Switzerland to exchange data and research materials quickly with other scientists. Many people believe the Internet and the Web to be one and the same, but this is not so.

The Web consists of **hypertext** and **hypermedia** documents. A **hypertext** document is a document that contains a **hyperlink** to another document located on the same computer or on another computer in any part of the world. Hypertext allows you to move easily from one document to the next. For example, if you have used the help files in any of Microsoft Office's application programs, you have already encountered hypertext. You may have asked for help with a certain topic and been shown an explanation, in which you saw certain words highlighted in blue. If you clicked on such a word, you would get an additional help screen. The word is associated with a hyperlink to somewhere else either in the same file or in a different file on the computer or on a web server.

Hypermedia is a general name for documents that contain links to text, graphics, sound or video files. A computer that stores and makes available hypertext and hypermedia documents is called a web **server,** and a computer that requests such a document is called a **client.** All the information that can be accessed using the

Internet is often referred to as **Cyberspace,** which is made up of all the websites and all the files accessible over the Internet.

Browsers

A web browser (see Figure 9.3) is software that lets you access the information available on the Web. Popular browsers include Microsoft Internet Explorer and Mozilla Firefox. All web browsers operate in a very similar manner and have similar features.

Figure 9.3 *A web page accessed using the Microsoft Internet Explorer browser*

Internet addresses

Each computer on the Internet has a unique address that identifies it. This unique address is a number called the **IP address (Internet Protocol address)**, which is a 32-bit address consisting of four sets of up to three digits each, separated by full stops, e.g. 196.161.232.4. The IP address could be **static** (it remains the same every time you connect to the Internet) or it could be **dynamic** (it is a temporary address that changes each time you connect to the Internet). To connect to a computer on the Internet, your computer needs to know its IP address.

Web addresses or URLs

The IP addresses used by software are difficult for humans to remember so URLs (Uniform Resource Locators) or web addresses are used instead. Every web address is unique and is constructed like this:

> TypeOfResource://HostComputer.Domain/Directory/SubDirectory/Filename.Extension

The different components are as follows:

- *TypeOfResource* identifies the type of resource. There are several different types; for example, **http://** identifies a web page and **mailto://** identifies an email address.

- *HostComputer* is the name of the host computer or web server. This must be unique within the domain.

- *Domain* identifies the type of organisation that owns the website. There are several different types of domain, for example:

  - **.com** identifies an international commercial organisation.
  - **.co.uk** identifies a UK-based commercial organisation.
  - **.ac.uk** identifies a UK-based university or other academic institution.
  - **.org.uk** identifies a UK-based non-commercial organisation.

- *Directory* is the directory or folder on the web server. The directory's name must be unique at its level of the directory structure on the server. It maybe followed by one or more subdirectories. Again, these must be unique at their own level.

- *Filename* is the name of the file.

- *Extension* identifies the type of file. There are several different types, for example:

  - **.htm** or **.html** identifies a file that contains HTML (Hypertext Markup Language).
  - **.doc** identifies a file that contains a document, that is, a word processing file with format information.
  - **.txt** identifies a file that contains only text, that is, a word-processing file without format information.

The filename and extension, taken together, must be unique within the directory or subdirectory containing the file.

For example, the web address

http://www.hud.ac.uk/schools/education/welcome.htm

is interpreted like this:

http://	The type of resource the address refers to is a web page
www.hud.ac.uk	The web server is called *www.hud* and it is run by a UK-based university or other academic institution; in fact, it is the University of Huddersfield web server
/schools/education/	On the web server, the file that will be displayed is in the directory called */schools* in a subdirectory called */education*
welcome.htm	The file is called welcome and contains HTML. The extensions **.htm** and **.html** are both recognised as files containing HTML.

What can you do on the Internet and the Web?

The following are some of the facilities and services that you can access on the Web using a browser:

- View hundreds of millions of web pages, all over the world.
- Use a search engine such as Google to find the pages you want.
- Send and receive email.
- Use online shopping and e-commerce – you can buy goods, pay for them online and have them delivered to your door.
- Do your banking.
- Access customer support – many commercial organisations support the sale and maintenance of their products by putting information about their features and how to maintain them on the Web. Company websites often have help and **FAQs** which support customers using their products.
- Software distribution – for example, you can download free software or purchase it online, and download printer drivers.
- Access and discuss information – mailing lists, bulletin boards and newsgroups provide you with the information you need.
- Join discussion groups and chat online.
- Participate in conferences – you can even use a sound card, speakers and a microphone to talk to other users.
- Browse web rings – these connect websites with similar themes or topics.
- Receive web broadcasting – you can hear radio programmes as they are broadcast and watch TV during transmission. You do not have to wait until all the information is downloaded.
- Advertise your business by setting up your own website or by purchasing adverts on other websites.
- Build your own website and upload it to the Web.
- Upload and download digital media, such as music, images and video, and publish these on the Web so that they can be shared with friends and family.
- Publish an online personal diary with narrative, pictures and hyperlinks. These online diaries are called web logs (or **blogs**).
- Describe and define particular topics in collaboration with other web users, using a **wiki.** An online encyclopedia could be a wiki, and you would find articles about history, science and many other topics that have been written by many different contributors.
- Use social networking sites to communicate with a closed circle of friends who can see the information about yourself that you upload.

Surfing the Web

Surfing means to search for information following whatever route you choose. It is the act of browsing through information on web servers throughout the world. You can do this by clicking on a hyperlink in your browser, entering the web address of a website, or by using one of the many search engines. Some of the best-known search engines are Google, Yahoo! and Bing.

Did you know?
Web 2.0 describes a trend in web design and development that is a second generation of web-based communities and hosted services. These include blogs, wikis, social bookmarking and social networking sites that aim to facilitate creativity, collaboration, and sharing between web users.

Finding information using a directory service

Some search engines, for example Yahoo!, provide users with a directory containing a list of the broad categories of information and services available, such as Arts and Humanities, Education, Recreation and Sports, and many more (see Figure 9.4). When you select a category, a list of subcategories is displayed, and selecting a subcategory can lead to further subcategories. You keep selecting deeper and deeper until you find the website you want. This makes it easier to find information. Figure 9.5 shows the results when the category 'Education' is selected, and Figure 9.6 displays the sites available when the topic 'Further and Adult Education' is selected.

Figure 9.4 *Yahoo! Directory's home page, showing a list of broad categories*

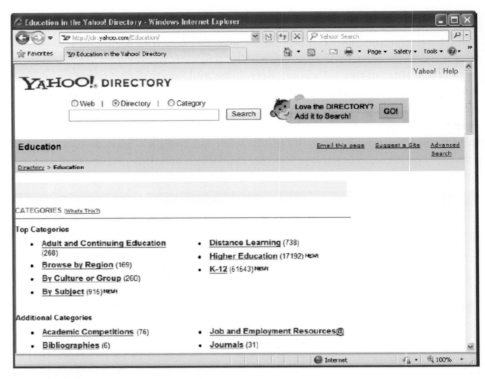

Figure 9.5 *Yahoo!'s listing of subcategories of 'Education'*

Figure 9.6 *The list of sites in Yahoo!'s subcategory for 'Further and Adult Education'*

Finding information using a web address

If you know the web address or URL of the website you want to visit, such as **http://www.edexcel.com,** you can type this into the **Address** field, which is located at the top of the browser window (just below the menu bar, if there is one). You type in the web address, press **Enter,** and the website is displayed (see Figure 9.7).

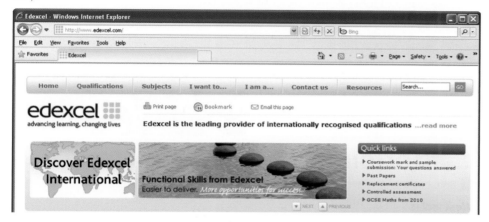

Figure 9.7 *Finding a web page having a known address*

Finding information using a search engine

The easiest way to access a search engine is by clicking the **Search** button on your browser toolbar. What happens after that will depend on which search engine is set as the default one for your browser to use. There are many search engines available, and you can use as many as you like until you find a website that you are interested in.

You can also go to search engines directly using their web addresses; for example:

- www.google.co.uk
- www.yahoo.co.uk
- www.bing.com
- www.altavista.com
- www.lycos.com
- www.excite.co.uk

Each search engine has its own database of web documents. Items are continually added to the database by a program called a **spider,** which searches the Web looking for new pages. Most search engines will allow you to submit the web address of your own website to make sure the spider visits it. Some search engines charge for this, while others provide this service free. In addition to giving access to information in its database, a search engine site may also provide services such as free email, chat rooms, news and facilities for online shopping.

Searching the Web using keywords

You can also find information by typing into a search engine one or more **keywords** or key phrases that indicate the topic you would like to search for. For example:

- Type one or more keywords or a phrase into the search box (e.g. 'West Indies cricket').

- Click on the 'Search' or 'Go' button.

- A list of sites that are related to the **search terms** will be displayed. Figure 9.8 shows one of the websites found by Excite when the words 'West Indies cricket' were typed in and the 'Search' button was clicked.

Figure 9.8 *A web page found by searching for 'West Indies cricket'*

Advanced search syntax

All search engines give you the option of an advanced syntax to narrow down searches, so that you can find specific information more quickly. The syntax used may differ between search engines, but here is some of the advanced search syntax used by Yahoo!

Required and specific search words

- Placing a plus sign (' + ') in front of a word tells Yahoo! that the word *must be* included in all search results.

- Conversely, placing a minus sign ('−') in front of a word specifies that the word *must not be* included in any of the search results.

Phrase matching

- Placing double quotes ("...") around a string of words tells Yahoo! that all search results must contain the string in that exact sequence.

Finding information using a web bot

Bot is short for *robot*, and a **web bot** is software that can run automatically on the Web once it has been set up. Web bots can be useful for searching the Web and alerting you if there is news you are interested in, books you may want to buy, or if information you gathered earlier has been updated. Some examples of web bots are:

- Copernic and WebFerret are search bots that will search many search engines from a single search condition. The results are ranked in order of relevance to the search condition.

- Various sniping tools can automatically place bids on auction sites in the last few seconds of the auction, so that you don't forget to bid for an item you want, and avoid price increases due to bidding against other buyers.

- Web Whacker and other similar tools will download a copy of an entire website and save it on a server or local hard disk so that it can be used when there is no web connection available or instead of connecting to the Web. When you do connect to the Web, your copy will be automatically updated. These tools can increase the speed at which you can view web pages and reduce the frequency of web access. Schools can significantly increase the speed at which web pages can be viewed using this software.

Task
Auction sniping
What are the advantages and disadvantages of auction sniping tools?

Intranets

An **intranet** is a local version of the Internet within a company or organisation. It offers many of the same features as the global Internet, but in a localised environment such as a factory site or an office. Many companies make large volumes of information – such as notice boards, staff directories, training manuals, company reports, job adverts, and newsletters – available to their employees on an intranet. An intranet allows information about organisational procedures to be centralised, leading to more consistent operations and the distribution of the forms used for record keeping from a centralised repository.

Authorised users within a company can use the company's intranet to find information easily and quickly. An intranet uses the same browsers, TCP/IP and other software as used for the Internet. If a company has an intranet and allows limited, secure access to it by people working off site, for example at home, the intranet is referred to as an **extranet.**

VPNs (Virtual Private Network)

A **VPN** is private network that runs within public networks. Conceptually it is similar to an extranet but network traffic will be encrypted and Internet protocols such as TCP/IP might not be used. It can be thought of as a separate 'pipe' inside the Internet. Network traffic inside the pipe is inaccessible to those outside the pipe.

Electronic mail (email)

Email is one of the most popular and widely used services on the Internet today. It enables users to send electronic messages to an individual or group, and to receive messages from others. Messages can include text, pictures and hyperlinks. An email can have other files of any type attached to it and sent with it.

Email is usually much faster than mail delivered by the traditional postal system. An email can be sent to an email subscriber in any part of the world in a matter of seconds (although this can sometimes take much longer). Apart from the cost of equipment and the fixed fee that a subscriber has to pay to an ISP for Internet access, sending email is free. You can send as many emails as you like at no additional charge and at your own convenience, any time of the day or night. This does not cause any problems for the person receiving it, who does not have to be present to receive the email.

In order to send or receive email, each user must have an **email address,** which is unique to the user and consists of two parts separated by the '@' ('at') symbol. The first part is the user name, which can be a real name, a shortened form of a real name or some made-up name. The second part is the location of the account on the Internet. For users living in Trinidad and Tobago who have the Telecommunications Services of Trinidad and Tobago (TSTT) as their ISP, their email addresses could look like the following:

- vern30@tstt.net.tt
- bobonline@tstt.net.tt

Internet users can also use the **free email services** offered by websites such as Yahoo! and Hotmail. You simply fill out an online form to open an account and get an email address. Examples of these addresses are:

- nick@yahoo.com
- kamo@hotmail.com

An **email server** is needed to send and receive email messages. This is a computer on the Internet that receives incoming messages and delivers outgoing messages. It allocates a certain amount of storage for registered users to store their email. The area of storage allocated to you is your **mailbox.** You can retrieve your mail by supplying your username and password. This is necessary to protect your email from unauthorised access.

To access your email, you can use webmail or an email client.

- **Webmail** runs within an Internet browser. Using the browser, you log on to a website to retrieve your email. You can access your email from any computer with an Internet browser installed that is connected to the Web. However, webmail tends to run more slowly than an email client and have a more restricted range of features. Examples of webmail are: hotmail (www.hotmail.com) and gmail (mail.google.com).

- An email client is a program that runs on your computer and enables you to read and compose email messages and to send and access email, e.g. Microsoft Outlook. An email client tends to run more quickly than Webmail and it will have a wider range of customizable options. An Internet browser does not need to be installed. However, the client software may need to be purchased and installed, and it can be more complex to set up.

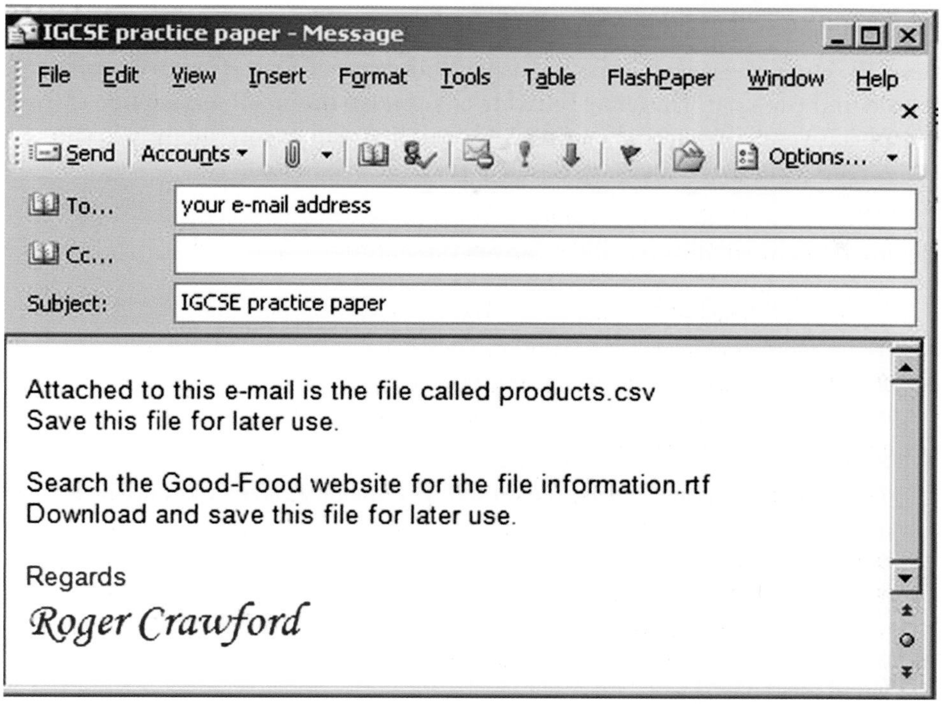

Figure 9.9 *An email message*

Sending an email message

In Microsoft Outlook, with the Inbox open on screen, click on the **New** button in the toolbar to open a new email message. Figure 9.9 shows the email screen for creating a new message. The format for other email software is similar.

To send an email:

● In the **To:** field, fill in the email address of the person you are sending it to.

● If you send a copy of the email to other people, enter their email addresses in the **Cc:** field.

● If you want to send a copy of the email to someone and want to hide this from others, enter their email address in the **Bcc:** field. This field may be hidden. To locate it, click on the **To:** field and it will be visible in the **Select Names** dialog box.

● In the **Subject:** field, enter a phrase that describes what your email is about.

● Type your message.

● You can also send **attachments** along with the original email. An attachment can be, for example: a word processed document, a spreadsheet file, a database file, a picture file, a sound file or a video file. When a file is attached, a new field showing the name and size of the file is displayed below the **Subject:** field. In Microsoft Outlook, to attach a file to an email, with the new email open, in the **Insert** tab, select **Attach File.** The **Insert File** dialog box appears. Locate the file and click on **Insert.**

● To send the email, click on the **Send** button in the toolbar and the email will be stored in the **outbox** ready to be sent. To send all your email, click on the **Send/Receive** button in the toolbar.

Receiving and replying to an email message

Open the email client and, if you are using Outlook, click on the **Send/Receive** button in the toolbar. The email software connects to the email server and downloads your email into the **inbox.** To read the email in your inbox, you can either read them in the preview section of the screen, or double-click on each email to open it.

Having read the email you could do any of these things:

- If the email has an attachment, open this and read it. In Outlook, double-click on the attachment.

- **Reply.** If you click on the **Reply** button, a new message opens. This is addressed to the person who sent you the original email.

- **Reply to All.** If you click on the **Reply to All** button, a new message opens. This is addressed to the person who sent you the original email and all email addresses in the Cc: field.

- **Forward.** If you click on the **Forward** button, a new message opens. You will have to fill in all the email addresses you want the message sent to.

- **Move** the email to a personal folder. To do this in Outlook, drag and drop the email message.

- **Delete.** Click on the **Delete** button in the toolbar to delete the email.

- If you reply to or forward an email, when you have finished writing your message, to send it, click on the **Send** button in the toolbar to store the email in the outbox ready to be sent. To send all your email, click on the **Send/ Receive** button in the toolbar.

Storing email messages

Outlook sets up folders to store email messages. You can see these folders in the **Navigation** pane. If this is not visible, in Outlook, in the **View** menu, select **Navigation Pane** and then **Normal.**

Here are some common folders:

- **Deleted Items.** When you delete an email, it is saved in the **Deleted Items** folder. If necessary, you can retrieve a deleted email from this folder. If you right-click on the folder and select **Empty 'Deleted Items' Folder,** all the emails in the folder are deleted.

- **Drafts.** If you save an email you are working on, it will be saved in this folder.

- **Inbox.** As emails are received, they are put in the inbox.

- **Junk Email.** Email can be filtered to remove spam and this is put in the **Junk Email** folder. You should check this occasionally to make sure that only junk email has been filtered out.

- **Outbox.** Email that is ready to send may be stored in the outbox. This email can be opened and re-edited if necessary – click on the **Outbox** folder and double-click on the email. To send email stored in the outbox, click on the **Send/Receive** button in the toolbar.

- **Personal.** It is likely that most of the email you receive will be deleted as soon as you have read it. If you need to save email, you can do this in the **Personal** folder. If you save a lot of email, you can organise this in sub-folders you can create. For example, you might have a sub-folder called *Shopping* where you put emails from online shops; or a sub-folder called *Finance* where you put emails from your bank or credit card issuer or other emails related to managing your personal finances; or a sub-folder called *Family* where you put emails from your family.

- **Quarantine.** A virus scanner may put in this folder emails that are found to have viruses.

- **Sent Items.** When email is sent, a copy could be placed in this folder.

Email messages are files and can also be saved on backing storage. You might find it convenient to store email messages received at school or work on a USB memory stick so that you can take them home. In Microsoft Outlook, select **File, Save As,** choose an appropriate location in the **Save As** dialog box and click on **OK.**

Contacts

Contacts are entries in an address book. In Microsoft Outlook, you can access your contacts by clicking on **To:, Cc:** or **Bcc:** in an open email message, or by clicking on the **Address Book** button in the toolbar. In the dialog box that appears, type the name of the contact you wish to access in the **Type Name** or **Select from List** field and the contact will appear automatically. Double-click on the contact to display the **Contact** dialog box (see Figure 9.10)

Address Book button in Microsoft Outlook

To set up a new contact for someone who sent you an email:

- Click on their email address in the **From:** field in the message, and select **Add to Outlook Contacts.** Alternatively, you could click on the **New** button in the Outlook toolbar and select **Contact.**

- Fill in the details you wish to record in the **Contact** dialog box (see Figure 9.10). The fields, such as **Full Name, Job title** and **Company** are pre-set. You can add notes and a photograph. The picture of Victoria Cave shown in Figure 9.10 would more usually be a picture of the contact. To change the picture, right-click on the picture and select **Change Picture.** A dialog box appears. Locate the new picture and click on **OK.**

To save the contact, click on the **Save and Close** button in the toolbar.

To delete a contact, open the contact and, in the **File** menu, select **Delete.**

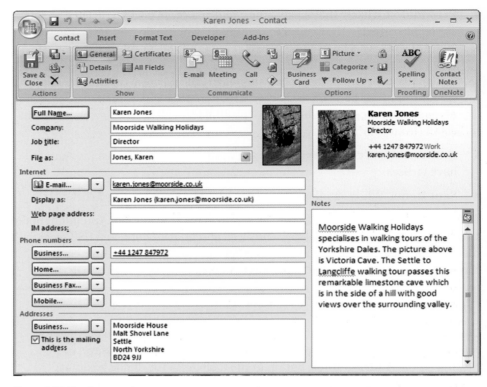

Figure 9.10 *The Contact tab*

A **distribution list** is a list of contacts that you wish to group together. You can send an email to everyone in a distribution list at the same time by selecting the list rather than each individual member. For example, an electrical store may set up a distribution list of customers and email the list with details of special offers. The store would address the email to the list not to each individual customer.

To set up a distribution list:

- Click on the **New** button in the Outlook toolbar and select **Distribution List.**

- In the **Distribution List** dialog box, click on **Select Members.**

- In the **Select Members** dialog box, enter the name of the contact in the **Type Name or Select from List** field. The contact will appear automatically.

- Select the contact, click the **Members** button and click on **OK.**

The contact is now a member of the distribution list. When you have selected the contacts you wish to be in the distribution list, click on **Save and Close.**

Fax

At its simplest, **fax** involves sending a document over the telephone lines from one fax machine to another. The telephone number of the receiving fax machine is entered on the sending machine to make the connection. Fax machines can scan and print documents. The sending fax machine scans the document and the receiving fax machine prints it.

However, this process can be more complex. The functions of a fax machine can be replicated by a computer connected to a scanner and printer. As a result, either or both of the sending or receiving fax machines can be replaced by a computer. In addition, the original document may not be scanned but created on a computer. The communication network is now likely to include the Internet as well the telephone network. Consequently, a fax can be sent from a computer to many fax machines. This enables, for example, the head office of a company to communicate more effectively with a large number of employees working remotely; however, it also enables spam to be sent to fax machines.

Online shopping

Online shopping is increasingly popular. You can order goods online and pay for them using a credit or debit card (see Figure 9.11). The goods will be delivered by post to the address you specify.

Online shopping can be very convenient. You can go shopping at any time of the day or night. You do not have to leave your home, travel to the shops and visit shop after shop until you find the goods you want, which can be unpleasant if the weather is bad. Online shopping is particularly helpful to those who have to stay at home because they are disabled or caring for someone else. A very wide range of goods is available online so that you can have a much wider selection. Local shops may only have a few different samples of a manufacturer's product range, but online the whole range will be available. You may find that specialist goods that are not on sale in your locality are available online as the potential market is much greater. In addition, you can get the goods you buy gift-wrapped and have them sent direct to a friend as a present.

Figure 9.11 *The ScrewFix online shopping site*

However, you cannot inspect the goods other than on screen. For example, you are not able to try on a jacket or judge the quality of its manufacture. If the goods are not satisfactory, you will have to post them back and claim a refund. It is often more difficult to get a refund from a distant website than from a local trader. You often have to pay by credit or debit card. This is impossible if you do not have one, and there is a risk of online fraud if someone steals your credit or debit card details and uses them to buy goods.

Online banking

Many people now have bank accounts that they can access using the Web instead of visiting the bank's branches. As a result, some banks have a much smaller number of branches, and others such as first direct have no branches.

Internet banking has similar advantages to online shopping. You can access your bank account at any time of the day or night and find out your balance, print statements, and set up direct debits in advance so that you do not have to remember to pay your bills – this is done automatically. You can send messages to your bank and receive their replies without having to visit a branch. Internet banking can have lower charges and pay you more interest on your money because the cost to the bank of providing the service is much less. One major disadvantage is that if others obtain your banking details they can operate your account and transfer money out of it, perhaps without being recognised.

Figure 9.12 *Online banking can be accessed from anywhere with an Internet connection*

Customer support

Many organisations now provide a range of customer support services over the Web. Many commercial organisations support the sale and maintenance of their products by putting information about their features and how to install and maintain them on the Web. This means that customers have much more convenient and faster access to a wider range of information and tools to support the installation, use and maintenance of a manufacturer's products. If such customer support was not available on the Web, obtaining it could be more time-consuming and more expensive, and there is a possibility that appropriate support would not be provided.

Computer hardware and software companies can provide information about their product range and specific technical details and support. For example, printer manufacturers can set up a website where you can download printer drivers, and software providers can provide help using their software. It is common for help installed with the software to refer to pages on the Web.

Software providers often supply free versions of their software that you can download over the Web. Sometimes the free version is a cut-down version of a full professional software package, or it may be useable for only a limited time (30 days is common). When you try out this software you may be tempted to buy it. While this is a sales strategy, it is also customer support. Sometimes the free version has been in use for a considerable time before the full version is purchased, and the user has become very familiar with how to operate the software. This makes learning to use the full version much easier.

Electronic discussion forums

Electronic discussion forums such as mailing lists, newsgroups, chats and bulletin boards are another very popular feature of the Internet.

Mailing lists

A **mailing list** is a group of people using email to communicate their views on common issues or interests. You **subscribe** to become part of the group. Not all groups are open to everyone: some might only allow professionals in a certain field. For example, a group discussing the genetic blueprint of humans may only want to include researchers in that field. When you become a member of a mailing list, you can send messages with your comments or views on some matter that is being discussed or to which you want an answer. A copy of your message is then sent to all subscribers on the mailing list. Some mailing lists only let subscribers receive messages but not send them. For example, there is a mailing list that sends a joke a day to its members, but the members cannot reply.

Newsgroups

A **newsgroup** or bulletin board enables a group of people with common interests to communicate with each other. There are thousands of newsgroups on almost every imaginable topic (see Figure 9.13). A subscriber to a newsgroup **posts** a message, which can vary from a few lines to whole articles; for example, a bulletin board for doctors may have substantial articles on the treatment of diseases. When other subscribers log on to the newsgroup, they can read the message and may or may not reply. A subscriber can look at a **thread** of the related messages that have been posted previously.

The main difference between newsgroups and mailing lists is the method of communication. Mailing lists use email to communicate with subscribers. If you want to send a message to the mailing list, you send it to its email address and the message is sent on to every subscriber's email address. Newsgroups post messages on the Internet for all the users to access. The messages are not sent out to subscribers; instead, users have to log on and read messages on the newsgroup.

Figure 9.13 *Newsgroups on Google*

Chat

Chatting on the Internet has become a favourite pastime for many users. A user can enter any one of the thousands of chat rooms that are present on the Web. A **chat room** is a group of people with common interests communicating with one another interactively, in real time. There are chat rooms for specific topics, but many chat rooms discuss a range of subjects. For example, a chat room for unemployed Internet users at home might discuss things like their children's education or possible opportunities for work.

Some of the different ways of chatting include the following:

- **Text-based chat –** This is the oldest and most common method of chatting. You enter a chat room and look at the comments posted about a topic. Everyone currently in the room is notified that a new person has entered the discussion. You are identified by a name, but many users prefer to use a **handle** (a name that they want to characterise their personality). You can see the comments made by other participants and can type out a reply on any of the comments to everyone who is connected at the time, or only to selected people in the group. You may wish to start a topic of your own. Users can enter and leave a chat room as they wish.

- **Internet Relay Chat (IRC)** – This is a real-time conference system that lets you talk with as many people as you like, grouped together on **channels** by topics, using text messages. Once you have accessed IRC, you can find out what topics are being discussed and how many users are involved. You can then search for a channel that suits your interest. IRC can be considered as a type of text-based chat where each chat room (channel) is dedicated to a specific topic, and where users are not allowed to discuss topics unrelated to the channel's purpose.

- **Instant messaging** – This enables you to chat privately with another person. Messages are sent instantly. Messages are usually in text and can be sent using a mix of email type systems and mobile phones.

- **Multimedia chat** – With multimedia software, you can use the microphone in a computer to talk to another user anywhere in the world over the Internet. If you each have a webcam connected to your computer, you will also be able to see each other.

Video conferencing

Video conferencing is essentially the same as multimedia chat but is likely to involve more people communicating at the same time. Video camera systems are often more sophisticated than a simple webcam and may have the facility to zoom out to see the whole group or to zoom in on an individual who is speaking. The video image is more likely to be displayed on a large screen or several monitors, so everyone involved can see it, rather than being displayed on a single monitor. Video conferencing technology tries to avoid problems with the speed of communication channels and bandwidth on the Internet by using private communication systems. These were originally analogue video and satellite links but increasingly they use compressed digital images transmitted over wide area networks or the Internet.

Web rings

A **web ring** is a way of interlinking a group of websites that have information on related topics or themes. The websites are linked so that you can visit each site one after the other, eventually (if you keep going) returning to the first website. Users can also elect to go backwards through the web ring or see a list of all the websites on the ring. A web ring is managed from one website that is able to omit websites that have dropped out or are no longer reachable. The advantage of a web ring is that if you are interested in the topic on one website you can quickly connect to another website on the same topic.

Web broadcasting

You can listen to radio programmes (see Figure 9.14) and watch television programmes and movies. These could be broadcast live or could be a recording. You can see and hear information as the programme is transmitted. You do not have to wait until all the information is downloaded before you can see and hear it. These new services are currently restricted by copyright problems, and low bandwidth and transmission speed. As these problems are overcome, there will be a wider choice of programmes.

Setting up your own website

You can advertise your business by setting up your own website. To do this you would create your own web pages and put them on the Web.

You can write web pages in **HTML (Hypertext Markup Language)**, or use software that generates HTML. HTML is a programming language that you can use to create web pages. It contains standard codes that are used to specify how a web page is structured and formatted. These codes determine the appearance of the web page when it is displayed by your browser. HTML also contains tags that are used to create hyperlinks to access related information on the Web.

Software is available that will help you write HTML by generating the structure of the code which you then fill in. You could use software that is specifically designed to help you write web pages in both HTML code and in a manner similar to using DTP software. Such software will also help you manage the structure of your website. Examples are Adobe Dreamweaver and Microsoft Expression Web (the replacement for Microsoft FrontPage).

Figure 9.14 *Broadcast radio from the BBC*

Many applications can produce output as a web page; for example, you can save Word files as web pages. Having written your website, you must upload it to a web server before it is generally accessible over the Web. More information on how to set up a website is given in the next chapter.

Web 2.0

Web 2.0 describes a trend in web design and development towards a second generation of web-based communities and services. These include blogs, wikis and social networking websites which aim to facilitate creativity, collaboration, and sharing between web users. They often have features in common but combine these in different ways.

For example, **Facebook (www.facebook.com)** states that it 'gives people the power to share and makes the world more open and connected'. It goes on to say: 'Millions of people use Facebook everyday [sic] to keep up with friends... and learn more about the people they meet.' Facebook allows members to set up a personal profile. Other members can be accepted as friends and will then have access to a member's personal profile. Members can upload text, images and videos to their personal profile and share links to other web pages from it. Similarly, **YouTube (www.youtube.com)** provides an online video streaming and sharing service that enables members to upload videos and allows anyone to view them. It also allows members to set up their own page with a personal profile, and there are community forums.

Upload and download digital media

Many sites allow digital media in the form of images or video or music to be uploaded and shared. For example, Facebook allows images and videos to be uploaded and shared as a part of a personal profile and sharing video is the main purpose of YouTube.

Some sites specialise in uploading and sharing images. For example, on **Worldisround (www.worldisround.com)** you can upload images and share them. Travellers could use Worldisround to make a record of their experiences around the world by uploading digital photographs so that friends and family back home could keep up with what they were doing. You could use Worldisround for other purposes, such as showing the world around the place where you live.

Downloading music is very popular and may replace the sale of music on CDs and other physical media. Websites such as **iTunes (www.itunes.com)** and **Napster (www.napster.co.uk)** sell digital music downloads, and these can be downloaded to portable devices so that music can be enjoyed on the move. iTunes also has features that allow users to organise and browse their entire collection of music.

Bit Torrent (www.bittorrent.com) is a peer-to-peer file-sharing service that allows users to share any digital content. This could be images, video or music. Files can be downloaded to any registered computer and any file can be made available for downloading.

Blogs

Blogs are online personal diaries with narrative, pictures and hyperlinks. Anyone can set up a blog and these could be on almost any topic.

Here are some examples:

- The Adam Smith Institute promotes free-market economic and social policies in its blog on **http://www.adamsmith.org/blog/**

- Warwick University has blogs by its staff and students on **http://blogs.warwick.ac.uk/directory/people/**

- There are many blogs about music on **http://www.blogtoplist.com/music/**

- There is a directory of blogs on **http://www.blogcatalog.com/directory/**

- You can create your own blog using a hosted service, for example on **http://www.blogger.com.**

Wikis

Wikis enable you to describe and comment on topics in collaboration with other web users. A wiki is a database of web pages that you can edit. You can also search the wiki's content, and view updates since your last visit. In a moderated wiki, the owner of the wiki can review edits before they become a permanent part of the wiki.

Here are some example wikis:

- **Wikipedia (http://www.wikipedia.org)** is an online encyclopedia with articles about a very wide range of topics, including technology, history, science and many other topics that have been written by many different contributors. Because anyone can contribute, a wide range of viewpoints can be seen. People contribute what they know and this is moderated so that what is available is usually reasonably accurate.

- There are wikis dedicated to gaming, sport, and toys on **Wikia (www.wikia.com).**

- **Wikitravel (http://wikitravel.org)** is a worldwide travel guide that has over twenty thousand destination guides and other travel articles that are written and edited by contributors around the world.

- You can set up your own wiki on any topic. For example, on **http://wiki.com**.

Social networking sites

There are many social networking sites where you can interact with a circle of friends, those with similar interests or a wider community. Members usually share some information about themselves, often setting up a personal profile page where personal information, images and video can be uploaded and displayed. There is considerable overlap in the features offered by different social networking websites:

- Members of **Facebook (http://www.facebook.com)** can join networks organised by workplace, school, city or region to communicate with other people. Members update their personal profile to notify friends about themselves and can add friends and send them messages.

- On **Friends Reunited (http://www.friendsreunited.co.uk),** you join networks grouped by school, college, university or workplace and can contact other members.

- On **Genes Reunited (http://www.genesreunited.com)** you can set up a family tree, research your genealogy and communicate with members and potential members of your family.

- On **LibraryThing (http://www.librarything.com)** book lovers review the books they read and can catalogue their personal libraries. They can communicate with other book lovers with similar interests.

Quick question
What other social networking sites do you know about?

Threats from the Internet and security

There are many threats to safe use of the Internet and some of these are described below. See also the section on Computer Crime in Chapter 12.

Viruses

A **virus** is software that is designed to be secretly loaded onto a computer without the user's knowledge for malicious intent. Viruses have many forms, and can do many things, such as type the same character no matter which key is pressed on the keyboard, and delete all the data on a hard disk. Many Internet users have had their computers crash from viruses that can attach themselves to emails and infect the computer when the email is opened. Viruses can also be transmitted by downloading programs or accessing backing storage. **Antivirus software** can check a computer for viruses and remove them.

Spam

Spam is unsolicited email and is the email equivalent of junk mail. It is an inappropriate attempt to use an email address, mailing list, newsgroup or other networked communications facility as a means of broadcasting the same email message to a large number of people who didn't ask for it and probably don't want it. Spam is generally sent by commercial operations that use the Internet to sell products and services. There is so much spam, much of which is pornographic, that it can obstruct the use of email by making it difficult and time-consuming to find legitimate email.

Spam can be removed using a spam **filter** that scans incoming email and removes unwanted email messages. Unfortunately, spam filters are unlikely to be entirely accurate and some legitimate email may be removed along with the spam.

Phishing

Phishing is an attempt to find out personal information, usually social security numbers, credit card numbers, or usernames and passwords for online banks. These are then used for identity theft and fraud.

A phishing attack is often made by email (see Figure 9.15). Typically, victims receive an email asking them to log on to their online bank and enter their username and password. A hyperlink in the email appears to connect to the online bank's website. However, clicking on this takes the victim to a fraudulent website not to the bank's real website. When the victim enters their username and password these are stolen and later used to steal money from the victim's bank account. The fraudulent website may be a good replica of the bank's real website so

> **Did you know?**
> What you see on the Web is not always what it appears to be. Don't assume everything you see is true. Remember that videos and photographs can be edited to show something that did not happen. To be safe, you should always ask yourself:
> - Can I rely on the information to be true?
> - Are the people who make the information available sufficiently knowledgeable?
> - Can I trust the source of the information?
> - Is the website of an organisation I trust?
> - Is the email or other communication from someone I trust?
> - Is the information biased or unreliable in some other way?
> - Is there a good reason why I am being asked for personal information?
> - Will providing this information put me at risk?

that the victim of a phishing attack is unaware of it until much later when they notice that money is missing from their account.

The bank is not responsible for sending phishing emails and cannot be responsible for the criminals who send them. Most banks do not send unsolicited emails to customers so that customers will know that a phishing attack is underway when they receive an email claiming to be from the bank.

Other phishing attacks may appeal to the victim's vanity. For example, they may be told they have won a prize in a competition but need to enter personal details to collect it.

You can recognise and deal with phishing attacks like this:

- Look for spelling and grammar errors in the email. A reputable bank is unlikely to make such errors.
- If you are worried your bank might really be trying to contact you, then contact them directly but don't click on the hyperlink in the email. Break your connection with the email.
- Check that you have an account with the bank named in the phishing email.
- Remember that you are unlikely to win a competition you haven't entered!

```
27 September 2008

Dear Lloyds TSB User,

We recently have determined that your Lloyds TSB account, needs to be
updated again. This update will help us in making our database more
secure. This procedure has become the standard and must follow way
for any Bank providing Online Banking services. activity. This new
security statement will helps us continue to offer Lloyds TSB as a
secure Online Banking Service. We appreciate your cooperation and
assistance.

Please click on continue, to the verification process and ensure your
Account information is entered correctly to get verified.
Continue To Internet Banking
http://www.navyhovik.no/images/kaz/www.lloydstsb.com/customer.ibc/onl
ine/banking/Update/LloydsTSB%20online%20-%20Welcome.index.htm


Sincerely,
Lloyds TSB Online Account Security.
_________________________________

Lloyds TSB Bank plc and Lloyds TSB Scotland plc are authorised and
regulated by the Financial Services Authority and signatories to the
Banking Codes. FSA authorization can be checked on the FSA's Register
at: www.fsa.gov.uk/register. Lloyds TSB Bank plc and Lloyds TSB
Scotland plc are members of the Financial Services Compensation
Scheme and the Financial Ombudsman Service. Lloyds TSB Group plc.
```

Figure 9.15 *A phishing email*

Pharming

Pharming is an attempt to collect personal information from users when they connect to a legitimate website. Unknown to the user, they have previously downloaded malicious software from the Internet and this is running on their computer. The software either records any information they enter while connected to the legitimate site, or when they enter the web address of a legitimate website they are re-directed to a fraudulent website.

Access to inappropriate information

Parental control or **filter software** can be used to monitor individuals' computer usage. This is often used by parents to monitor and control their children's access to the information on the Internet. Some examples are CYBERsitter, Net Nanny and Cyber Patrol. An advantage of parental control software is that children can be allowed unsupervised access to the Internet, but a disadvantage is that it could slow down the speed of Internet access.

Features of parental control software are as follows:

- **URL filtering** – the URL or web address of all the websites accessed is checked against a list of undesirable sites and access to these can be blocked; for example, children can be prevented from accessing adult websites.
- **Keyword filtering** – the content of web pages, chat rooms, email, newsgroups, bulletin boards, pop-up windows and other Internet content can be monitored against a list of undesirable key words and communication can be blocked.
- **Customised filtering** – this caters for the individual maturity and sensitivity of each family member. It could be possible to allow access, warn of undesirable content or block access for each filtered item.
- **Activity reporting** – you can view a log of what each individual has been doing on the computer, which could include details of where they have been on the Internet and what has been said in chat rooms.
- **Notification capability** – parents could be notified by email while on holiday, at work or at home that unauthorised access or blocking is occurring.
- **Remote management** – parents should be able to change the filter settings over the Internet, from work or while on holiday.
- **Personal information blocking** – an effective filter will block personal information, such as addresses and phone numbers, from leaving the computer.

Unauthorised access

The first precaution against unauthorised access is to use a **username** and **password** to access all computer systems. You will be given a username but will be able to decide on your own password:

- A password should be easy to remember but hard to guess. Passwords that are at least eight characters long and made up of upper case and lower case letters and numbers are likely to be more secure than, for example, the name of your pet.
- Don't tell anyone your password and don't write it down.
- Change your password regularly so that if someone does find out your password, they will not be able to use it for very long.
- Turn away when others are typing in their password. You may be curious to find out the password of your friend or teacher but avoid this as it is bad etiquette.

Even with a good password, it is possible that someone else on the Internet could maliciously access your computer when it is connected to the Internet. A **firewall** is a combination of hardware and software that prevents unauthorised access to and from a LAN (or an individual computer), especially from the Internet. It is installed between the LAN and the rest of the Internet. Firewalls help prevent external Internet users from accessing files other than those that are publicly available, and shield the LAN from unauthorised users, preventing them from making use of the LAN's computer resources. This helps protect the network against external attacks.

Firewalls have been extended and developed to include a range of features, including parental control software, which enables you to manage your web access. For example, a firewall might also include the following:

- **Parental control software** to block access to particular sites.

- **Antivirus** software to detect and delete viruses.

- **Pop-up blocker** to block pop-up adverts on websites. Some websites finance their operations by selling advertising. When you are connected to a website, windows with adverts in them continually pop up. You can disconnect from these sites but if you are interested in the information on them, frequent **pop-up adverts** can be irritating. The pop-up blocker prevents pop-up adverts appearing.

- **Keyword alert** so that you can be warned if particular words or content appear on a website.

- **Cookie manager** so that you can block cookies or edit those copied to your computer. Cookies are saved on your hard disk by websites and contain personal information that can be accessed by the website.

Exercise 9.2

1.

A	Modem
B	Browser
C	Keyboard
D	Printer

Put a cross in one box to show which hardware is needed to access the Internet.

☐ A

☐ B

☐ C

☐ D

2. Many individuals and organisations are connected to the Internet.

 a) Describe what is meant by the Internet.

 b) Describe what is meant by an **Internet Service Provider** and explain why you would need one.

3. Describe what is meant by **narrowband** and **broadband.**

4. Many people use email.

   a) Describe what is meant by **email.**

   b) Discuss the advantages and disadvantages of email compared with the post.

   c) Discuss the advantages and disadvantages of using email compared with the telephone.

   d) You receive an email with an attachment and want to send this to a friend. Describe what would happen if you forwarded the email

   e) Describe what is meant by **email contacts** and say how these could be useful when sending an email.

5. Describe what is meant by a **mailing list** and a **newsgroup.** Identify the differences between them and discuss their advantages and disadvantages.

6. Describe what is meant by the following:

   a) Hyperlink

   b) Web ring

   c) HTML

7. Describe what is meant by **chat** and explain why you might want to use it.

8. a) Describe what is meant by a **search engine.**

   b) Write down the web addresses of three popular search engines.

   c) Describe how information can be found on the Web by entering keywords in a search engine.

9. a) State the name of a browser.

   b) Describe the purpose of a browser.

   c) List the main features of a browser and briefly describe what each is used for.

10. Describe what is meant by **online shopping** and discuss its advantages and disadvantages.

11. Describe what is meant by **online banking** and discuss its advantages and disadvantages.

12. Explain the difference between **uploading** and **downloading**.

13. With the aid of examples, explain what is meant by **phishing.**

14. Describe each component part of this URL: http://www.pearsoned.com/community/index.htm

15. a) Describe the benefits that can be gained by a company setting up its own website.

    b) Describe what is meant by an **intranet**, and explain how this differs from **the Internet.**

    c) Describe the benefits that can be gained by a company by setting up an intranet.

Exercise 9.3

You are to compare the advantages and disadvantages of sending messages, large documents and otherwise communicating by a variety of mailing and communication systems. You will need to read this chapter thoroughly and answer the following questions carefully.

1. In this question you will compare sending messages and larger documents by post and email.

    a) You are going to send a short written message of around 50 words to a friend who lives in the same street:

    i   Describe how you would you do this. Consider each of post and email and explain which of these methods you would use (if any). Give reasons for your answer.

    ii State which method would be faster. Give reasons for your answer.

    iii State which method would be cheaper. Remember to take into account the total cost when assessing which method is cheaper. For example, each email is free to send but you have to buy all the equipment and subscribe to an ISP for an Internet connection.

    iv State which method would be more convenient. Give reasons for your answer.

    v   State which method would be the most secure. Give reasons for your answer.

    b) You have produced a word processed leaflet of four pages advertising your business, and want to send this to the print shop, which is 100 kilometres away. State whether you would use post or email. Consider which method would be faster, cheaper, more convenient and more secure, giving reasons for your answers.

    c) You have produced a substantial word processed report of 150 pages which includes statistical tables and graphs from a spreadsheet. You want to send this to a university in another country. State whether you would use post or email. Consider which method would be faster, cheaper, more convenient and more secure, giving reasons for your answers.

    d) You have received a substantial printed report of 50 pages by post, and want to send copies of this to colleagues who work:

    i   in the same building

    ii at the head office of your company in a city 150 kilometres away

    iii at an overseas branch of your company in a major industrial nation

    iv at an overseas branch of your company in a developing country.

    Describe how you would send the report to each of the above using post and email. Consider which method would be faster, cheaper, more convenient and more secure, giving reasons for your answers.

2. In this question you will consider how you communicate by telephone, chat and video conferencing.

a) Describe how each of telephone, chat and video conferencing allows you to communicate instantly with another person.

b) Find out the cost of installing and running the technology needed to allow you to communicate by each of telephone, chat and video conferencing.

c) State which of these methods of communication gives you the most personal contact. Give reasons for your answer.

d) You are working on your computer preparing a word processed essay. You want to communicate with a friend as you are doing this. State which of these methods of communication you would use. Give reasons for your answer.

e) You are working at home and want to communicate with a colleague at your head office. State which of these methods of communication you would prefer to use. Give reasons for your answers.

f) You are working on a product design with others in your project team. The team wants to talk to a technical design expert who has expertise that the team does not have. All the team wants to ask the expert questions. State which of these methods of communication you would use. Give reasons for your answer.

g) A class of school pupils wants to talk to another class in a school on the other side of the world. State which of these methods of communication you would use. Give reasons for your answer.

End of Chapter 9 Checklist

1. A **local area network (LAN)** is a collection of computers connected together within a small geographical area so that they can share information and peripherals and also communicate with each other.

2. **A wide area network (WAN)** can connect computers and peripherals across a large geographical area, including internationally.

3. **The Internet** is a network of networks that connects computers around the world. To connect to the Internet you need a personal computer or workstation, a **modem,** a communications link such as a telephone line and access to an Internet Service Provider (ISP).

4. An **Internet Service Provider (ISP)** is a company that has a direct connection to the Internet and gives users access to it, usually for a fee.

5. To transfer data from one computer to the next, computers must follow a set of rules called a **protocol.** The protocol used over the Internet is **TCP/IP (Transfer Control Protocol/Internet Protocol),** which allows operating systems software from different computers to communicate.

6. The **World Wide Web** consists of many millions of **web pages.**

7. You need a **browser** such as Microsoft Internet Explorer or Mozilla Firefox in order to view web pages.

8. Web pages are written in **Hypertext Markup Language (HTML).**

9. You can view a web page by entering its web address or **URL (Uniform Resource Locator)** in a browser.

10. Search engines, such as Google, enable you to find information quickly by entering keywords.

11. These are some of the services available on the Internet and the Web:

   ✓ Search engines.

   ✓ Email.

   ✓ Online shopping and banking.

   ✓ Customer support.

   ✓ Software downloads.

   ✓ Mailing lists, bulletin boards and newsgroups.

   ✓ Chat and conferencing.

   ✓ Web rings.

   ✓ Web broadcasting.

   ✓ Sites where you can upload and download digital media, such as music, images and video, and publish these on the Web so that they can be shared with friends and family.

   ✓ Blogs – online personal diaries with narrative, pictures and hyperlinks that you can publish on the Web.

   ✓ Wikis, where you can describe and define particular topics in collaboration with other web users.

   ✓ Social networking sites where you can communicate with friends.

12. **Web 2.0** describes a trend in web design and development towards a second generation of web-based communities and hosted services. These include blogs, wikis and social networking sites which aim to facilitate creativity, collaboration, and sharing between web users.

13. An **intranet** provides many of the features of the Internet within a company or organisation. An **extranet** extends an intranet so that there is restricted remote access; for example, for employees working at home. A **VPN** (Virtual Private Network) is an especially secure extranet.

14. Viruses can be spread by downloading infected email or programs from the Internet. They can be removed using **antivirus software.**

15. Spam is unsolicited email that can be removed using a spam filter.

16. Phishing is an attempt to find out personal information, usually social security numbers, credit card numbers, or usernames and passwords for online banks. These are then used for identity theft and fraud. Phishing is done by sending a fraudulent email that pretends to be from the bank.

17. Pharming is an attempt to collect personal information from a user when they connect to a legitimate website. Malicious software running on their computer records information they enter or when they enter a legitimate web address they are re-directed to a fraudulent website.

18. Parental control software can be used by parents to control their children's access to information and services available on the Internet.

19. A **firewall** is a combination of hardware and software that protects a LAN or an individual computer from unauthorised access by external Internet users.

Chapter 10: Web authoring

Publishing a website

If you want to publish a website you must follow these steps:

● Create the web pages that will be part of the website.

● Link them together.

● Upload these pages to a web server.

Creating web pages

We will briefly look at how to create web pages using these methods:

● Using applications software, such as Word, Excel and Access.

● Writing the HTML directly using a text editor such as Notepad.

● Using web authoring software, such as Adobe Dreamweaver, that allows you to write web pages as they appear on screen and in HTML, and that provides you with tools to manage a website.

Most web pages are saved as HTML (Hypertext Markup Language) files; however, you do not have to create them by writing HTML as there are many ways that web pages can be created. Such web pages will have filenames ending in **.htm** or **.html.** It is good practice for HTML files to have filenames that:

● Are in lower case

● Have no spaces in them

● End in .html.

A **website** is a group of web pages linked together. It is best if this is done in a structured way, because this makes navigation easier. The structure of many websites is broadly hierarchical but there are nearly always links from each page to a range of other pages.

Creating web pages using applications software

You can create a web page by saving a word processing document as an HTML file that can be opened in a web browser.

For example, in Microsoft Word:

● Click the Office button and select **Save As.**

● In the **Save As** dialog box, give the document a filename.

● Set **Save as type** to **Web Page (*.htm; *.html).**

● Click **OK.**

This method can also be used to save a spreadsheet as an HTML file in Excel.

You can create a web page in most applications software but the method is sometimes slightly different. For example, in Access to create a static web page that displays a database table, on the **External Data** tab, in the **Export** area, click on **More** and select **HTML Document.**

Inserting links

If you intend to save a document as a web page, you may need to insert links to other web pages. In Word, on the **Insert** tab select **Hyperlink,** and the **Insert Hyperlink** dialog box appears (see Figure 10.1). This is used as you would use it in PowerPoint.

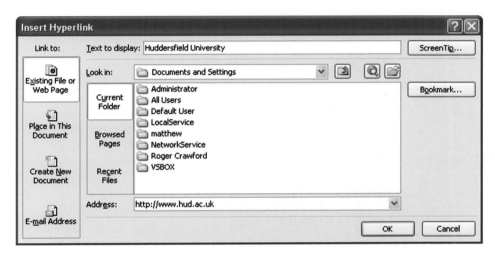

Figure 10.1 *Insert Hyperlink dialog box*

Opening a web page in a browser

A word processed document saved as a web page can be displayed in a web browser, although you may find that some features of the word processing software do not work. To do this in Internet Explorer, in the **File** menu select **Open** (if you cannot see the **File** menu, press the **Alt** key). In the **Open** dialog box, click the **Browse** button and find the word processed document that you have saved as an HTML file. Click **OK** and the file is displayed in the web browser. This method can be used to display any HTML file in a browser.

Writing HTML using a text editor

In Exercise 10.1, you are going to create a simple web page by writing an HTML program in a text editor (for example, Notepad). A **text editor** is very basic word processing software.

Exercise 10.1

You are going to create a web page that will have a title, a picture and some descriptive text. To do this you should carry out the following instructions very carefully.

1. You will need a picture of your house saved as **myhouse.jpg.**

2. Open **Notepad** from the **Accessories** menu in Windows.

3. Type into Notepad the following HTML exactly as it appears in the first column below. **Do not type in the notes in the second column,** which explain what you are doing.

HTML	Comment
<html>	<html> is a tag. This tells the browser it is looking at HTML. At the end of the program </html> tells the browser that all the HTML has been seen.
<head>	Tags frequently come in pairs. <head> and </head> indicate the start and end of the heading section.
<title>My house</title>	Whatever is between the <title> tags will appear in the browser's title bar (see Figure 10.2).
</head>	
<body>	This is the start of the <body> section where what is displayed on the main part of the browser's screen is described.
<h1>This is my house</h1>	An <h1> tag indicates that the text up to the </h1> tag is a heading in large text. An <h2> heading would have slightly smaller text, and so on.
<img src="myhouse.jpg">	This tag inserts a picture. The picture file, myhouse.jpg, should be saved in the same folder as the web page that displays it.
<p>My house is built of stone. There are two very tall chimneys and a big garden round the back. The garden wall has a cast iron fence. I have my own bedroom but I have to share the bathroom with my brother and sister. My parents have their own bathroom next to their bedroom.</p>	The <p> tags indicate a paragraph of text.
</body>	
</html>	

4. Save the file giving it a filename ending in **.html**; for example, **myhouse.html**.

5. Open this file in a browser and you should see a web page similar to Figure 10.2.

Hint!

You can take a picture of your house with a digital camera and then transfer it to your PC.

Figure 10.2 *A web page created using HTML*

Formatting text

You can change the size of the text, its colour, and the font using these tags within the **<body>** section:

<font size="2" color="green" face="times new roman">insert your text here</font>

Links

You can insert a hyperlink to another web page using these tags within the **<body>** section:

<a href ="http://www.hud.ac.uk">The University of Huddersfield</a>

The target web page will open in a new window if you use:

<a href ="http://www.hud.ac.uk" target="new" >The University of Huddersfield</a>

When the web page with the hyperlink is opened in a browser, the link will be displayed as:

The University of Huddersfield

and when you click on it the University of Huddersfield web page will be displayed.

Hint!
If you want to put comments into HTML, enclose these between **<!-–** and **–->** tags.

Activity
In **myhouse.html** change the text size to 7, the colour to blue, and the font to Arial. Try out different sizes, colours and fonts.

Activity
Use a search engine to find the URL of a local estate agent.
In **myhouse.html** insert a link to this website.

Exercise 10.2

1. Write a web page using HTML and Notepad that provides information about your neighbourhood. Put links in the web page to the web pages for each of the shops you use.

2. The table below shows the income, expenditure and profits made by a holiday company.

The Blue Skies Holiday Company		
Year	Income	Expenditure
2000	£600,500	£500,200
2001	£700,300	£600,100
2002	£800,600	£550,000
2003	£600,900	£200,000
2004	£500,300	£100,950
2005	£600,200	£100,900

a) Enter this data in a spreadsheet.

b) Include a column to calculate profits.

c) Produce a graph which contrasts income and profits from 2000 to 2005.

d) Save the spreadsheet as a web page.

e) Using word processing software, write a report about the economic health of the tourist industry. This report should refer to the spreadsheet and the graph.

f) At an appropriate point in the word processed report, insert a link to the spreadsheet data and the graph.

g) Save the report as a web page.

h) Open a browser and open the word processed report as a web page. Follow the link to the spreadsheet data and the graph.

Web authoring software

HTML quickly becomes more complex, and there is more and more room for errors when you are entering the HTML statements. Using **web authoring** software that allows you to write web pages both as they appear on screen and in HTML may be easier. In addition, web authoring software often provides tools for managing your website. An example of such software is Adobe Dreamweaver (see Figure 10.3), formerly developed by Macromedia. Another example is Microsoft FrontPage, which is being replaced by Microsoft Expression Web.

Notice that the work area in Dreamweaver is divided into Code View and Design View. The balance of this division can be changed by dragging up or down the horizontal line that divides the views. In **Code View** you can write HTML, and in **Design View** you can work on the appearance of the web page as you would in word processing software. Because each view is of the same web page, as you work in Code View or Design View they are each kept up to date with the alterations you make.

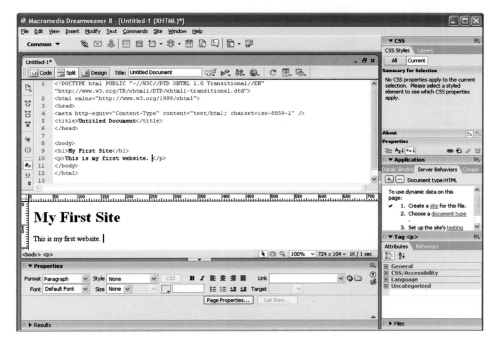

Figure 10.3 *Dreamweaver*

Creating a new website

Before you can write a web page in Dreamweaver, you need to start a new website. In Dreamweaver, in the **Site** menu select **New Site,** and the **Site Definition** dialog box appears (see Figure 10.4). You should fill in this information:

- **Site Name:** Give the site a name, for example, *myfirstsite.*

- **Local Root Folder:** This is the folder on the local hard disk where you will store all the files used in your website.

- **Default Images Folder:** It is good practice to keep all your pictures and graphics in a separate folder. It is usual to call the folder *images.*

- **HTTP Address:** This is where you will enter the web address of your site on the web so that it can be easily updated; however, it is not required when you are initially setting up the website.

Click on **OK** and a new blank web page appears.

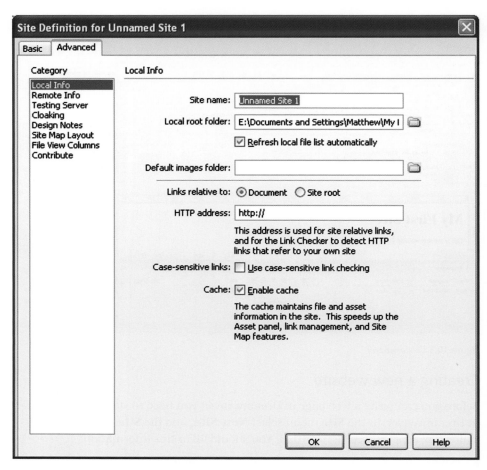

Figure 10.4 *The Site Definition dialog box*

Creating a new web page

In the **File** menu select **New,** and the **New Document** dialog box appears (see Figure 10.5). Click the **General** tab to choose from a wide variety of templates by selecting different categories and page designs. Your choice is shown in the **Preview** pane.

When you have made your choice, click on **Create**. The new page is shown. This will have dummy text which you can replace with your own. Generally, it is easier to use Design View to do this.

Save your new page, which will appear in the Site Panel. The **Site Panel** (titled **Files** and shown in the bottom right of Figure 10.3) shows the location of all the pages and other resources used in your website. As you add more web pages, the **Site Panel** becomes a useful way of accessing your web pages. You can open an existing web page by finding it in the **Site Panel** and double-clicking on it. When you have more than one website, you can switch between these using the drop-down menu in the **Site Panel.**

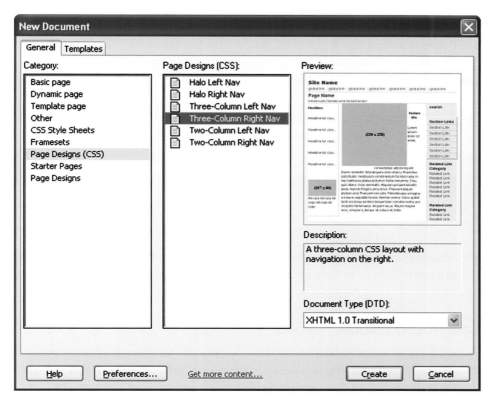

Figure 10.5 *The New Document dialog box*

Images

To insert an image or picture in a web page in Dreamweaver:

● If necessary, create a folder called *images* in your website folder.

● Using Windows Explorer, save the picture file in the images folder in your website folder.

● Using Dreamweaver, find this file in the **Site Panel**, and in Design View drag it across on to the web page.

ALT text

Alternate (or **ALT**) text associates a text description with an image. The text is downloaded and displayed on the web page before the image. When you point at the image, the text is displayed but otherwise it is not shown.

To associate ALT text with a picture in a web page in Dreamweaver:

● In Design View, select the image and in the **Properties** panel, type in the text in the **ALT** box.

● Alternatively, you can insert HTML code in Code View, for example:

> **<img src="images/myhouse.jpg" width="285" height="405" align="center" alt="The house where I live">**

Hint!
Alternatively, you can insert this HTML code in Code View: **<img src="images/ yourpicturename.jpg" width="285" height="405" align="center">**. The size of the image on the web page is given by the width and height, and its position is given by align.

The advantages of using ALT are as follows:

- Disabled people may find text on your web page easier to see than images, or they may use software that can read out the descriptions to them.

- If the image is not displayed, the text will be displayed. This can be very helpful; for example, some email software will block images to speed up the downloading of email. The ALT text downloads quickly and tells the user what the image is. If the user wants to look at the image, they can choose to download it. This avoids wasting time downloading unwanted images.

- A few browsers are text-based and these do not download images, for example, Lynx.

- You can use ALT text to point users to other interesting features of your web page.

- Search engine spiders recognise the content of text but not images. Web pages are more likely to be fully indexed in the search engine if images have ALT text.

Background colours

Box for selecting a colour in Dreamweaver

To set a **background colour,** in Dreamweaver in the **Modify** menu select **Page Properties.** The **Page Properties** dialog box appears (see Figure 10.6). Click the drop-down box next to **Background color** and select a colour. Click on **OK.**

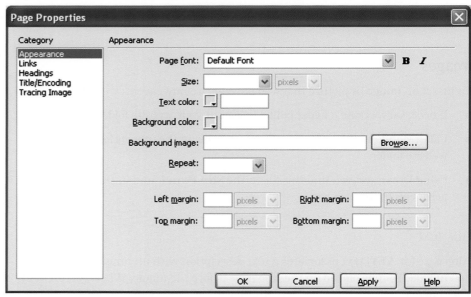

Figure 10.6 *The Page Properties dialog box*

To set a **background image,** in Dreamweaver in the **Modify** menu select **Page Properties.** The **Page Properties** dialog box appears (see Figure 10.6). Browse to find a background image (in the *images* folder) and click on **OK**. The image is tiled over the background.

Text

To change the **size** of text, in Dreamweaver in Design View, highlight the text. In the **Text** menu select **Size,** and select the size of text you want. Click on **OK.** The text changes to the size you chose.

To change the **colour** of text, in Dreamweaver in Design View, highlight the text. In the **Text** menu select **Color.** The **Color** dialog box appears. Select the colour you want and click on **OK.** The text changes to the colour you chose.

To change the **font** of text, in Dreamweaver in Design View, highlight the text. In the **Text** menu select **Font,** and select the font you want. Click on **OK.** The text changes to the font you chose.

Links to other web pages

To insert a link to another web page in Dreamweaver, in Design View in the **Insert** menu select **Hyperlink.** The **Hyperlink** dialog box appears (see Figure 10.7). Fill in the **Text** box with the text to be displayed, and the **Link** box with the full web address of the web page to go to, and click **OK.** The example shown in Figure 10.7 would create a link shown as <u>Google</u> on your web page. If the page was running in a browser, this would link to the Google search engine.

In HTML code, this has the same effect:

<a href="http://www.google.co.uk">Google</a>

To insert a **graphic link** to another web page, in Dreamweaver, in Design View, insert the graphic, highlight it and enter the full web address of the web page to go to in the **Properties** panel in the **Link** box.

In HTML code, the following creates a link to the web address **http://www.pearsoned.com** from the image **myhouse.jpg** which has been inserted on the web page.

<a href="http://www.pearsoned.com"><img src="myhouse.jpg"></a>

Figure 10.7 *The Hyperlink dialog box*

> **Did you know?**
> The HTML tag for a link is **<a>...</a>**, which stands for **anchor**. You can think of the page you are linking to as being anchored to the underlined text in the page.

Links within a page

Links within a page are useful for navigating within large pages. A typical page where links within a page could be used is shown in Figure 10.8. The letters of the alphabet are shown across the top of the page and each of these is a hyperlink to a jump point lower down the page. Lower down the page, there are hyperlinks back to the top of the page.

For example, suppose the page has been saved as **glossary.html.**

The letter B is a hyperlink to a jump point called **Bwords** lower down the web page where the words beginning with B start. The HTML code is:

<a href="glossary.html#Bwords">B</a>

Clicking on B navigates to the start of the words beginning with B at the jump point called Bwords, which is marked by the code:

<a name="Bwords"></a>

At the end of the words beginning with B, there will be a hyperlink back to the top of the page:

<a href="glossary.html#Top">Top of Page</a>

At the top of the page is the jump point Top:

<a name="Top"></a>

This coding is done for each letter of the alphabet and provides an easy way to navigate within a page.

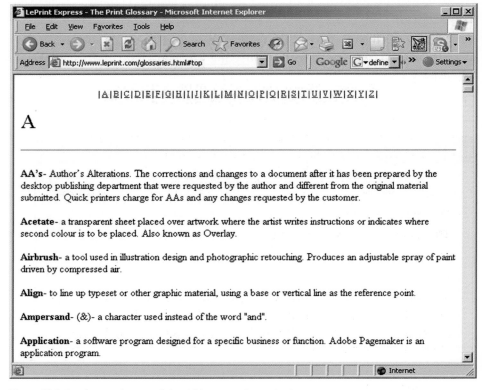

Figure 10.8 *A web page that uses links within a page for navigation*

Email links

In Dreamweaver, to insert a link that loads an email client, in the **Insert** menu select **Email Link.** Enter the text to be displayed and the address the email will be sent to. Click on **OK**.

The HTML code for this is, for example:

<a href="mailto:customerservices@pearsoned.com">Contact Customer Services</a>

The text displayed is <u>Contact Customer Services</u> and this opens an email which is automatically addressed to **customerservices@pearsoned.com.**

Thumbnails

Thumbnails are very small versions of a picture that link to a full-sized copy of the same picture. You can display several thumbnails on a web page; the user clicks on a thumbnail if they want to see a bigger copy of the picture.

To do this in DreamWeaver, in the **Insert** menu, select **Image.** Choose the picture file you want to insert. Next select the image in Design View and make it much smaller by resizing it. While the image is selected, right-click and select **Make Link.** Choose the same picture file.

This is the easiest way to create a thumbnail. However, your web page will load faster if you create two copies of the picture file: one should contain a small version of the picture to be used as a thumbnail and the other a larger version for a full-screen display.

Tables

Tables are very useful for controlling the layout of a web page, because the position of blocks of text and images can be easily controlled.

To insert a table, in Dreamweaver, in Design View position the cursor where the table is to be placed. In the **Insert** menu select **Table.** The **Table** dialog box appears (see Figure 10.9). Set the features of the table and click on **OK.** The table outline appears in Design View. Click in a cell and enter text. You can also insert images in a cell.

The features of a table that you can set in the **Table** dialog box in Dreamweaver are as follows:

- **The number of rows.** Enter the number of rows in the **Rows** box.

- **The number of columns.** Enter the number of columns in the **Columns** box.

- **Table width.** This can be a fixed width stated in pixels and your table will always be the same size on screen. It can also be a variable width stated as a percentage of the screen width: 100% would be across the entire screen, whereas 50% would occupy half the screen width.

- **Border thickness.** Enter a number of pixels. If this is set at zero, the border will not be visible.

> **Did you know?**
>
> Some people choose not to use **mailto** links because of the increased risk of receiving spam. Instead, they may choose one of the following techniques to hide their email addresses from spambots:
> - using javascript programming code to generate the link when the page is loaded
> - using an image instead of text to show the email address
> - using a feedback form instead of publicising their email address.

```
<table width="50%"
        border= "1" cellspacing = "2"
        cellpadding = "3">
        <caption>The table's title
        </caption>
        <tr>
        <th scope = "col"> </th>
        <!--these are the table header
        tags -->
        <th scope= "col"> </th>
        </tr>
        <tr>
        <td> </td>
        <td> </td>
        </tr>
</table>
```

Did you know?

The code ** ** means to insert a non-breaking space. This is used as a placeholder in table cells that would otherwise be empty, because older browsers were unreliable when drawing the borders of empty cells.

- **Cell padding.** This is the amount of space between the cell border and the cell content.

- **Cell spacing.** This is the amount of space between the cells in a table.

- **The position of the row or column headers.**

- **Caption.** This will appear above the table. Enter the title of the table.

If you look in Code View, you will see HTML code similar to that on the left-hand side of this page at the top of the table. The code can be edited to alter the initial values set in the **Table** dialog box.

Cell content can be edited either in Design View, or in Code View by replacing ** ** with meaningful text.

Two columns are shown and this can be edited by changing the number of pairs of **<td>** and **</td>** tags between the **<tr>** and **</tr>** tags.

The number of rows can be edited by changing the number of pairs of **<tr>** and **</tr>** tags.

You can merge adjoining cells on the same row using **Colspan.** The code below is equivalent to two pairs of **<td>** and **</td>** tags. If you want the table to have the same shape then reduce the number of pairs of these tags.

<td colspan="2"> </td>

You can also merge two adjoining cells in the same column using **<th rowspan="2">.**

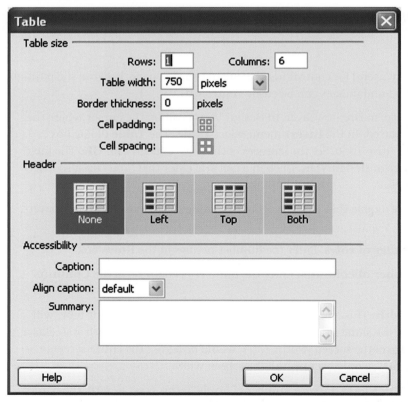

Figure 10.9 *The Table dialog box*

Using styles

Styles are used to control the appearance of text and can help with consistency. They can be applied to the text in specific heading tags, throughout a web page, or throughout a website.

Inline style declarations

An **inline style declaration** will affect only the text in the tag. For example, to change the colour of the text to red and the background to silver for the second largest heading tag, insert this HTML statement:

<h2 style="color: red; background-color: silver">write your text here </h2>

Embedded style declarations

An **embedded style declaration** will affect all the relevant tags within a web page. However, an inline style declaration will override an embedded style declaration.

For example, to ensure that all second-level headings in a web page are blue, insert this HTML between the **<head>** and **</head>** tags in the header section of an HTML file:

```
<style>
        h2 {color: blue}
</style>
```

You can add more than one style declaration. These are added between the same **<style>** and **</style>** tags.

For example, to ensure that all level-one headings are in the Arial font, green, large, centred and bold, insert this HTML statement between the same **<style>** and **</style>** tags:

h1 {color: green; font-family: arial; text-align: center; font-size: 48pt; font-weight: bold}

Similarly, if you also wanted to set the appearance of the text between all the **<p>** and **</p>** paragraph tags to font Arial, size 12 pixels, background colour red and font colour white, then insert this HTML between the same **<style>** and **</style>** tags.

p {font-family:Arial; font-size:12px; background-color:red; color:white}

External stylesheets

An **external stylesheet** can be used to create a consistent appearance on several web pages. To do this, set up a stylesheet and link each web page to it. This applies the styles defined in the stylesheet to each linked web page. However, inline or embedded style declarations will override the external stylesheet.

Set up an external stylesheet by creating a text file called **style.css,** for example, with these or similar statements in it:

h2 {color: red}

p {font-family:Arial; font-size: 20; background-color: cyan; color: white}

Save this file in the same folder as the web pages that will use it.

Every web page in your website will have a consistent style if you link them all to the external stylesheet. You can link a web page to the external stylesheet by inserting this HTML code between its **<head>** and **</head>** tags:

<link rel="stylesheet" type="text/css" href = "style.css">

Inheritance rules

The browser first loads the external stylesheet and applies it to the page. Next it applies any embedded style declarations, leaving unchanged external styles that have not been affected by these. The browser finally applies inline style declarations. Again, unchanged styles are not affected.

Uploading a website

You have to copy your website to a web server before it is available over the Internet. Many Internet Service Providers (ISPs) offer hosting on their web servers and the tools to move your website to their web server.

Promoting a website

Because there are so many websites, search engines may not find your website or rate it very highly. You can improve visibility on the web as follows.

Use meta tags

For example, the following tag provides the short description that is displayed when you point at search results.

<meta name="description" content="Hazel Cottage for holidays in Settle, Yorkshire">

This tag provides keywords so that search engines can relate the web page to a search.

<meta name="keywords" content="Yorkshire, holiday, accommodation, self catering">

Submit your website to search engines

Submit the address of your website to individual search engines. For example, to submit to Google go to **http://www.google.com/addurl**

Submit the address of your website to multiple search engines. For example, go to **http://www.addpro.com/submit30.htm**

Exercise 10.3

1. Using web authoring software such as Dreamweaver, write a website for your school.

On each page include suitable text, images and links to other web pages.

Include the following:

a) A home page that introduces the school and provides links to the other pages in the website.

b) Other web pages as follows:

✓ An introduction from the head teacher (include a picture of the head teacher and a background which is a photograph of the school)
✓ Contacts, including the postal address, telephone number and email address of the school, and a map of how to find it
✓ Latest news about school sporting and other events (include pictures)
✓ A timetable of forthcoming school sporting and other events
✓ The school curriculum
✓ Summaries of school results in examinations and tests
✓ The latest school inspection report
✓ A staff list
✓ Local information, including links to websites for the local council, estate agents and doctors.

c) The curriculum web page should explain briefly how the curriculum is organised and provide links to pages for each subject studied, which should show:

✓ The staff who teach the subject
✓ A description of the curriculum followed
✓ A description of the rooms and resources used
✓ Examples of the work students do.

d) Draw a structure diagram showing the links between the web pages.

e) Upload your website to a web server and check that it is accessible.

2. **Extension exercise.** Use tables to control the layout of some of the web pages you built in Question 1 above. For example, to lay out the timetable of forthcoming school sporting and other events, and your summary of school results in examinations and tests.

3. **Extension exercise.** Generate graphs in a spreadsheet and include these in the website built in Question 1. For example, write a page on healthy eating at school and include a bar chart showing the number of packets of crisps sold from the school tuck shop over a period of two weeks.

4. **Extension exercise.** Include a page of thumbnails in the website built in Question 1; for example, for pictures of a sporting event.

5. Set up a website on a topic of your choice.

End of Chapter 10 Checklist

1. All web pages are saved as **HTML (Hypertext Markup Language) files;** however, you do not have to create them by writing HTML as there are many ways that web pages can be created. You can create web pages using these methods:

    ✓ Using application software, such as Word, Excel and Access.

    ✓ Writing HTML using a text editor such as Notepad.

    ✓ Using web authoring software that enables you to write web pages as they appear on screen and in HTML, and provides you with tools to manage a website; for example, Dreamweaver.

2. Whatever method you use you should be able to create web pages that have these elements:

    ✓ Text in different sizes, colours and fonts.

    ✓ Graphics.

    ✓ Links within the web page.

    ✓ Links to other web pages.

    ✓ Email links.

    ✓ Backgrounds that are different colours or graphics.

    ✓ Thumbnails.

    ✓ Tables.

    ✓ Styles determined by inline, embedded and external style controls.

3. A **website** is a group of web pages linked together. It is best if this is done in a structured way because this makes navigation easier. The structure of many websites is broadly hierarchical but there are nearly always links from each page to a range of other pages.

4. You have to copy your website to a **web server** before it is available over the Internet. Many Internet Service Providers (ISPs) offer hosting on their web servers and the tools to move your website to their web server.

5. You can promote your website by submitting its web address to **search engines**.

Chapter 11: Data input and output

Input

Data capture is collecting data for input to a computer. We try to make sure that the data we collect is accurate and that it is input to the computer without mistakes. There are various ways of doing this which are based on the different peripheral devices used to input data into the computer.

Data capture forms

Data can be collected using a **data capture form** or **source document**; for example, a questionnaire.

Data written on a questionnaire can be collected by:

- Observing an individual's behaviour and making notes
- Interviewing individuals and making notes
- Asking individuals to fill in the questionnaire.

These methods are still widely used although they are now avoided if possible because they are slow and expensive. An example of a form that might be filled in when joining a sports club is shown in Figure 11.1. After the form has been filled in, the data on it is typed into the computer using a keyboard and the input saved on disk.

When designing a questionnaire or data capture form you should:

- Clearly state why the information is being collected. This could be done using a meaningful title and a short introductory paragraph explaining what the information will be used for.
- Use simple language so people can easily understand it.
- Lay out the form in a straightforward and uncluttered way so that it is easy to see what must be filled in.
- Say clearly and unambiguously what information must be provided and what is optional.
- Provide help in answering or examples of how to fill in the form if necessary.
- Provide enough space for the answer.
- Show how much space is available for the answer so that users can tailor the length of their answer to the space available.
- Collect all the information needed, but no more.

In this chapter you will learn about ways to prepare and process data input to a computer system in order to ensure it is accurate. After this, you will look at factors that affect the design of the output.

Chapter 11: Data input and output

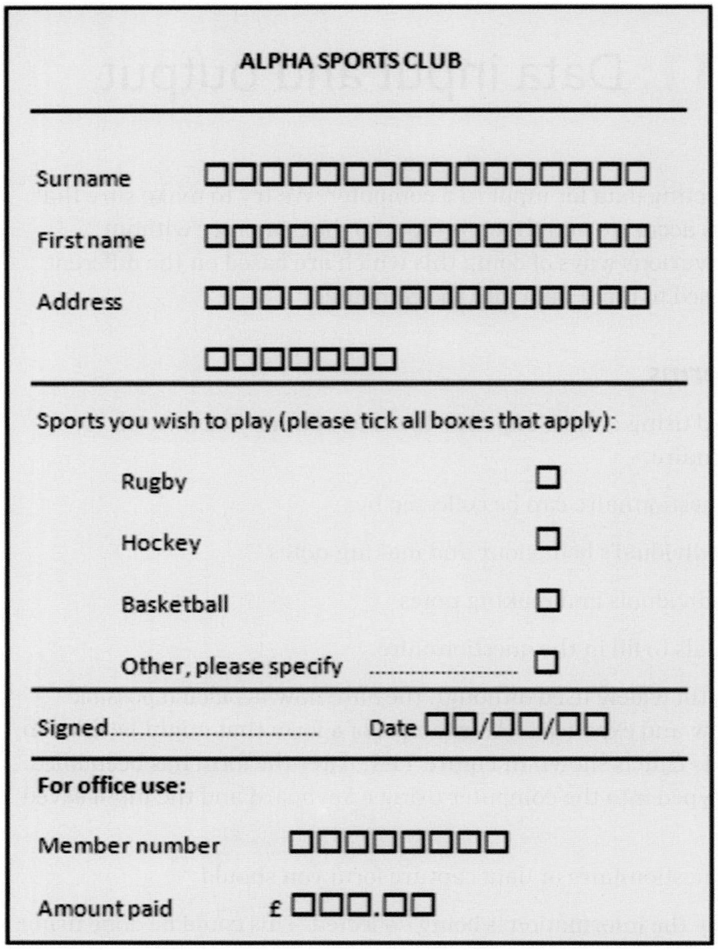

ALPHA SPORTS CLUB

Surname ☐☐☐☐☐☐☐☐☐☐☐☐☐☐☐☐

First name ☐☐☐☐☐☐☐☐☐☐☐☐☐☐☐☐

Address ☐☐☐☐☐☐☐☐☐☐☐☐☐☐☐☐
☐☐☐☐☐☐☐

Sports you wish to play (please tick all boxes that apply):

Rugby ☐

Hockey ☐

Basketball ☐

Other, please specify .... ☐

Signed............................ Date ☐☐/☐☐/☐☐

For office use:

Member number ☐☐☐☐☐☐☐☐

Amount paid £ ☐☐☐.☐☐

Figure 11.1 *A questionnaire filled in when joining a sports club*

- Avoid asking questions that may not be answered truthfully.

- Collect the information in a way which assists computer input. For example, use tick boxes or character boxes, or code the information (see Figure 11.2).

- Request the information in an intuitive logical order, e.g. name, date of birth, address, telephone number, fax number, email address.

- Encourage people who fill in the form to write their name clearly, and to sign and date the form. This helps ensure that they will fill in the form accurately.

- Allow people who fill in the form to give you their preferred contact details. This could be an address, telephone number or email address. Doing this will enable you to contact them if they raise issues that need a response.

- Make it easy for people who fill in the form to submit it. Provide instructions on the form that clearly state how the form can be submitted for processing. For example, on a printed form sent by post you would need to provide the name and address of the person the form is to be returned to, and you would get a better response rate if you included a stamped addressed envelope recipients could use to return the form.

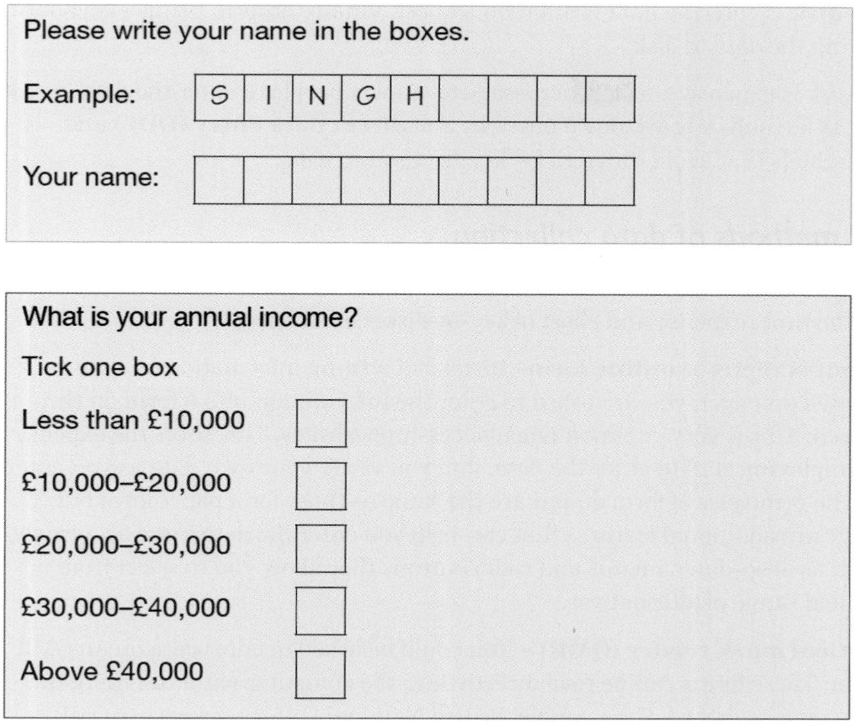

Please write your name in the boxes.

Example: | S | I | N | G | H | | | | |

Your name: | | | | | | | | | |

What is your annual income?

Tick one box

Less than £10,000 ☐

£10,000–£20,000 ☐

£20,000–£30,000 ☐

£30,000–£40,000 ☐

Above £40,000 ☐

Figure 11.2 *Character boxes and tick lists*

Verification

The data on a questionnaire or form has to be entered into a computer. Verification ensures that this is done accurately. There are two main approaches to verification. The double entry method is the most accurate but the most expensive.

Visual verification

After the data has been typed into the computer, the person who entered the data checks that the data displayed on the monitor screen is the same as that written on the form, and corrects any errors. The accuracy of this method depends on the person being thorough and conscientious.

Double entry verification

The **double entry verification** method uses three steps:

- The data is typed into the computer and saved as version 1.

- The data is typed into the computer again by someone else and saved as version 2.

- The computer compares version 1 and version 2. If these are the same, the data has been transferred accurately. If they are not the same, a mistake has been made and this will be corrected by referring back to the form. This method is much more accurate but is more expensive because of the need to employ two people, and more time-consuming because it takes twice as long.

Key-to-disk is entering data written on a questionnaire or form using a keyboard and saving the data to disk.

Key-to-disk is expensive, as it is necessary to employ people to enter the data, and it is slow. As a result, it is avoided if possible, and **direct data entry (DDE)** and other methods that avoid the need for key-to-disk are used.

Other methods of data collection

Direct data entry (DDE) allows data to be entered directly into the computer, saving the time, expense and effort of key-to-disk. For example:

- **Input screens** or **online form–** Instead of writing information on a form printed on paper, you are asked to enter the information into a form on the screen. This is very common when accessing websites. This saves the expense of employing staff to enter the data, and you verify your own data as you enter it. The principles of form design are the same as those for a paper form but there are additional features that can help you enter the data more accurately, such as drop-down menus and radio buttons that allow you to select from a limited range of alternatives.

- **Optical mark reader (OMR)** – You could be asked to enter data on an OMR form. These forms can be read directly into the computer without typing the data on a keyboard. For example, British National Lottery tickets use OMR.

- **Card reader** – A stripe card or a smart card is a more secure and accurate method of entering personal data than typing this in using a keyboard.

- **Sensors** – Sensors can input information at times and in locations where it would be difficult or dangerous for a person to do this. For example, a temperature sensor is more reliable and can be read more frequently in more remote locations at a lower cost than sending a person to read the temperature using a mercury thermometer.

- **Bar code reader** – Bar codes can be read using a bar code reader. This process is much faster and more accurate than entering product codes using a keyboard.

- **Radio frequency identification (RFID)** – RFID microchips are very small and inexpensive. They can be embedded in garment tags and other forms of product labeling. They have been tried out for several applications, including stock keeping in supermarkets as a replacement for bar codes. They can be read wirelessly as a customer passes through a gateway. Potentially, they overcome the need to queue at supermarket checkouts because shoppers simply wheel their trolleys through the RFID gateway. The cost of the goods in the trolley is automatically charged to their credit card.

These features of online forms help you fill them in:

Radio Buttons

Please show your family income:

- ● £40,000 or above
- ○ £30,000 or above
- ○ £20,000 or above
- ○ £10,000 or above
- ○ Less than £10,000

Drop-down menus

Please show the area you live:

North East
North East
North West
Yorkshire and Humberside
Midlands
South East
South West

Validation

Validation checks help ensure that data that has been input and stored on a computer is reasonable.

Validation checks include the following:

- **Field length** – The field length is the number of characters that are allowed to be stored in a field. A field length check makes sure that the number of characters of data in a field is no longer than the maximum number of characters allowed. For example, if a student number 6 characters long was expected by the software and you had typed in 8 characters, then this would be rejected by a field length check.

- **Type check** – This makes sure that the data is of the type expected. For example, if a number is expected, then '89' would be acceptable but 'AB89' would not be acceptable. Similarly, if only alphabetic characters are expected, then 'Tom Smith' would be accepted but '5 High Street' would not as this is **alphanumeric** data.

- **Format check** – This makes sure that the data is in the expected format. For example, a date may have to be entered in dd/mm/yyyy form for the UK. Dates not entered in this form would be rejected. If you entered the 3rd of September 2005 as *3/9/5*, then it would be rejected because two digits are expected for the day, two for the month and four for the year.

- **Range check** – This makes sure that the data falls within a sensible range. For example, a date entered in dd/mm/yyyy form would have to comply with these range checks:

  - ❑ 0<dd<32 – this means the minimum value is 1 and the maximum value is 31.

  - ❑ 0<mm<13 – this means the minimum value is 1 and the maximum value is 12.

  - ❑ The range that the year could fall within would be determined by the application.

- **Presence check** – This makes sure that data that is required is entered. For example, many web forms cannot be submitted unless the person filling in the form provides their name and email address.

- **Check digit** – This is used in specialist applications to detect transposition errors. A **transposition error** is when digits are swapped – it is very easy to do this without realising it. For example, compare the number 0631900578 with 0631900587. There has been a transposition error in the two rightmost digits. This could be detected using a check digit.

  Check digits are often used with bar codes to help ensure that these have been accurately read. The use of a check digit is explained in more detail below.

Check digits (Extension material)

A **check digit** is an extra digit added to a number. The check digit is calculated in a prescribed way that is known to the computer system. Every time the number is input to the computer system or transferred within it the check digit is recalculated. If the correct check digit is not obtained from the recalculation then an error has been made and the data must be rechecked.

Check digits are used with the bar codes that identify books. The International Standard Book Number (ISBN) contains a check digit in the rightmost position. You will find an ISBN on every published book including this one! ISBNs used to be 10 digits long, but now new books are published with 13-digit ISBNs. The example described below is based on a10-digit ISBN.

The ISBN has a weighted modulus 11 check digit. The check digit has a value that makes the sum of the products of the digits in the ISBN and the weights exactly divisible by 11. It can take the values 0 to 9 and 10 (which is represented by an X). In this example the check digit has the value 8. When the products are calculated and added, the answer is 176, which is exactly divisible by 11. The calculation is as follows:

Index	1	2	3	4	5	6	7	8	9	Check digit
ISBN	0	6	3	1	9	0	0	5	7	8
Weight	10	9	8	7	6	5	4	3	2	1

Quick question
Which of these is a correct ISBN?
ISBN 0-781-37388-8
ISBN 0-582-47388-8
ISBN 0-582-47388-X

Calculation

$$0 \times 10 + 6 \times 9 + 3 \times 8 + 1 \times 7 + 9 \times 6 + 0 \times 5 + 0 \times 4 + 5 \times 3 + 7 \times 2 + 8 \times 1 = 176$$

If any of the digits in the ISBN were changed then it is unlikely that the answer would be 176, although this is possible.

Limitations of verification and validation

Even after rigorous verification and validation checks, we cannot be entirely certain that the data is correct. A **verification** check ensures that input is accurate; that is, that what is presented for input into the computer is saved on the computer. It does not necessarily ensure that it is correct. A **validation** check is a further check that the data that is already stored on the computer is reasonable. Even so, not all errors in the data will have been detected.

For example, in the UK dates are input in dd/mm/yyyy form but in the USA dates are input in the form mm/dd/yyyy. If a UK citizen input a date in the UK format into software that expected dates in the USA format, not all of these errors would be detected (see below):

Quick question
What date is 04/05/2006 in the UK?
In the USA?
Is 05/14/2006 a correct date?

Input to USA software	Response of software
03/04/2005	No error would be found by the software. The UK citizen meant the 3rd April 2005. The USA software would interpret this as 4th March 2005 but this would not be detected.
24/11/2005	If the UK citizen input the 24th November 2005 like this, the USA software would indicate an error because 24 would be outside the range expected in the leftmost two digits.

Exercise 11.1

1. This is part of a questionnaire:

Where were you born? (please tick one)

☐ Yorkshire

☐ Lancashire

☐ Other, please state:...........................

Put a cross in one box to name the part of the questionnaire.

☐ A   Tick list

☐ B   Radio buttons

☐ C   Drop-down menu

☐ D   Character boxes

2. Students have to provide an emergency contact.

a) Design part of a data collection form for collecting a person's name, address and telephone number.

b) Design part of a data collection form for collecting information about the relationship of the student to the emergency contact. You should use character boxes and code the information.

3. Key-to-disk is used to transfer data written on a questionnaire into the computer.

a) Describe what is meant by key-to-disk.

b) Give an example of the use of key-to-disk.

c) Explain why it is best to avoid the use of key-to-disk.

4. The accuracy of data entry can be checked by visual verification or double entry verification.

a) Describe what is meant by **visual verification.** Describe an example of its use, and justify this.

b) Describe what is meant by **double entry verification.** Describe an example of its use, and justify this.

c) Discuss the advantages and disadvantages of visual verification.

d) Discuss the advantages and disadvantages of double entry verification.

5. *a)* Explain why verification is not used when data is entered using:

    ✓ OMR

    ✓ A bar code reader

    ✓ A temperature sensor

b) Describe the advantages and disadvantages to an organisation if data is entered into a form on a web page rather than written on a questionnaire.

6. People who want to join a local sports centre have to fill in an application form.

   a) Design a membership application form for the sports centre. Make sure your design makes input to the computer easier.

   b) There are only two or three new membership applications each month. The form will be input to a computer by typing it in on a keyboard. Describe suitable verification procedures.

   c) It has been suggested that the form could be input using OMR. State whether this is appropriate in this application, giving reasons for your answer.

   d) Applicants have to write their date of birth on the application form. Describe the validation checks that should be done on the date.

7. A large national organisation for people who enjoy gardening keeps membership records on a database. Membership application forms are posted to new members. Design the membership application form.

8. You have been asked to carry out research into the lifestyles of young people.

   a) Design a data collection form that could be used.

   b) Describe how you would make this form available to young people and explain how this affected the design of your form.

   c) Select a suitable method of inputting the data and justify your choice.

   d) Describe what verification and validation checks would be done.

9. Give three examples of data that could be incorrect but that would not necessarily be detected by verification or validation checks.

10. Some of these ISBN numbers are incorrect. Identify those that are correct and those that are incorrect.

   a) 1-902505-51-4

   b) 1-85828-442-3

   c) 0-415-10735-0

   d) 0-582-30494-5

   e) 0-582-05187-X

Output

Many factors influence output design. One very important constraint is that output is dependent on the availability of the data it is derived from. If this is not already stored within the ICT system when output is requested, then the required output cannot be generated.

General guidelines for output design are given below, and there is discussion of some issues relating to the following:

- audience
- using tables, diagrams and graphs
- layout
- timing
- accessibility.

Output design guidelines

- State what information is being output. This could be done using a title and a short introductory sentence explaining what information is being provided.

- Use simple language so people can easily understand. Avoid jargon.

- Each page or screen should have a title even if this is only a part of a larger report.

- Lay out the output in a straightforward and uncluttered way so that it is easy to find the information required.

- The information output should be balanced across the page or screen. If there is only a small amount of information to be displayed, this should not be grouped in a corner with most of the output area blank.

- There should be sufficient output to fill the output area without making it look too crowded.

- Tailor the detail and complexity of the output to the needs of the target audience.

- The information in outputs should follow an intuitive logical order, e.g. customer name, customer number, address, telephone number and email address.

- The output should be sorted into an order which makes finding information easier.

- Use tables and graphs to summarise. These should be clearly labelled and legends should be provided for all abbreviations. There is more discussion of tables and graphs on the next page.

- Use codes to reduce the volume of output, especially when these are well known. For example, you could code gender as 'M' or 'F', which most people would easily interpret as Male or Female. Doing this reduces the number of characters that have to be displayed.

- The information that users need should be available without their having to do further analysis or calculation.

- Use hyperlinks to web pages providing more detail, or appendices in a printed report, to provide more extensive detail that might otherwise disrupt the simplicity of a summary or overview.

- Navigation should be straightforward whether this is a website or a printed document.

- Provide all the information needed, but no more unless there is a good reason to do so.

- Graphics should reflect the nature of the information. For example, on a website, information about forests may be accessed via a graphic hyperlink which is a small picture of a tree.

- Avoid techniques and technologies that do not add to the information provided, for example graphics and video. Colours and fonts should be consistent and not interfere with ease of access to the information.

- On web pages, consider whether to provide a facility to print the information displayed on the screen.

- Use screen templates or pre-printed stationery to minimise the time and effort involved in producing repetitive output.
- State the source of the information so that users can evaluate whether it is reliable.
- State the time and date the output was produced.

Audience

For an organisation there are three types of output in relation to the audience:

- **Internal** – This type of output is produced for the audience within the organisation.

- **External** – This type of output is produced for the audience outside the organisation.

- **Turnaround** – This type of output is produced for the external audience but it is expected that they will add data to it and return it to the organisation. An example of a turnaround document is a printed questionnaire or data capture form.

The target audience for the output will affect some features of the design. For example, less care may be taken over the graphic design of screen layouts intended for internal use than over the design of web pages to be accessed externally by potential customers.

Even within an organisation, different users will have different needs. For example, summary reports, graphs and charts may be used to present information for managers who need an overview, but these may be produced as complex tables of statistics for employees who need more detailed information. Similarly, managers may need **exception reports** that filter out normal activity and focus only on deviations from expected performance rather than comprehensive statistics.

Using tables, diagrams and graphs

Tables, diagrams and graphs can be used to summarise information. They should be clearly labelled, with legends provided for all abbreviations.

Tables are often produced in spreadsheets and exported to other applications. For example, the table in Figure 11.3 shows the takings from the sales of different types of meal in a restaurant. The title of the table is on the first row and it tells us what information we can expect to find in the table. Each column has a meaningful title at the top. The titles are in bold so that they stand out. This is a very straightforward way of summarising and displaying this information. However, although the information is accurate, the table does not help us interpret it.

Takings from the sales of meals in a restaurant			
Meal	Quantity sold	Price	Takings
Meat Bhuna	2	£4.50	£9.00
Chicken Tandoori	5	£5.00	£25.00
Lamb Balti	3	£6.50	£19.50
Vegetable Curry	4	£3.25	£13.00
Total takings			£66.50

Figure 11.3 *The takings from the sales of meal in a restaurant*

A **pie diagram** (see Figure 11.4) gives us information about the relative importance of the takings from the sales of the different types of meals. Notice that there is a meaningful title and each slice of the pie has been labelled with the name of one of the meals. The size of the angle at the centre of each slice of the pie is proportional to the takings for a meal. It is clear that the takings from the sales of Chicken Tandoori are much greater than the takings from Vegetable Curry. If you were particularly interested in the sales of Vegetable Curry, you could offset the slice to emphasise this. However, there is no information about the actual takings on this pie diagram. These could be added but this would make the pie diagram look more cluttered.

A **bar chart** (see Figure 11.5) is slightly more complex than a pie diagram but provides more information. Notice that there is an overall title, and that each axis and each bar is labelled.

The height of each bar is proportional to the takings for the type of meal. The relative value of the takings for each type of meal is clear, and it is also possible to estimate the actual value of the takings from the vertical scale. For example, it is much clearer that sales of Chicken Tandoori have a greater value than sales of Lamb Balti, and it is possible to estimate the actual value of the takings from Chicken Tandoori as £25.00. Even so, it would be difficult to obtain from this bar chart the exact value of the takings for Lamb Balti given in the table.

The bars on a bar chart could be horizontal or vertical. Microsoft Excel refers to bar charts with vertical bars as column charts, and to those with horizontal bars as bar charts. However, apart from the orientation of the bars, the charts are used in an identical way.

Bar charts should not be used when the information on the horizontal scale is continuous. It is easy to know whether information is continuous. You look between two known points and try to find another meaningful point. If you can do this (and carry on doing it) the information is continuous; if you cannot, it is not continuous. For example, looking between the bars for Meat Bhuna and Chicken Tandoori, we don't know if this represents a blend of the two dishes (is it Meat Tandoori or Chicken Bhuna?). In fact, there is no dish between the two bars; if there were, it would be shown separately.

When the information on the horizontal scale is continuous, you should use a **line graph** (see Figure 11.6). Time is shown on the horizontal scale.

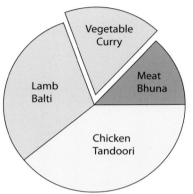

Takings from the sales of meals

Figure 11.4 *A pie diagram*

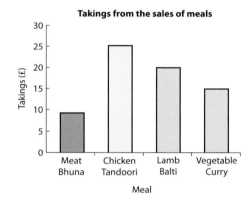

Takings from the sales of meals

Figure 11.5 *A bar chart*

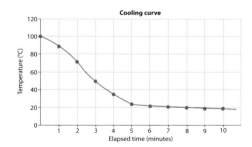

Figure 11.6 *A line graph*

Between any two times there is always another time, so time is continuous and it is appropriate to use a line graph. The graph shows the temperature as a flask of boiling water cools to room temperature. The temperature was taken at one-minute intervals and the graph plotted. Even though the temperature was only measured at one-minute intervals, you could use the graph to estimate the temperature at any time between these measurements. Notice that there is an overall title and each axis is carefully labelled.

Layout

The characteristics of the output device constrain the layout of the output. For example, if a map is being output, less detail can be shown if it is output on the screen than if it is printed on an A3 sheet of paper.

Some information may be better printed in landscape or portrait orientation but changes between these should not be frequent. Printed output can be designed using a **printer spacing chart** (see Figure 11.7).

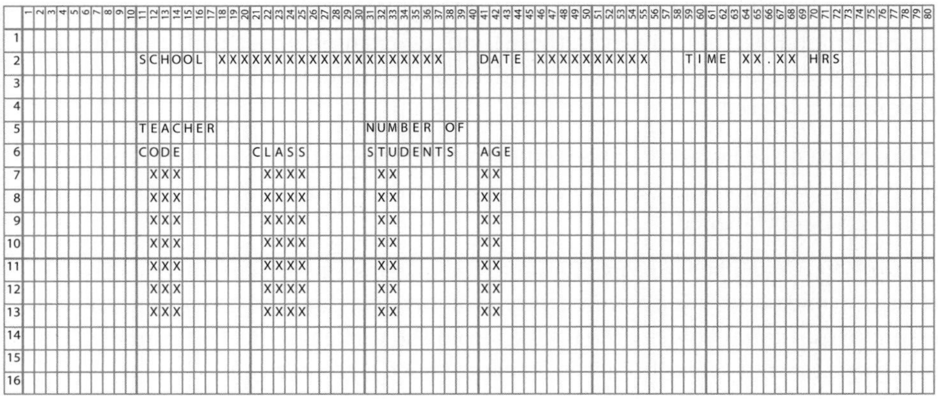

Figure 11.7 *A printer spacing chart used for layout design*

Output on a monitor screen will present less immediately visible detail than printed output but can include features such as hyperlinks to more detailed information, animation, sound and video. Users' monitors will have different screen resolutions. Much less information can be displayed on a monitor with a screen resolution of 800×600 than one with a 1024×768 screen resolution. Screen output can be designed using a **screen spacing chart**. This is similar to a printer spacing chart but the number of columns and rows would be different.

A familiar example of how the characteristics of the output device constrain the layout of the output is the **point of sale (PoS)** terminal used at supermarket checkouts. This has a very small screen built into the till and a small printer to print receipts. The physical size of the output limits the information that can be displayed. Consequently, the design of screen displays for the checkout operator and receipts for customers focuses more on providing the information needed than on the attractiveness of the graphic design.

Timing

Here are some guidelines for timing:

- The output provided should be the most up-to-date available.

- Output should be provided as soon as possible after the relevant inputs are available. This is particularly important for real-time applications.

- The speed at which output can be generated affects its usefulness. Users will not wait long periods of time for output, especially if the output has a limited usefulness.

Accessibility

Output should be easily accessible to users. It is necessary to consider whether users will be able to receive the output in the form in which it is provided. There could be various limiting factors:

- **Connection speed –** The lack of availability of an Internet connection of sufficient speed to download the output within a reasonable waiting time could reduce accessibility. For example, output intended for those with access via a 56K modem and a telephone line must present the output without any features which may take too long to download, such as video. Such features may not be problematic for users with broadband. The form of the output should take into account different connection speeds.

- **Physical access –** Not everyone has easy access to communication and distribution systems. It should be remembered that some people do not have physical access to computers at school, at home, in cyber cafés or in libraries or other public access areas. Particularly in developing countries, people may have no opportunity to use a computer connected to local and international networks. Access to postal delivery services can also be very restricted. Only a few people receive a delivery of post more than once each day, and users in very remote areas may not have access to reliable daily postal services. The form of the output should take into account the availability of communication and distribution systems.

- **Disability –** People with disabilities – for example, restricted vision or hearing, or the physically disabled – may have difficulty accessing output. If output is to be used by disabled people, particular care needs to be taken to ensure that it is accessible to them. Some guidelines for improving accessibility to information on the Web are:

    1. Create a style of presentation that is consistent across pages.

    2. Ensure that all information conveyed with colour is also available without colour.

    3. Ensure that foreground and background colour combinations provide sufficient contrast when viewed by someone having colour deficits or when viewed on a black and white screen.

    4. Avoid causing the screen to flicker, for example by using animations that blink.

    5. Clearly identify the target of each link.

> **Did you know?**
> Very detailed design guidelines for improving accessibility are available at the World Wide Web Consortium's website **(http://www.w3.org)**.

6. Provide a text equivalent for every non-text element, including for images, maps, audio, video or animation.

7. Provide auditory descriptions of important visual information.

8. Provide customisable features that can be adjusted to compensate for individual disabilities. Each person's disability will be different and so it is important to design output that can be customised by them. For example, partially sighted people may find it helpful to be able to enlarge the text on the screen, whereas this might not be very useful to people who are deaf.

Encoding data

When data is input to a computer it is often encoded. **Encoding** is using a brief **code** to represent a more detailed and lengthy description. This is something that we do frequently when we communicate. For example, when sending text messages on a mobile phone, words and phrases are often abbreviated. The code 'lol' could be used to mean 'laughing out loud'.

The American Speech-Language-Hearing Association (ASHA) describes on its website at **www.asha.org** how disabled people who find it difficult to communicate encode their language to make communication easier.

Codes can be used to represent lengthy snippets of language. For example:

- '1' could mean 'Can you switch the television on?'

- '2' could mean 'Which channel would you like to watch?'

- '3' could mean 'I'd like to have pasta for dinner!'

Computers encode the language we use. You type the letter 'A' on your keyboard but it may be represented as a binary code in ASCII so that the computer can store and process it. The binary code is decoded before it is displayed for you to read.

Some codes are well known and widely used. Gender can be encoded as 'M' for 'Male' and 'F' for 'Female'. Many people would recognise this without the code being interpreted for them. This encoding is often used on data capture forms as it speeds up input by reducing the number of characters that have to be typed in, and less space is needed to store the information on backing storage. There is very little loss of meaning if this code is used in printed output or on a screen display. If you type 'F' instead of 'Female', you notice immediately how much faster and easier this is. If you had to do this several thousand times this would be a considerable saving of time and effort!

Validation checks on codes are often much easier. You could easily set up a validation check to make sure that only 'F' or 'M' were entered. Similarly, 'Male' and 'Female' could easily be validated if this was being entered in an interactive form on a website. You would most likely find that there would be a drop-down list that would not allow you to choose other alternatives. On a paper-based questionnaire, if you did not code gender, you might get a wide variety of different responses. Some people would write 'boy' or 'girl' and many responses would be spelt incorrectly. If these responses were accurately copied from the form when they were input, it would be very difficult for a computer to know what was a reasonable response, particularly where words are misspelt.

Codes are widely used in ICT systems. Another example would be a database for a school library where books are classified as 'fiction', 'non-fiction' or 'reference', and there are other resources such as 'CDs', 'DVDs' and 'magazines' that can be borrowed. Coding these as 'F', 'N', 'R', 'C', 'D' and 'M' would speed up data input, reduce the space needed on backing storage and make output more concise. Library staff would understand these codes because they would use them frequently. There would be some loss of meaning for borrowers and other library users; however, they may not need to use the codes. Validating the codes would be much easier. If you were allowed to type in text rather than a code, some people might enter 'computer magazine' or the name of a magazine, such as 'Autotrader', and there would be many misspellings. It would be much more difficult for a computer to know what was a reasonable response than if it was told to accept one of 'F', 'N', 'R', 'C', 'D' and 'M' and no others.

Sometimes, having to select a code helps clarify what data needs to be entered. For example, in Figure 11.2, when you fill in the tick list this is effectively coding the data. The different ranges of annual income could be entered as '1' meaning 'less than £10,000', '2' meaning '£10,000 to £20,000' and so on. You could find it easier to estimate your income within a given range, and this groups the data for later statistical analysis and also helps preserve your privacy. If you are asked to tick a box instead of entering your annual income in full, this is much easier and faster. Validating these codes would be much easier. A computer could easily be set up to validate a '1', but if you were asked to enter your actual income, setting up a validation check (for example, for '£9,000', '9000', '£9000.00', '£8943.45') would be much more difficult. Less space would be needed to save a '1' on backing storage.

Codes should be meaningful and as brief as possible. They are used because:

- data entry is easier
- data entry is faster
- less space is needed to store the data on backing storage
- setting up validation checks is easier
- privacy can be preserved
- output can be more concise.

Exercise 11.2

1. A newspaper shop prints a list of customers' names and addresses and the amount they owe for papers that have been delivered to their homes.

This is some of the data:

Fran Jones of 3 Main Street owes £4.50; Simon Gower who lives at 237 Allerton Road owes £6.72; David Wilson – 78 Poplar Avenue owes £8.50; Manish Patel of 16 Greystones Drive owes £6.90.

a) Design a suitable table to display this information for the newspaper shop. The design should take into account that there could be a large number of customers. The table will be printed on A4 paper. You may find it helpful to use a printer spacing chart.

b) Make sure there is a suitable title at the top of the page.

c) Use the headings *name*, *address* and *amount owed* in your table.

d) Sort the table into a sensible order so that employees of the newspaper shop can find customers easily.

e) Customers order many different newspapers. Design a code for the newspapers.

2. A school outputs information about pupils in different ways. This information could be included in the output: date of birth; address; name; target grades for Mathematics, English and ICT; class; teacher; name of school; date; and gender.

a) Design a code for each subject studied at the school.

b) Some other items of data can be coded. Design a code for these.

c) Design a suitable output format for printing all the assessment information for one class on A4 paper.

d) Design a suitable output format for printing the information about one pupil on a monitor screen. You may find it helpful to use a screen spacing chart.

3. A student uses a search engine to find sources of information about agriculture. Brief details of each source are output by the search engine: the URL or web address, a hyperlink to the website, a description of the content and a link to similar websites. Several hundred of these sources of information might be identified by a single search. Design an output screen to display this information.

4. Design graphics (icons) to link to web pages that have information about:

a) The weather

b) Sheep farming

c) Volcanoes

d) Government information about education

e) An online bank.

5. Each week 1000 people attend a sports centre. Of these, 250 people go swimming, 50 use the weight lifting equipment, 300 attend aerobic exercise classes, 195 use the sauna and 205 use the Jacuzzi.

a) State the type of table, diagram or graph which would be easiest to understand and would show that aerobic exercise is the most popular activity.

b) State the type of table, diagram or graph which would be easiest to understand and would show that weight lifting is the least popular activity.

c) Explain why a line graph would not be appropriate.

d) Design a code for the activities people do at the sports centre.

6. An organisation produces information for employees and for customers. Describe differences in the presentation of the output to each of these groups.

7. A website gives the weekly results of football league matches. It is updated each month. Explain why football fans might prefer to access a website that was updated more frequently.

8. You are going on holiday and have to leave home for the airport in an hour. You can get a detailed weather forecast for your holiday destination posted to you if you telephone the travel agent.

a) Explain why this way of getting a weather forecast might not be very useful to you.

b) Describe another way that could be more useful.

9. The characteristics of an output device can constrain the form of the output produced. For example, supermarket receipts are printed on very small printers and, as a result, the printed output is unlikely to contain detailed graphics. For each of the following, describe how the characteristics of the output device constrain the form of the output.

a) PDAs and smartphones

b) Speakers

c) Data projectors

d) Plotters

e) Electric motors.

10. Some people find it difficult to access information on the Web.

a) State what features could be used on a website to make it more accessible to partially sighted people.

b) State what features could be used on a website to make it more accessible to deaf people.

c) Design a coding system that would enable people who are unable to speak to communicate their everyday needs concisely.

1. Data can be collected using a **data capture form** or **questionnaire** that is printed on a piece of paper and filled in using a pen or pencil.

2. When designing a questionnaire or data capture form you should:

✓ Clearly state why the information is being collected.

✓ Use simple language.

✓ Lay out the form in a straightforward and uncluttered way.

✓ Say clearly and unambiguously what information must be provided.

✓ Provide help in answering.

✓ Provide enough space for the answer.

✓ Collect all the information needed.

✓ Collect the information in a way which assists computer input.

✓ Provide space for users to sign and date the form.

3. **Key-to-disk** is typing in data written on a questionnaire or form and saving it on disk.

4. Written data can be collected by asking individuals to fill in a questionnaire or form, or by someone doing this while observing or interviewing people.

5. **Verification** ensures that data is accurately entered into a computer.

6. With **visual verification,** the person who entered the data checks that the data on the monitor screen is the same as that written on the form.

7. With **double entry verification,** the data is entered twice by two different people. The computer compares version 1 and version 2. If these are the same, the data has been transferred accurately.

8. Methods of data collection include input screens, OMR, bar code readers, stripe card readers, sensors and RFID.

9. **Validation checks** help ensure that data that has been input and stored on a computer is reasonable.

10. Validation checks include:

✓ A **field length check** makes sure that the number of characters of data in a field is no longer than the maximum number of characters allowed.

✓ A **format check** makes sure that the data is in the expected format. For example, a date may have to be entered in dd/mm/yyyy form for the UK.

✓ A **range check** makes sure that data falls within a sensible range. For example, a date entered in dd/mm/yyyy form would have to have $0<dd<32$.

✓ A **presence check** makes sure that data that is required is entered.

✓ A **check digit** is an extra digit added to a number and is calculated in a prescribed way that is known to the computer system. Every time the number is input to the computer system or transferred within it, the check digit is recalculated. If this is incorrect then an error has been made and the data must be rechecked. Check digits are often used with bar codes to help ensure that these have been accurately read.

11. Output design guidelines:

✓ Provide a title and a short description of the information provided. Each page or screen should have a title.

✓ Use simple language.

✓ Lay out the output in a straightforward way and balance this across the page or screen.

✓ Navigation should be straightforward.

✓ The detail and complexity of the output should take into account the needs of the target audience.

✓ The output should be sorted to make finding information easier.

✓ Use tables and graphs to summarise.

✓ Use hyperlinks or appendices to provide more extensive detail.

✓ The information that users need should be available without their having to do further calculation.

✓ Provide all the information needed, but no more.

✓ Graphics should reflect the nature of the information. For example, on a website, information about forests may be accessed via a graphic hyperlink which is a small picture of a tree.

✓ Colours and fonts should be consistent and not interfere with ease of access to the information.

✓ State the source of the information so that users can evaluate whether it is reliable.

✓ State the time and date the output was produced.

12. Internal output is for the audience within an organisation. **External output** is for the audience outside the organisation. **Turnaround output** is for the external audience but they add data to it and return it to the organisation.

13. Tables, diagrams and graphs can be used to summarise information.

✓ **Tables** are a very straightforward way of summarising information and are often produced in spreadsheets. Each table should have a title, and the columns and rows should have labels that make it clear what information is being shown.

✓ A **pie diagram** (see Figure 11.4) shows the relative importance of each component part of the information displayed. There should be a title, and each slice of the pie should be labelled.

✓ A **bar chart** (see Figure 11.5) should have an overall title, and each axis and each bar should be labelled. The height of each bar is proportional to the component part of the information displayed.

✓ A **line graph** (see Figure 11.6) should be used when the information on the horizontal scale is continuous.

14. Printed output can be designed using a **printer spacing chart** (see Figure 11.7). Screen output can be designed using a **screen spacing chart,** which is very similar.

15. The characteristics of an output device constrain the layout of the output. For example, a supermarket checkout has a very small screen and a small printer, and this affects what is printed on receipts and displayed on the screen.

16. The **timing** of the output affects its usefulness. Output should be up to date and produced quickly when requested.

17. Accessibility is affected by connection speed, physical access and disability. People with restricted vision or hearing or the physically disabled may have difficulty accessing output. If output is to be used by disabled people, particular care needs to be taken to ensure that it is accessible to them.

18. Codes should be meaningful and as brief as possible. They are used because:

✓ data entry is easier

✓ data entry is faster

✓ less space is needed to store the data on backing storage

✓ setting up validation checks is easier

✓ privacy can be preserved

✓ output can be more concise.

Chapter 12: Applications and effects

A typical day

Ian's bedside radio/alarm clock goes off at precisely 6.30 a.m. on weekdays to wake him up to go to school. The alarm was set at the beginning of the month and the information was stored in the chip that is in the clock. The clock is powered by electricity, which is controlled by an ICT system that adjusts the power in the grid to suit fluctuating demand.

Ian's mother heats up the pizza left over from last night for Ian's breakfast, using a microwave oven. She specifies the length of time to heat up the pizza by pressing on the keypad. The chip inside the oven stores the value and turns off the power when the time is up.

Ian gets a lift to school in his father's new car. The car uses fuel injection; this means that there is a microchip built into the engine that controls the fuel consumption, based on load and speed. It also controls most of the displays on the digital panel on the dashboard.

At school Ian studies English, Mathematics, ICT and some other subjects. Ian is not performing well in his Mathematics class and his teacher has suggested that he tries using a Computer Assisted Learning (CAL) program to try to improve his grades.

After school, Ian goes to the shopping mall with his mother. Ian's mother works in a local warehouse that stocks parts for radios and she has just been paid. She wants to withdraw some money, so she takes out her bank card and inserts it into a cashpoint/ATM located in the mall. She enters her PIN and, after the computer to which the ATM is connected approves the transaction, she withdraws some cash.

Before leaving the mall, Ian and his mother decide to go to the supermarket to purchase a few items. They pick up the items and go to the checkout counter. The cashier passes the items over the bar code reader to record what is being sold. Ian's mother pays for the items using her credit card. The card is inserted in a card machine and the amount of money is keyed in. The machine is connected to a computer in the credit card centre that has to approve the transaction. Once the transaction is approved, the amount of money, the time and date, and the name of the supermarket are recorded by the computer and a receipt is issued for Ian's mother.

Ian and his mother make a quick visit to the hospital to check on Granny, who is very ill. She has a number of sensors from different devices attached to her. The equipment is part of a patient monitoring system that tracks all her vital signs and alerts the staff if there are any significant changes. After the visit Ian goes to the video arcade to play computer games and his mother goes home.

At home, Ian's mother uses the Web to book and pay for the flights and accommodation for the family holiday in the USA this summer. She has to go to a training day at her employer's national head office the following week and she books and pays for the train tickets.

In this chapter you will learn about the ICT applications we make use of in our daily lives

Did you know?
An **ATM** is an automated teller machine, also known as a *cashpoint*.
A **PIN** is a *personal identification number*. Because you must enter a PIN to withdraw money, this helps to prevent fraud if the card is lost or stolen.

Ian gets home later at around 6.30 p.m. and telephones some friends and his aunt in the United States. The telephone calls are made using VoIP. He starts his homework at about 7.30 p.m., using an encyclopedia that is stored on a CD-ROM and has to be read using a PC. He connects to the Internet and searches the Web to find more information. Ian also emails friends abroad and accesses a chat site to see what is being discussed. He completes his homework and goes to sleep.

This general scenario is increasingly familiar; whether we are aware of it or not, we are affected in much of our daily living by Information and Communications Technology (ICT). This chapter describes several common applications of ICT that affect people's lives and more generally considers the social impact of the widespread use of ICT.

Payroll

One of the oldest and most common commercial applications of ICT is payroll processing. Every company or business has to pay its employees. Although this is a fairly straightforward task it has to be done frequently and accurately. Employees will be annoyed if they are not paid the correct amount of money at the appropriate time. However, it is not a task that needs to be done instantaneously, which is just as well because a large company may need to process a very large amount of data. The data to be input is readily available when required and it might be possible to do the processing needed over a few days or longer. Provided the ICT system is well organised and the payroll applications software works, all should be well. In following through the description of the payroll system it would be useful to refer to the systems flow chart (see Figure 12.2).

In a warehouse, employees each have their own swipe card, which identifies them (see Figure 12.1). Each employee has a unique employee number and this is recorded on their swipe card. When employees arrive at work they *clock in;* that is, they put their swipe card in a slot in a machine that records the time they arrived. When they leave work they *clock out by* putting the swipe card in the slot again so that the time they finished work is also recorded. Workers have to be present to use their swipe card and will be fired immediately if they swipe any card other than their own.

The information about an employee that is **input** to the ICT system each day is:

- employee number
- clock-in time
- clock-out time.

Figure 12.1 *Warehouse employees often have their own swipe cards used for clocking in*

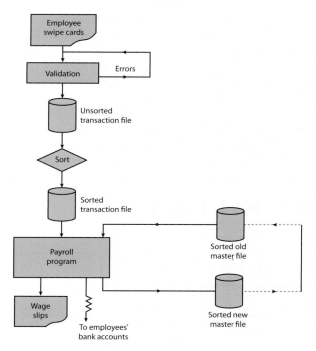

Figure 12.2 *An ICT system for payroll processing*

Workers are paid a week in arrears; that is, they are paid for the week before the one they have just worked. This means that there is one week in which to process the payroll data.

Validation checks are made on all the data input to the ICT system. Employee numbers can be checked against a table of known employee numbers (**table look-up**); the clock-in time and clock-out times can be checked to see if they are in a reasonable range (**range check**) – for example, between 7.00 hours and 19.00 hours. The clock-in time should be less than the clock-out time; the hours worked each day should usually not exceed 10 hours; the total hours worked each week should usually be less than 45.

Invalid data must be corrected before further processing, but data that has been successfully validated is written to the transaction file. This is the data about employees that changes daily.

The data that does not change so frequently is saved on the **old master file.** There is one record on the old master file for each employee. A record on the old master file contains the following:

- employee number
- employee name
- address and other contact details
- hourly rate of pay
- details of the tax to be paid
- cumulative totals of the tax paid during the current tax year
- employee's bank account details.

For each employee, the record on the transaction file and the record on the old master file must be quickly matched so that all the data for an employee is available when the payroll program is run.

Now that the data to be processed has been captured and validated, it can be input to the payroll program. In the **payroll program** each transaction file record will be matched with the corresponding old master file record. A **new master file** record is created containing the amended data. The payroll program prints a wage slip to give to each employee so that they have all the information they need about how their pay is calculated (see Figure 12.3), and the payroll program pays each employee directly into their bank account.

RADIO U.K. LTD. ⚛		
Name: A. Jones	Employee number: 86502	Date: 10/07/92
Hours worked: 45	Hourly rate of pay: £3.50	
Gross pay: £157.50		
Tax: £26.25	Tax paid this year:	£240.75
National insurance: £17.40	National insurance paid this year:	£136.14
Net pay: £113.85		

Figure 12.3 *A wage slip printed by the payroll system*

Backups of files for security purposes can be generated as a consequence of the need to create a new master file each time the payroll program is run. The **ancestral backup system** normally provides three levels of backup (see below); however, this could be extended to four or more levels.

Son	New master file – will become the old master file the next time the payroll program is run
Father	Old master file – stored securely but accessibly, possibly on site
Grandfather	Previous old master file – stored securely, probably off site

Corresponding copies of the sorted transaction file must also be kept so that if the current files are lost they can be recovered by repeating previous runs of the payroll program. Backup copies of the old master file and the transaction file can be used to restore the current file.

The system described above is a known as a **batch processing** system because the data captured can be divided into batches before processing. It is characteristic of batch processing that all the data to be processed is available before processing begins and that there is no need to process the data immediately. The system can be run **off line**; that is, it is not interactive. Once the data has been captured, there is no need for additional input from users while the payroll program is running.

The hardware needed to run the system will include:
- Swipe card readers – to read employees' swipe cards
- Printers – with the capability to print wage slips
- Disk drives – additional disk drives may be required.

Airline booking system

A large airline keeps details of flight schedules and passenger bookings on a **mainframe** computer (see Figure 12.4). Passengers may make enquiries over the Web or at travel agents anywhere in the world at any time to find out if a seat is free on any of the flights operated by the airline. Passengers require immediate up-to-date information. Online contact with the airline's computer is made using a desktop PC and a broadband connection. This gives immediate access to the flight information and booking file stored on hard disk on the airline's mainframe computer.

The airline's computer should support **multi-access** because there may be a large number of passengers wanting to make enquiries at the same time. The flight information and booking file must be held on magnetic disk because data held on disk can be read by direct or random access. **Direct access** (or random access) means that any record on the file can be read without having to read previous records. Consequently, direct access to a record is usually much faster than serial access. Access to the flight information and booking file must be made using direct access for high-speed data retrieval so that the information requested can be displayed instantaneously and kept up to date while displayed on the screen.

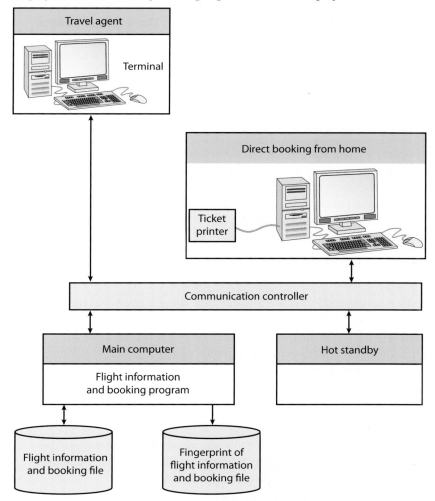

Figure 12.4 *An airline booking system*

Figure 12.5 *Booking a flight with a travel agent*

The passenger may decide to book a seat on a flight and this is booked online. Once a seat has been booked the flight information and booking file must be updated immediately so that further enquiries show the seat as already booked. When the flight information and booking file is being accessed to book a flight, to avoid double booking, all other attempts to book the seat must be locked out. Tickets for booked seats may be printed out on the spot or may be sent to customers at a later date. Payment may be made in cash at the travel agents, online using a credit card, or passengers may be sent the bill by mail some days later. There should also be a facility for cancellation and refund of payments online. Security of access to the system is maintained by giving each travel agent a unique username and password.

Since the ICT system needs to be online 24 hours a day, it is very important that the computer is not out of action for any time due to mechanical breakdown. This is avoided by having two identical computers: the main one in use and an additional computer available as a **hot standby** to be used if the main computer breaks down. This helps the airline make its booking system available 24 hours each day.

As the ICT system is in constant use, file **backups** cannot be done in the usual way by copying all the files onto a backup disk at regular intervals; for example, each evening. This would mean halting the flight information and booking program while the backups are done. Instead two disks are used, both having copies of the flight information and booking file on them. Any changes that are made to the file are made on both disks at the same time. This technique is known as **finger-printing.** It ensures that if one disk becomes faulty there is an exact copy of the file immediately available on the other disk.

This is a highly specialised ICT system. The computer hardware and software involved are only used for running the airline booking system. Any other data processing required must be done on other ICT systems.

An online booking system such as the one described above is an example of a **real-time** processing system. It is so called because processing is in real time; that is, as data is input it is processed, before any further input can be processed. A real-time ICT system must be fast enough to ensure that input data is processed immediately so that the results can influence any further input. Typically, data can be input to a real-time ICT system at any time, from a variety of sources. Even so, processing must be instantaneous and immediate.

The hardware needed to run the system will include:

- Terminals – networked PCs and dedicated thin client terminals. These will be needed throughout the world in order to access the booking system. Dedicated terminals will be needed in locations where there is a high volume of bookings. Elsewhere, the booking system may run on travel agents' computers as one of many networked applications.

- Computers – two are needed: one to operate as the main computer and one as a hot standby. These need to be sufficiently fast to handle high volumes of booking requests immediately.

- Disk drives – two are needed: one to store the main flight information and booking file and the other as fingerprint backup. The capacity of these disk drives depends on the volume of data being handled.

- Communication – a specialised computer will act as a communication controller.

Supermarket stock control

A large modern supermarket will have an ICT system similar to that shown in Figure 12.6. At the checkout, the **point of sale (POS)** terminal has a laser scanner that is used to read the bar code printed on items sold by the supermarket. The POS terminal also has a keyboard for entering the product details of the few items that do not have bar codes printed on them. A small screen is used to display messages sent from the central computer to the POS terminal, and a small dot matrix printer built into the terminal is used to print receipts for customers.

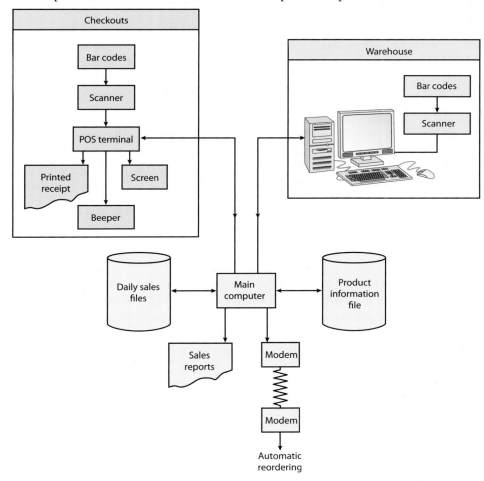

Figure 12.6 *A supermarket stock control system*

There will be several checkouts in the supermarket, all connected to the supermarket's main computer located in the store. This computer also has terminals in the warehouse and elsewhere. There are disk drives, a printer and a broadband link to other computers via the telephone network. This is a **general purpose** ICT system and is used for all the data processing done by the supermarket, including payroll; however, we are only going to look at its use for stock control.

Most products sold by the supermarket have on them a bar code. The data held on a bar code identifies the product and includes a product code and a check digit. When an item is sold, the bar code is read by the laser scanner and the data on it is transmitted to the main computer. Here the **check digit** is recalculated from the product code and then checked against the check digit received from the POS terminal. If these are not the same, the bar code must be re-entered. If both check digits are the same, the product code is checked against the product information file. A record on this file contains the following fields for each product:

- Product code, e.g. 152907

- Name of product, e.g. baked beans 570g

- Price.

If the bar code received from the POS terminal is not on the product information file, it may have been entered incorrectly. In this case, the bar code must be re-entered. When it is necessary to re-enter a bar code an error message is displayed on the screen of the POS terminal. If the bar code has been damaged and cannot be read, the checkout operator can type in the number printed under the bar code. The entry of valid bar codes is indicated by a loud beep.

The product code that is input from the bar code is used to find the corresponding record in the product information file. The name of the product and the price contained in this record are sent to the POS terminal from the main computer and these are printed on the customer's receipt.

For every item sold, the price is added to the total for the customer and this is printed on the receipt when all the customer's purchases have been processed. Access to the product information file must be fast enough so that customers are not kept waiting and, in consequence, it must be a direct access file on disk.

The sales made at each checkout are recorded in the daily sales file as the goods are sold. It is sufficient to record the product code and quantity sold. At the end of each day the individual product codes are read from this file, the total quantity of each item sold is calculated and a report is printed showing the product code, the name of the product and the total number of each product sold. An extract from this report follows:

Sales Report Wed 23rd March		
Product code	**Name of product**	**Total number sold**
152907	baked beans 570g	500
923673	pea soup 300g	258
025993	peaches 420g	367
300609	pasta 500g	124
007085	tomato puree 50g	356

This information is also used to update the stock control file. The stock control file contains a record for each product with fields as follows:

- Product code, e.g. 152907

- Number in stock, e.g. 1200

- Reorder level, e.g. 1000

- Reorder quantity, e.g. 800.

For each product, the total number sold that day is subtracted from the number in stock, which is updated. In the above example, the total number of baked beans

Did you know?

It is a very common belief that the bar code contains the name of the product and its price. This is not so. These are kept in the product information file and transferred to the POS terminal when required.

570g sold on Wed 23rd March is 500. The number in stock is 1200 so the updated number in stock is 1200 less 500, i.e. 700.

The supermarket has to be careful that it does not run out of stock because this will annoy customers and sales and profits will be lost. Periodically a stock report will be printed showing existing stock levels as recorded on the stock control file. Those products that have a lower number in stock than their reorder level will be emphasised in the report. The supermarket manager will go through the report and reorder those products that are needed. If the manager wishes, items can be reordered automatically when the stock control file is updated. For these products, if they have a lower number in stock than their reorder level, the manufacturer is contacted and asked to send more of the product. This is done automatically using email sent by the supermarket's computer to the manufacturer's computer. In the example, 800 (the reorder quantity) baked beans 570g should be reordered because the number in stock (700) has fallen below the reorder level (1000).

When items that have been ordered arrive at the supermarket they are received by the local warehouse. At the warehouse the goods are checked as they arrive and stored until they are moved into the supermarket to be sold. As they arrive, the warehouse manager enters the quantity of each product that is delivered at the terminal in the warehouse. This data is used to update the stock control file. For example, if 800 cans of baked beans 570g are delivered then the number in stock is updated to 700 plus 800, i.e. 1500, bringing the number in stock above the reorder level. Using this system the manager can control the flow of stock into the supermarket in response to sales of stock to customers.

The above description focuses on one basic aspect of a stock control system. In practice, the same system would be used to do a range of additional tasks. For example:

- The number of items sold and the takings at each till could be recorded and used to monitor the performance of checkout operators.

- The rate of sales of each product could be calculated and used to increase the choice of popular goods or to reduce stocks of unpopular items.

- The pattern of sales of every product could be recorded so that stocks are not held at times of the year when they are unlikely to sell.

- The effectiveness of sales promotions (see Figure 12.7) could be monitored.

- Goods that have high profit margins could be stocked in preference to those with lower profit margins.

To keep business expenses to a minimum, stocks of goods should be kept as low as possible. If a maximum stock level is recorded for each product on the stock control file then the quantity reordered can be adjusted so that this level is not exceeded when new supplies arrive at the warehouse. This maximum stock level can be adjusted so that the extra costs involved in frequent reordering are balanced against the expense of storing larger quantities of a product in the warehouse.

The system can be also be used to determine the extent of theft from the supermarket and to improve security. If the actual number of each product in stock is counted and found to be less than the number in stock on the stock control file then this difference is due to loss of stock. Loss of stock can be due to damage or theft. If damages are recorded as they occur then loss due to theft can be

Quick question
What other tasks could a stock control system be used for?

Figure 12.7 *A sales promotion in a supermarket*

calculated. This information can also be used to identify high-risk products so that security can be improved.

ICT systems for stock control allow managers to monitor stock levels very closely and to exercise greater control over the business. This allows the manager to increase the profitability of the business and to improve customer service. Prices can be kept lower and customer service is quicker because of the speed of the POS terminals. The customer's receipt is itemised and fewer mistakes occur at the checkout. However, the purchase cost of the ICT system is high and it will be necessary to train employees to use it. Because the productivity of checkout employees is increased, there may be a reduced number of employees at the supermarket.

The stock control system described above is an online interactive multiprocessing ICT system. **Online** systems use checkouts and other terminals connected to a computer. These interact with the ICT system, sending data to it and receiving data from it. A real-time system is an online interactive system but not all such systems are real time. The stock control system described here is not real time.

In order for an itemised receipt to be printed showing the description and price of every item sold, this data must be found in the product information file, using the product code contained in the bar code input by the laser scanner at the checkout. As a result, interactive processing is necessary because an interchange of data takes place. However, there is no need to immediately update the stock control file at the moment goods are sold. It is quite acceptable for recorded stock levels to be an hour or so out of date because this is unlikely to significantly affect the business. The expense of a specialised real-time system cannot be justified in these circumstances.

Many supermarkets combine sales to customers through their shops with online sales (see Chapter 9). Customers place an order online and this order is put together by pickers working in the supermarket alongside ordinary shoppers.

Only simple outlines of the payroll, airline booking and supermarket stock control ICT systems have been described above. In reality these ICT systems are much more complex than described here. For example, the hardware, networks and data structures will be more extensive than can reasonably be described in this textbook. It is also most likely that, in practice, an ICT system will be a hybrid involving some batch and online interactive processing with links to a real-time system where one is in use. For example, both payroll and stock control could be run by the supermarket on the same computer.

The supermarket ICT system will include:

- POS terminals at every supermarket checkout, operated by employees of the supermarket. These are used to record sales to customers and payments. They are likely to include a bar code scanner, small screen, receipt printer, beeper, smart card reader and arrangements for handling cash or paying by credit or debit card.

- Hand-held terminals. These are used by the customer to scan product bar codes as purchases are placed in their shopping trolley. The hand-held terminal is read very quickly at the checkout and this helps to speed up purchasing and to reduce queues.

- Self-service POS terminals. Customers check out their own purchases. For example, a touch screen is used to help the customer start, operate and end the purchasing process. A customer scans each item and places it on scales. The terminal checks the weight on the scale to make sure there is no fraud. The customer pays by credit or debit card, or the POS terminal can accept bank notes and dispense change.

- Mobile terminals – for use in the warehouse and elsewhere for recording deliveries and for stock-taking. These will be built to be robust and are likely to incorporate a bar code scanner, touch screen and stylus.

- Communications network – an internal network based on the main computer and external access to the Internet for general email, etc. and automatic reordering.

- Main computer – this might be a general computer used for a range of applications. Even so, it must have sufficient capacity to handle communications from all the POS terminals and sufficient storage to record details about all the products for sale.

Banking

ICT systems are used throughout banking. Banks use ICT for storing customer information, processing transactions and in almost all aspects of banking operations. This improves the competitiveness and efficiency of the banking industry and provides greater convenience for customers. Many banks also offer home or Internet banking. A customer has to be able to connect to the Internet to use this (see Chapter 9 for more details).

Automatic teller machines (ATMs)

ATMs or cashpoints are electronic terminals (see Figure 12.9) that allow routine banking transactions at almost any time. They are situated in the walls of banks, in shopping malls, supermarkets, bus stations and other suitable locations. Most ATMs can be used by customers of any bank to access their accounts and carry out transactions, although a fee may be charged.

ATMs can be used to:

- Withdraw cash

- Make deposits

Figure 12.8 *An ATM*

- Transfer funds between accounts
- Obtain account balances
- Pay bills.

Using an ATM

To use an ATM, a customer must have an **ATM card** issued by a bank. This card stores the customer's account number. Debit and credit cards can be used in ATMs.

- When a customer inserts a card, the ATM reads the information from the card and communicates with a central computer to access the customer's account. The information may be recorded on the card on a magnetic stripe or on a microchip embedded in the card.

- A message appears on the ATM's screen asking for a personal identification number (PIN).

- The customer enters the PIN using the ATM's numeric keypad.

- If the PIN does not match the one stored in the computer's memory, the customer is given several chances to enter the information again. If the correct PIN is still not entered, the ATM keeps the card and the customer cannot carry out any further transactions.

- If a match is made, the customer is asked to select a transaction from a list displayed on the screen. In the case of a withdrawal or transfer of funds, the computer checks the customer's account to determine if sufficient funds are available for the transaction.

- If there are sufficient funds, the account will be updated immediately to reflect the transaction. The customer can be issued with a receipt showing the date, time, amount and type of transaction, and the transaction will be shown on the customer's bank account statement. Otherwise the customer will get a message saying that the transaction has failed.

Electronic Funds Transfer (EFT)

Many supermarkets, gas stations, hotels and other businesses use **electronic funds transfer (EFT)** as a means of transacting business. EFT is the movement of funds from one account to another electronically. Typically, funds are transferred from a customer's account to the retailer's account when the customer pays using a debit or credit card. When this occurs at the point of sale or checkout, the process is known as **electronic funds transfer at point of sale (EFTPOS).**

The use of **debit and credit cards** and EFT is a step towards the 'cashless society'. Debit and credit cards are issued by banks or by independent companies such as Visa, MasterCard or American Express, and are fast becoming one of the most frequently used methods of payment for goods and services. These cards usually contain a magnetic stripe at the back or a microchip that holds the customer's account number, which is also stored by the bank or the credit card centre.

When a customer pays for goods or services using a debit or credit card, this process takes place:

- The customer gives the merchant the card and this is read by the merchant's EFT machine (see Figure 12.9). The account number stored on the card is read and used to access the customer's bank or credit account.

- The merchant enters the amount of money to be paid.

- The customer enters the PIN used with the card, or signs a receipt.

- If the account has sufficient funds to pay for the transaction (if a debit card is being used), or a sufficiently high credit limit (if a credit card is being used), the money is deducted from the customer's account immediately using EFT and deposited into the merchant's account. The customer is issued with a receipt as proof of the transaction.

- If the customer fails to enter the correct PIN or has insufficient funds, a 'failed transaction' message will be displayed.

Smart cards are predicted to be the means by which most payments will be made in the near future. Smart cards are more technologically advanced versions of debit and credit cards. Whereas debit and credit cards usually have magnetic stripes on them, smart cards have a microchip built into them. While a magnetic stripe can be altered or forged, it is more difficult to tamper with the microchip in a smart card. As a result, smart cards can provide better security. Microchips also have a larger memory capacity than magnetic stripes do. Eventually microchips on smart cards will store biometric data such as voiceprints, fingerprints and retinal scans, and it may be possible to have one card per person rather than the variety of cards that people currently have.

Figure 12.9 *An EFT machine*

Engineering and Manufacturing

Computer-aided design (CAD)

A CAD system uses computer hardware and software in the drawing of engineering or architectural designs. A CAD package is designed to make it easier to produce detailed plans and accurate technical drawings. It contains software that provides a set of standard components and basic elements such as points, lines, circles, shapes and solids, from which CAD drawings can be constructed. CAD programs can produce three-dimensional drawings that can be rotated and viewed on screen from many different angles. In addition, the computer keeps track of design dependencies, so that when a value is changed all other dependent values are automatically changed.

A CAD package can be run on most PCs but a high-resolution graphics monitor is needed to show sufficient detail. The input devices required for a CAD system include a light pen or digitising tablet for drawing. A special printer or plotter is required for printing detailed design specifications on large sheets of paper.

CAD has considerable advantages:

- Designs can be produced faster, reducing cost.

- It is easier to make changes to the original design.

- It is easier to make duplicates.

- Documentation is generated with the design.

- Standard components can be used, which reduces construction time and costs.

There are many types of CAD software that are used to design products, buildings and parts in the automotive, aerospace and consumer electronics industries. They include CATIA® (developed jointly by Dassault Systemes and IBM) which is a general purpose CAD, testing and manufacturing system used in the automobile and aerospace industries; and CADdy® (now owned by the German company DataSolid) which is used in areas such as architecture, electronics, engineering and manufacturing.

Computer-aided manufacture (CAM)

Computer-aided manufacture (CAM) refers to the use of a computer to control manufacturing plant and equipment in a production system. It is used in applications where precision and accuracy are important, including processes such as welding, paint spraying, cutting and polishing (see Figure 12.10).

CAM software generates instructions for the computerised control of machines. These **CNC (Computerised Numerical Control)** machines include computerised lathes for turning and drilling and machines for cutting and polishing large stones for building purposes.

The advantages of CAM include:

- Faster production of parts and products

- Production of a more consistent product

- The ability to better control and maintain the quality of a product

- Production of more complex designs and mouldings.

Figure 12.10 *Computers are used in the steel industry*

CAD/CAM systems

CAD/CAM systems are used to integrate design and manufacturing. Engineers use the system to create product designs, and then to control the manufacturing process. Two CAD/CAM software packages currently available are SolidWorks® and MasterCAM®. They can create drawings, model trajectories (develop and work out the movement) of cutting tools, and develop numeric control programs. They support 3D modelling, sheet metal punching and bending, and plasma and laser cutting.

Computer-aided engineering (CAE)

Computer-aided engineering (CAE) systems analyse engineering designs produced by CAD systems, and simulate a variety of conditions to see if the design actually works. CAE features are found in most CAD packages. One CAD/CAM/CAE package is hyperMILL®.

Weather stations

Weather stations (see Figure 12.11) are used to collect information about the weather. They may have sensors that measure, for example, the temperature, wind speed, wind direction, whether it is raining, and how much rain has fallen. This information may be collected from a weather station by a computer communicating with it using the telephone network. The computer will automatically collect the information and record it on backing storage. This is an example of **data logging**. The information collected can be useful in many ways; for example, for weather forecasting.

Local councils may find it useful to have weather stations. These will tell them if the temperature is likely to fall below freezing point so that they know when and where to grit the roads. Using weather stations spread throughout the district helps them save money because grit may not be needed everywhere. Having reliable records of past usage helps them predict future demand.

Local radio stations often provide information to car drivers commuting to work. Weather stations can give them information about driving conditions; for example, whether it is foggy; if there are high winds; whether it is raining or snowing; and if the roads are likely to be icy.

Traffic can sometimes avoid these hazards if they are localized. For example, Queensbury is on the top of the hills overlooking Bradford and Halifax in Yorkshire in the UK. It is often very foggy when surrounding areas have good visibility. Some commuters find it convenient to drive through Queensbury on their way to work. However, many would choose to take a different route when it is foggy. The local radio station could use the information from a weather station to find out if it is foggy and let drivers know.

The data provided by a weather station could be collected by a computer communicating with it over the telephone network. The computer could automatically contact a number of weather stations spread over a wide area. It might contact them in rotation, collecting the information as often as possible. Alternatively, it might contact each weather station at particular times each day. The frequency of sampling might be designed so that a good illustration of the

Figure 12.11 *A roadside weather station*

weather conditions throughout the day was recorded but data collection by the computer was kept to a minimum. This would provide useful information while keeping costs as low as possible.

If up-to-date information was not needed immediately, details of the current weather conditions could be recorded on backing storage at the weather station. The computer might communicate with the weather station very infrequently, perhaps only once or twice a year. When the weather station and the computer were in contact, the information recorded on **backing storage** at the weather station would be transmitted to the computer.

Weather stations are simply groups of sensors that provide useful information about the weather. They are only one of many data logging applications where information is collected and recorded automatically from remote, widely dispersed or dangerous locations. Other groupings of sensors can provide information about different environmental conditions. Here are some examples:

- sensors on icebergs can provide scientists with information that helps them understand how they formed and what becomes of them

- sensors underground can record information about earthquakes

- sensors on space vehicles can provide information about the atmospheres on different planets.

Weather forecasting

Weather forecasting tries to predict what the weather conditions will be by measuring and observing the current weather around the world and supplying the data collected to a supercomputer. Weather forecasting on a global scale uses highly developed methods for collecting data, such as the following:

- Weather balloons at many locations around the world. The instruments in weather balloons are similar to those in weather stations but are more complex and varied.

- Satellites orbiting high above the earth. These allow meteorologists to observe clouds across the entire globe.

A supercomputer uses mathematical models of the atmosphere to make its predictions. Computer models are programs that contain complex mathematical equations and that try to predict what weather conditions will be like, based on historical data. However, even with the fastest computers, meteorologists cannot forecast day-to-day weather for more than about a week ahead. The models used are constantly being improved and new models are developed. Some of these will help to forecast tropical features such as hurricanes. Other models will help to forecast smaller-scale features such as thunderstorms and other outbreaks of severe weather. As these models become more developed, forecasters are able to issue more accurate and timely warnings.

Figure 12.12 *The inside of a weather room, with the computer showing different feeds from a satellite*

Robots

Robots are hardware devices that perform physical tasks. These tasks may be complex industrial or manufacturing tasks. Robots are used for welding, paint spraying, assembling products, packaging, handling dangerous substances and assembling cars (see Figure 12.13). They have many different shapes and sizes but they all work in similar ways.

Specialised robots have been developed for a number of tasks:

- Robots are used to enter active volcanoes to gather information.

- **Remotely-operated vehicles (ROVs)** are robots that can perform tasks such as searching for and recovering ship and plane wreckage, and the repair of underground telecommunication cables.

- Robots can clean up hazardous waste sites and handle wastes that might be too dangerous for humans.

- Robots can decontaminate and dismantle radioactive devices, and measure levels of radioactivity at waste sites.

- Robots can mine for metal and coal.

- Robots can paint bridges.

- Robots can deactivate bombs.

Figure 12.13 *Robots at work in an assembly plant*

Robots can be programmed to do tasks by using programming languages or teach and learn methods. Using a teach and learn method, you program a robot under the control of the computer one instruction at a time. You watch what the robot does as it performs the instruction. If it is what you want the robot to do, you can save the instruction. If not, you can try again. In this way you can build up a complete program to control the robot. You can also program a robot by physically moving it through the actions you want it to do; the computer converts these actions into a program and saves it.

Process control

Process control refers to the use of digital computers in industrial settings, such as chemical plants, steel mills and oil refineries, to monitor manufacturing processes closely and take corrective action to prevent malfunction if necessary. The computer inputs data such as temperature, pressure, flow and volume from the process using sensors.

Process control systems still require human supervision because unusual or unforeseen developments might not be adequately managed by a computer-controlled system. Even so, there are many advantages:

- Data from the process can be stored and displayed. This is useful if there has been an industrial accident and investigators are trying to find out what went wrong. The data can also be used to improve the operation of the process.

- Safety can be ensured by constant monitoring and the automatic sounding of an alarm and closure of the process if there are problems.

- Product quality can be maintained.

Figure 12.14 *A computerised control room showing the control board and an operator*

- Employees can have better working conditions.

- Operating costs are lower because the system is more efficient.

Flight simulators

Flight simulators (see Figure 12.15) are used to train pilots to fly aircraft. They are very complex constructions involving a wide range of computer control subsystems with highly developed interacting feedback loops. A trainee pilot using a flight simulator experiences what it is like to fly an aircraft without actually having to fly one. While 'flying' the simulator, trainees can explore what the aircraft can do without risk to themselves or to an aircraft, and they can learn to fly a variety of aircraft and practise landing and taking off from different airports.

A flight simulator will have a cockpit the same size and shape, and with the same controls and seats, as those in the real aircraft. A computer controls the view the trainee sees through the cockpit windows which is a projected video image, and gives the trainee a realistic feeling of how the real aircraft would move. The simulator is mounted on mobile legs, which are used to alter the position of the cockpit. The computer moves the legs when the pilot moves the simulator's controls. The trainee pilot feels the simulator move in the way the real aircraft would move.

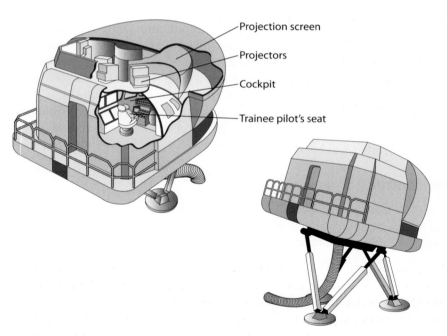

Figure 12.15 *A flight simulator*

Trainees can be given experience of unusual circumstances and emergencies. Fire can be simulated by introducing smoke into the cockpit and programming the cockpit display to mimic a real aircraft on fire. Similarly, the reaction of the simulator to the pilot's controls can be modified to represent bad weather.

Exercise 12.1

1. Figure 12.11 shows a roadside weather station. One sensor attached to it is used to record the temperature at midday. The council uses this data to predict when the roads will be icy so that they can grit them. Sometimes the council grit the roads when it isn't necessary and this wastes time and money.

   a) Describe three types of sensor that could be attached to the weather station and describe how the data recorded by them could be useful to the council.

   b) Describe how the council could improve the accuracy of their predictions of when the roads will be icy.

   c) The council used to send an employee to the weather station to collect the data that had been saved on a local backing storage device. The weather station is now connected to a computer network. Discuss the advantages and disadvantages in using the council's computer to collect the data using this network instead of sending an employee.

   d) A CCTV (closed circuit television) camera is attached to the weather station. Describe how this might be useful to the council and others.

   e) There are CCTV cameras in other places and all of these send pictures to a control centre where they are recorded and monitored. Discuss the advantages and disadvantages of this use of CCTV cameras.

2. **a)** Describe what is meant by process control.

   b) Name two industries that use process control.

   c) Discuss the advantages and disadvantages of process control.

3. **a)** Describe what is meant by a robot.

   b) State two industries that use robots.

   c) State three functions of robots in one of the industries named in your answer to 'b'.

   d) Describe the advantages and disadvantages of using robots.

Logistics

Logistics was developed to organise the supply, movement, and maintenance of an armed force under operational conditions. The type and scale of the forces that can be delivered to a battlefield, supported in battle, and the pace of the battle are dependent on effective logistics. **Logistics** is the organisation of the supply of, for example: ammunition; specialist personnel, such as mechanics; fuel; spares; food; soldiers and weapons.

The civil application of logistics ensures that complex supply chains deliver the required products or services. Logistics is used to plan, implement and control the effective delivery and storage of goods and services between the point of origin and the point of consumption in order to meet customer requirements. For example, effective logistics ensures that customers' shopping needs are met when they visit the supermarket.

Logistics could involve the organisation of:

- Information – the integration and coordination of information about customers' needs. For example, in a supermarket, this might be collected from loyalty cards and an analysis of sales.

- Transport – the transport of a wide range of goods to the supermarket from different suppliers; for example, fresh vegetables from local farms and flowers flown in from Kenya.

- Materials handling – organising the movement of goods so that materials are moved to where they are needed, when they are needed.

- Packaging – ensuring that all the goods in store are saleable and fresh, and have appropriate packaging.

- Stock control – ensuring that sufficient goods are in stock to meet demand.

- Warehousing – making sure that warehouses can store sufficient goods in conditions that prevent damage to them.

- Security – for example, to prevent the theft of goods.

Logistics is complex and logistics software is used to model, analyse, visualise, organise and optimise the supply chain. For example: ForwardOffice software from Forward Computers Ltd. is a comprehensive freight management system and MiKroaid Ltd produce logistics software for warehouse management and stock control.

Education

ICT is widely used in schools, colleges and universities, both to help students learn and for management of the institution.

Many students now learn how to use ICT at school or college, and use ICT to learn about other subjects. Perhaps because of the widespread use of ICT in education, there has been a shift to a more student-centred approach. Some teachers have changed their focus from being dispensers of knowledge to being facilitators of learning. Many teachers now use ICT to support teaching and learning.

The Internet and the Web are invaluable tools for researching and gathering data. Students can search remote databases and the Web, and choose what they need from millions of pages of information. Students can also communicate and collaborate with other students by email or through chat sites.

The Web is a very useful tool for finding information but schools often wish to structure students' learning so that it is more focused. **Virtual learning environments (VLEs)** help students access a range of specific learning resources in school, college, university and at home and in other places where there is web access, and **computer-aided learning (CAL)** software helps students learn specific skills.

Virtual learning environments (VLEs), such as Blackboard (see Figure 12.16) and Moodle, have a range of different functions that help teachers teach and support students with their studies. These are a few examples of what may be done using a VLE:

- **Learning resources can be made easily available** anywhere there is Web access; for example, in class at school and at home. This makes access much easier. Students who are ill can keep up with schoolwork and homework can be done online.

- Students can **study at any time,** at their own pace and for as long as they wish.

- Students can **break off their studies and return to them** at any time.

- **Learning resources can be well organised** so that students can find worksheets, help sheets, task sheets, homework, simulation programs, and any other materials the teacher makes available to help students.

- Students can have access to **wikis, blogs, podcasts, web links** and **glossaries** that are especially relevant to their studies and they can contribute to them.

- **Digital drop boxes** can be used to store work and to submit it by uploading it.

- Students can find out their **grades** online when the teacher has assessed their work. There is no need to wait until the next class.

- Teachers and students may look at **grade profiles** for the student and the class and see what progress they are making.

- There are online surveys to help students and teachers with their research.

Computer-assisted learning (CAL), also known as **computer-aided instruction (CAI),** can be generally described as the use of ICT to help students to further their skills, knowledge and understanding of a specific part of a subject. CAL programs are usually designed to develop a very narrow range of skills, knowledge and understanding.

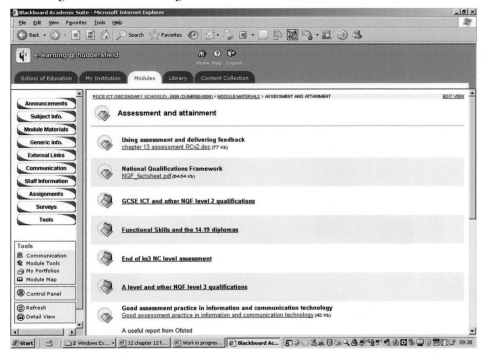

Figure 12.16 *A page from the Blackboard VLE*

Most CAL programs fall into three categories:

- **Drill and practice.** This type of CAL is used to complement a teacher's instruction – to reinforce old lessons rather than teach new ones. Most drill and practice programs enable individual students to practise skills and knowledge. This has been found to be a useful approach where material has to be memorised, such as when learning vocabulary work. The computer generates questions in a random order chosen from a stored set, and the student is required to answer them. Some programs keep scores and enable the student's progress to be tracked.

- **Tutorials.** These are self-instructional programs designed to introduce and teach new material to students. The computer acts like a tutor and allows students to move at their own pace. Many tutorial programs can assess a student's competence level and adjust the course accordingly. They are very useful for introducing and reviewing new topics.

- **Simulations.** These predict the outcome of a real-life situation by using a computer-based model of the situation. Simulation is one of the most effective CAL tools available for teaching students, since it provides the opportunity to vary situations in order to see different outcomes without any risk to the students or wastage of materials. Simulation packages are available in subject areas like physics, chemistry, biology and geography. Simulation software is sometimes used to prepare learner drivers for their first trip in a car.

CAL has many advantages:

- CAL can provide immediate feedback to students, who are able to tell immediately whether they understand the topics.

- CAL enables students to recognise their own weaknesses, and provides the opportunity to work on strengthening them.

- Most CAL courseware encourages students by displaying a congratulatory message for each correct response. This helps to motivate students to continue studying and move on to more complex material.

- CAL may be embedded in a learning programme accessible using a VLE.

Figure 12.17 *Students at work using a CAL package*

School information management systems (SIMS) are widely used to help with the day-to-day running of schools. They can be used for various purposes: to store students' records, to produce class lists, to register students, to produce reports, to manage book loans from the school library, to construct the school timetable and for many other tasks.

The advantages of SIMS are as follows:

- They support automatic reporting. For example, attendance at school can be tracked and the SIMS can automatically inform parents of the absence of their son or daughter using email, letter or telephone. Similarly, school library systems can automatically inform students that books are overdue.

- Communication with parents can be personalised using, for example, mail merge.

- The quality of communications with parents can be monitored. For example, standard forms and letters can be used, and school reports can be compiled using statement banks that have been vetted for appropriate language and content and accuracy of spelling and grammar.

- Access to information is faster.

- Statistics and accounting information can be generated automatically and quickly.

The disadvantages of SIMS are as follows:

- The data stored on the system must be kept up to date and this can be expensive. For example, office staff are needed to ensure that students' records are accurate. This is essential so that, for example, students' progress can be tracked and accurate progress reports sent to their carers. Another alternative is to allow carers or students to keep their personal information up to date using a web-based system with password protection; however, in this case, the school cannot be sure the information is up to date.

The law

Law enforcement

ICT systems are an important tool for the police and law enforcement officers in their fight against crime. National databases have been set up to hold information such as criminal records, profiles of wanted persons, data on stolen cars, DNA patterns and fingerprints of convicted individuals, and drivers who have had their licences suspended or revoked. These databases, such as the National Crime Information Center (NCIC) in the United States and the Police National Computer (PNC) in the United Kingdom, can be accessed by law enforcement officers throughout the country.

Police and other law enforcement officers also use the computers available in local police departments for a wide range of functions such as the following:

- Preparing reports.

- Tracking the history of telephone calls from a particular address.

- Managing cases.

- Identifying trends and patterns of criminal behaviour, and carrying out statistical analysis.

- Tracking parolees (criminals who have been released before the end of their jail term because of good conduct).

- Posting surveillance photos of wanted criminals and missing persons.

- Developing contacts with other police organisations, including transmitting, exchanging and obtaining information from other police officers in other departments or other countries.

- If a witness sees but cannot identify a criminal, the police can use appropriate software to compose a picture of the alleged criminal, based on the witness's description. This is called *profiling.* This picture can then be compared with one that is stored in the national database.

- A device attached to a computer is used to digitise and store an individual's fingerprint. The computer can then compare it with those stored in national or local databases. If a match is found, the individual's record is then retrieved.

- Holding equipment inventories.

Figure 12.18 *The control room at a police station*

In some countries, police officers can use laptop computers from their patrol cars to make online enquiries about vehicle registrations and drivers' licences from national and local police databases. The laptops are mounted in police cars and there is a wireless network link to a central computer in the police department headquarters. This enables officers to access information quickly, and has been instrumental in many arrests.

More recently, some police forces are using video glasses. A pair of spectacles has a very small video camera or webcam built into them and communicates wirelessly with the local police station. A high proportion of what a police officer sees is videoed and recorded for later use in prosecutions. Also, a police officer dealing with difficult circumstances can be advised by remote experts.

Law firms

Law firms have found that the productivity both of attorneys and of other staff increases with the use of ICT. Tasks such as reviewing case status and deadlines and preparing legal documents can be very time-consuming if ICT is not used.

ICT usage in law firms falls into two main categories: business management and practice management.

In the area of **business management**, ICT can be used for:

- Word processing – typing legal documents and other documents. Detailed templates of legal documents can be set up and quickly adapted for specific clients.

- Data storage and retrieval – storing information about clients.

- Spreadsheets – for accounting purposes such as billing, income and expenses.

Practice management software helps lawyers practise law. It includes:

- Software that offers expertise in a substantive area of law such as bankruptcy, family law or personal injury.

- Software to help with case management and document assembly. This can enable lawyers to find information easily on past cases and judgements to use as precedents in their arguments in cases with which they are currently dealing.

- Legal research websites, such as Westlaw and Quicklaw, help lawyers and law students obtain comprehensive information about case law and legislation from many countries around the world.

Some websites help members of the public prepare their own legal documents. This reduces the cost of legal assistance.

Healthcare and medicine

The use of ICT in healthcare and medicine is becoming more prevalent as ICT systems are developed that help doctors provide better medical care for their patients.

Computerised patient records

Many hospitals and doctors' offices still use paper-based systems for storing patients' medical records. A doctor writes notes (symptoms, diagnosis and drugs prescribed) on a patient's card while attending to the patient, with the card being filed away until the next visit. The same procedure takes place in the hospital. This can be very inefficient and cumbersome. It is not uncommon for hospital clerks to tell patients that their files cannot be found or that information from a file is missing. Manual files only enable doctors in one institution at a time to view patient information. This method of storing patient information may not lead doctors to make the best diagnoses, since they may not have all the information at hand.

To alleviate some of the problems of manual patient files, some institutions in the United States have introduced ICT systems to handle patient records. One such system allows doctors at over 120 different locations simultaneous access to patients' records stored on a central database. Each patient has a card with an ID number, which doctors can use to access a lifetime record that contains the notes from all the doctors and institutions that the patient has attended. This system enables doctors to easily find and send reminder notices to patients who may need follow up treatment. It also gives them a way of comparing methods of treating illnesses and, based on responses from many patients, deciding which is the best method of treatment in a particular case. It can also be used to identify patients taking a particular drug that new research has shown could be dangerous.

Patient monitoring

Patient monitoring systems help doctors treat patients by providing a twenty-four hour service and reducing false alarms. Some surgery patients and very ill patients must be continuously monitored in an intensive care unit. These patients are fitted with sensors connected to a computer, which record vital signs such as blood pressure, heart rate, temperature and blood oxygen levels. If a particular vital sign goes below or above the preset range, an alarm is sounded to alert nurses and doctors. The information obtained during the monitoring can also be stored on hard disk and analysed later.

Magnetic resonance imaging (MRI)

Magnetic resonance imaging (MRI) machines scan the body using very large magnets. A patient on a table is moved into a large magnetic machine, which scans a small area at a time and sends the image (also called a *slice)* to an MRI computer. This reconstructs the image in a two- or three-dimensional form so that it can be viewed.

MRI images are excellent for showing abnormalities of the brain such as strokes, tumours, infections and haemorrhages, and can be used to detect diseases of the neck and spine.

Computer axial tomography (CAT) scanning

The CAT scan machine is basically an X-ray tube that rotates in a circle around the patient, taking as many as 30 pictures in a few seconds as it rotates. The multiple X-ray pictures are reconstructed by a computer in three-dimensional axial slice images. Each slice can then be examined separately. It is very useful in detecting brain tumors.

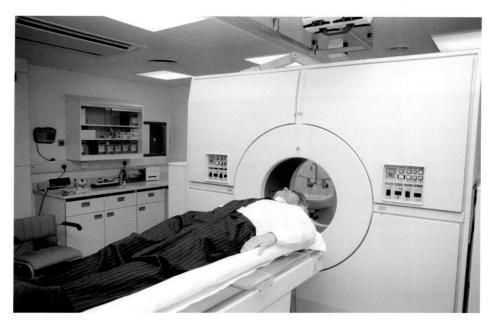

Figure 12.19 *A CAT machine*

Medical expert systems

An **expert system** or **knowledge-based system** is a program that analyses questions input by a practitioner and provides answers at the level of an expert in a particular field. An expert system is useful in providing support for making decisions and can also 'suggest' alternatives or other issues to be considered. It consists of two parts: the **knowledge base** and the **inference engine.** The knowledge base contains a large volume of information in a particular field – for example, the different types of diseases, symptoms and possible treatments. The inference engine of an expert system analyses the input data using *reasoning* methods and the knowledge base to arrive at a conclusion. It also provides the user with an explanation of how it arrived at its conclusion.

The Quick Medical Reference (QMR) system (available from the Camdat Corporation) is a medical expert system that performs differential diagnosis in many areas of internal medicine. Other examples of expert systems are Mycin and Dendral.

A medical expert system has the following advantages:

- It can indicate the range of possible health problems based on the known symptoms.
- It gives support in making decisions about which a doctor may be unsure because of a lack of knowledge or lack of experience.
- It can help experts arrive at an accurate solution much faster.
- It can be developed and kept up to date as new discoveries are made and knowledge is advanced.
- It can show the concepts it used to arrive at its conclusions.

A medical expert system has the following disadvantages:

- It lacks judgement and intuition, which are sometimes vital in diagnosis.
- It cannot learn from mistakes.

Telemedicine

Computers and the Internet are being used to allow scarce and expensive human and other medical resources to be shared around the world. Many rural residents in large countries such as the United States and Australia have difficulties in obtaining proper healthcare services because they live in very remote areas where there is a lack of medical facilities. Patients can visit a doctor online and doctors can treat their patients at a distance. Doctors are able to send X-rays to radiologists hundreds of miles away, and transmit video images of patients to specialists for instant consultations. Doctors can match their patients' radiographic information with data in a distant laboratory to help determine diagnosis and treatment.

Besides giving invaluable help to patients, the Internet also allows doctors to search for Internet sites that help them stay informed and involved with healthcare topics.

Libraries

Libraries use ICT systems to keep track of books and other resources they lend to borrowers (see Figure 12.20). Using an ICT system for a library, it may be possible to do these tasks:

- Store and access the personal details of borrowers.

- Store and access a catalogue of books owned by the library.

- Search the catalogue to see if the library has a book in stock.

- Reserve a book either from the library's stock or from another library.

- Keep track of which borrowers have which books. This is usually done by scanning the borrower's identification number on a membership card and the identification number of the book being borrowed.

- Send reminders to borrowers who have not returned books.

- Keep track of fines paid by borrowers.

Such an ICT system is commonly used in school, college and university libraries, public libraries and other types of library. Database software can be used to produce such an ICT system. At its simplest, there are likely to be three tables in a **relational database**:

Figure 12.20 *ICT system in a library*

Borrowers table	Book catalogue table	Books borrowed table
Borrower identification number	Book identification number	Borrower identification number
Name	Title	Book identification number
Address and other contact details	Author	Date borrowed
Other details	Location	Other details
	Reviews and other details	

The records in the **books borrowed** table are produced by reading the borrower's identification number off the membership card and the identification number of the book as it is borrowed. When the book is returned, it is only necessary to find the record in the **books borrowed** table and delete it, so only the identification number of the book is needed. This is why when you borrow a book you have to take your membership card and the books to the library desk so they can be issued. In contrast, in some libraries, when you return a book, it is possible to put the book into a post box when the library is closed, because your membership card is not needed to identify the record in the books borrowed table and delete it.

Entertainment and leisure activities

ICT can be a source of entertainment and support a wide range of leisure activities. Some examples are:

- **Communicating** with friends and family. Applications such as Skype allow you to talk to someone while looking at them in real time on the screen. If both you and the person you are speaking to have Skype then the call could be free. This helps people keep in touch with friends and family who live in different parts of the world.

- **Games**. Many people play a wide range of computer games. At the time of writing the Facebook game *FarmVille* has over 60 million active users and the online game, *World of Warcraft*, claims up to 1 million players every day. There are many genres: action games, adventure games, construction and management simulations, vehicle simulations, role-playing games, keep fit games and strategy games.

- **Media streaming**. You can listen to media, such as music and the radio, look at photographs and watch TV, video and films on your computer or on mobile devices such as smart phones. The media could be stored on the computer or mobile device you are using but it can also be streamed from another computer, often using a wireless network or the Internet. For example, you could watch video stored on your computer on your TV in any location in your house. Streaming media players connect to your TV and enable you to stream multimedia files from networked PCs, hard disks and the Internet. One example is the Netgear Digital Entertainer. In contrast, Spotify is a web-based, peer-to-peer, **music streaming** service that gives users access to their playlists and music from connected devices such as computers and smart phones. At the time of writing, Spotify had around 7 million users.

Exercise 12.2

1. An ICT system is used to print pay slips and pay workers.

    a) Explain why payroll is a common application.

    b) Explain what is meant by a **transaction file.**

    c) Describe what is meant by **batch processing.**

    d) Explain why batch processing is appropriate for payroll.

2. An ICT system is used to book airline tickets.

   a) Describe how you could book an airline ticket.

   b) Explain why an ICT system for airline booking should be multi-access.

   c) Describe what is meant by real-time processing.

   d) Explain why real-time processing is appropriate for an airline booking system.

   e) Explain how backups can be done on a real-time ICT system.

3. An ICT system is used for stock control in a supermarket.

   a) List the hardware used at a POS checkout in a supermarket.

   b) State the information input at a supermarket checkout from a bar code.

   c) Describe how the name and price of each item purchased can be printed on an itemised receipt for each customer.

   d) Explain how the ICT system knows when to reorder goods.

   e) Describe the advantages of using an ICT system for stock control.

   f) Describe three other tasks that could be done using the information generated by an ICT system for stock control.

4. *a)* Describe what is meant by **computer-aided design (CAD).**

   b) Give two examples of where CAD would be used.

   c) Describe three benefits of using CAD.

   d) Name three peripheral devices that are used with a CAD ICT system.

5. *a)* Explain what is meant by **computer-aided manufacturing (CAM).**

   b) Describe two benefits of using CAM.

   c) List two industries where CAM systems are used.

6. Banks issue customers with plastic bank cards that have magnetic stripes or microchips on them. These can be used to withdraw cash from an automatic teller machine (ATM).

   a) State one item of information that is stored on the magnetic stripe.

   b) Explain how a customer would use a bank card to draw money from an ATM.

   c) Explain why a customer has to enter a PIN when withdrawing money from an ATM.

   d) Describe how the bank could prevent customers from withdrawing more money than they have in their account.

7 *a)* Describe what is meant by **electronic funds transfer (EFT).**

   b) Explain how EFT is used when purchasing goods and services.

   c) Discuss the advantages and disadvantages of smart cards in comparison with magnetic stripe cards.

8. *a)* Explain what is meant by a **VLE.**

   b) Describe an example of a VLE that you are familiar with.

   c) List two advantages of a VLE for a student.

   d) List two advantages of a VLE for a teacher.

   e) Give two reasons why a teacher may not use a VLE in the classroom.

f) Describe how the Internet can be used to assist teaching and learning in the classroom.

9. ICT systems are useful tools for law enforcement officers in their fight against crime.

a) Describe how ICT systems can be used by police officers to fight crime.

b) Describe how ICT is used by law firms to manage the firm itself and to practise law.

10. ICT systems are used in healthcare and medicine.

a) Describe the information about patients that would be stored in an ICT system for keeping medical records.

b) Describe three advantages to doctors of using an ICT system for patients' records.

c) State three measures you would put in place to prevent unauthorised users from accessing patients' records.

d) Explain what is meant by a **medical expert system.**

e) Describe two advantages and two disadvantages to doctors of using a medical expert system.

f) State three other ways ICT can be used in healthcare and medicine.

The social impact of ICT

The widespread use of ICT has a significant impact on society. ICT permeates society and as governments, companies and individuals increasingly rely on ICT systems and devices, important social issues arise. There is a **digital divide** where some people have easy access to the wide range of goods and services available using ICT while others have limited or no access. ICT also has an impact on employment and workers' health; individual privacy is threatened and computer crime has increased.

The effects of ICT on employment

Job losses

The introduction of ICT systems has resulted in the loss of jobs in many companies. Heavy job losses in the automobile industry came with the introduction of automated assembly lines when robots were installed to do jobs previously done by humans.

ICT systems for process control have also resulted in the loss of many jobs. Chemical plants and oil refineries use ICT systems to monitor and adjust plant and machinery to control processes. Workers previously did these jobs.

Changes in job skills

With the introduction of computers in the workplace, many workers have had to acquire new skills or upgrade existing ones. A secretary who once used a typewriter now has to become proficient in the use of word processing packages and other applications. Designers and architects are now required to be able to use

CAD packages. Even workers in the computer industry have been affected because of the rapid introduction of new technologies which require new skills. Workers in almost every industry at almost every level have to keep up with technological developments or face unemployment.

Job creation

The introduction of ICT systems has directly and indirectly been responsible for many new jobs. Jobs created directly in the ICT industry are in areas such as research, design, manufacturing, sales, training, programming, communications, education and consultancy. Jobs created indirectly include those in the areas of video and CD production, and the production of magazines and books.

Changes in work patterns

ICT has changed the way people do their jobs. For example:

- A journalist can work from home, or sit in a train or on a bus and complete an article using a laptop while on the way to work, instead of having to be at a desk in the newspaper's offices.

- A teacher can have an entire class work on a VLE or CAL software and provide very little input during the session, although considerably more planning and preparation may be needed prior to the lesson.

- A police officer can access information on criminals and stolen vehicles from a police car, instead of having to go back to the police station to do this.

- Workers can telecommute (see below) instead of having travel to work every day.

Teleworking

Many office workers spend much of their time at the office using ICT. However, computers are relatively cheap and can be found in many homes, so that instead of going to the office, many workers now work at home some or all of the time, and communicate with the office using a network such as the Internet. This is called **teleworking** . Many companies use this method of employment, and there are many benefits for the worker and for the company.

Advantages for workers include:

- Reduced stress – no need to drive long distances to work or get up early to avoid congestion on the way to work
- The time that would have been spent on commuting can be spent working or relaxing
- Reduced expenses for travel and clothing
- Flexibility – you can work at your own convenience
- Working in the comfort of your own home
- Supervising a babysitter and working at the same time.

Disadvantages for workers include:

- Distractions from family members, neighbours and household chores

- Lack of social interaction with other workers

- Lack of access to specialist facilities and advice that may only be available at the office

- A feeling that you might be overlooked for promotion.

Advantages for the company include:

- A perk to attract and retain good workers

- The ability to employ workers who live a long way away, perhaps in another country

- Reduced sick leave – many telecommuters continue to work despite illnesses such as colds

- Increased productivity – employees are more relaxed at home and therefore work more effectively

- No stoppage of work because of floods or snowstorms

- Less expensive overheads in areas such as the purchase or rental of floor space and equipment.

Disadvantages for the company include:

- Management of the task rather than the worker may be more complex and time-consuming

- Managers may feel they do not have sufficient control over what workers are doing during working hours

- Workers may not be available when the company tries to contact them.

Effects on employees' health

As employees spend more time at work using ICT, there is a greater likelihood that this will affect their health. **Ergonomics** is important in reducing injury to people using computers. This includes:

- The design and arrangement of the seating and the computer system, especially the keyboard and monitor.

- Arrangements to support someone using the computer; that is, foot and wrist supports.

- Rules governing the user's behaviour when using the computer; for example, how often to take breaks.

The health risks associated with intense and prolonged computer use are:

- **Repetitive strain injury (RSI)** to the hands and arms. RSI is a painful condition that occurs because of damage to tendons, nerves, muscles and soft body tissue, and can be caused by the repetitive use of a keyboard and a mouse. It can be avoided and its effects reduced by taking regular breaks, using a specially adapted ergonomic keyboard and a wrist support (see Figure 12.21).

- Eye problems such as soreness, lack of focus and eye dryness can arise from staring at a monitor all day. Potential problems can be avoided by taking regular breaks, having regular eye examinations by an optician and using antistatic and other screen filters. Monitors should be positioned to avoid light reflecting on the screen, and interior lighting should be shaded and directed to avoid reflections. Using a larger screen can also help.

- Backache and similar problems. These can arise through sitting in an inappropriate posture for long periods of time. The solution is to use a purpose-designed operator's chair with adjustable height and backrest, and a footrest, and to take regular breaks.

- Fatigue and headaches. Again, part of the solution is to take regular breaks.

- Trip hazards. These are associated with trailing cables and should be reduced by putting cabling in trunking or where it is not likely to interfere with the user's movement.

- Electric shock. This can be minimized by the use of a **RCD (residual current device)** on the main power supply to the computer. This is designed to turn off the power if the user receives an electric shock.

Figure 12.21 *A wrist support can help to prevent RSI*

Privacy

Many businesses, organisations and governments hold personal information about individuals. This personal information is stored on ICT systems, and could be easily copied and transferred around the world across international networks from one organisation to another. Different countries have different laws and so the ways in which personal data can be legally processed will vary around the world. These developments raise questions about how to ensure the individual's right to privacy. **Privacy** refers to the right of individuals to determine what information is stored about them and how that information will be used.

In the United Kingdom, the **Data Protection Acts** (1984 and 1998) set out principles to make sure that personal information is handled appropriately. Organisations in the UK that store personal information must, by law, keep to these principles. These principles include:

- Data must be fairly and lawfully processed.

- Data must be used only for its intended purpose.

- The data collected must be adequate for its intended purpose, relevant to it and should not be excessive.

- The accuracy of the data must be maintained – it must be kept up to date and complete, the data must not be kept for longer than is necessary and the data must be processed in line with your rights – for example, unauthorised people should not be given access to it.

- The data must be stored securely and protected from unauthorised access and use.

- Personal data must not be transferred to countries that do not have similar rules to protect personal privacy.

Many other countries have recognised the need for such legislation.

Computer crime

Computer crime – that is, crime that is only possible because of the widespread use of ICT systems and networks – has increased in variety and extent. In this section, some computer crimes are briefly described.

Software piracy

Software piracy is the unauthorised copying, using or selling of software without an appropriate licence. It includes copying CDs with software or music on them, and downloading software or music without paying for it. These activities are effectively software theft.

Copyright violation

Using the Web you can download music, pictures, animated graphics, videos and books, as well as software. The copyright to some of this material is restricted to its owners. They may sell you the right to copy it, but if you copy it without permission this is effectively theft. The profitability of the music industry has been badly affected by music being freely copied and downloaded over the Web.

Hacking

Hacking means gaining unauthorised access to an ICT system, and an individual who does this is referred to as a **hacker.** Many hackers break into ICT systems just for the challenge or as a prank. This might seem harmless, but it can cause considerable damage and is illegal in many countries.

The reasons why criminally minded hackers gain unauthorised access to ICT systems include:

- To steal data – this may have a security classification or could be commercially sensitive.

- To alter data or destroy data, by deletion or by installing a virus to destroy or corrupt it. This may be done in order to disrupt legitimate commercial or governmental activities.

- To steal money by transferring it from one account to another using EFT.

Hackers who break into ICT systems across external networks are relatively rare. Most fraud carried out using ICT occurs when a person within an organisation makes changes to information in a computer without authorisation, for personal benefits or for malicious reasons. For example, when someone working in a company, who has access to payroll files, changes details on these to increase his or her salary, or when bank employees make fraudulent changes to bank accounts.

Identity theft

When you are connected to the Web, **spyware** may be installed on your computer without your knowledge. This could send information about your computer to others who may have malicious intent. For example, they may want to know when your computer is online so they can use it to send spam without your knowledge, or they might collect information about you and your online bank accounts so that

Figure 12.22 *Shred anything with your address on before putting it in the rubbish*

they can steal your identity, pretend to be you and steal your money or buy goods in your name. Such **identity theft** is an increasing problem.

Anti-spyware software, such as *Spybot – Search & Destroy,* can be used to remove spyware but information about you may not only be stolen when you are online. Thieves sometimes collect addressed envelopes, bank statements and credit card receipts in household rubbish and, consequently, it is advisable to shred these. The information on them can be used to commit thefts online.

Phishing

A **phishing** attack is when you receive an unsolicited email inviting you to a response that involves you entering your username, password and other personal details. For example, a phishing email may direct you to a website for online shopping. This might be a website criminals have set up for a bogus company. Users can view items on this website that are apparently on sale. In order to pay for goods being purchased, the customer fills in a form with information such as name, address, telephone number, email address and the item number and quantity desired. The customer then enters a credit card number and other details to pay for the item. Internet fraud occurs when the bogus company bills the unsuspecting customer for the purchase, collects the money and does not deliver the items purchased. More seriously, the bogus company may have been set up to lure individuals into giving their credit card numbers in order to steal even more of their money.

A variety of this scam is when you receive an email which appears to be from your bank asking you to access a particular website and to enter your bank account details so that the bank can confirm that these are correct. When you do this, the criminals operating the scam will steal money from your bank account. To help avoid this type of scam, do not access your bank's website using the link in the email. Always open your browser and access your bank's website independently. This breaks the link with the fraudulent website.

The Nigerian scam

You receive an email that looks something like Figure 12.23. The senders of this email, who may or may not be Nigerian, are making you think that you are going to scam the Nigerian Government when in fact the senders are going to scam you. They hope you will be so interested in earning US$4 million that you fail to notice that this is a scam. If you give them your bank account details, they will transfer money out of it. If you meet them in Lagos, there will be a delay, and then a requirement that you pay additional money to clear up the delay, and then another delay and more money, and so on until your money is exhausted, or you give up and leave.

FROM: Mr. Ben Ahore
Central Bank of Nigeria
Lagos, Nigeria

Dear Sir:

   I have been requested by the Nigerian National Petroleum Company to contact you for assistance in resolving a matter. The Nigerian National Petroleum Company has recently concluded a large number of contracts for oil exploration in the sub-Sahara region. The contracts have immediately produced moneys of US$40,000,000. The Nigerian National Petroleum Company is desirous of oil exploration in other parts of the world; however, because of certain regulations of the Nigerian Government, it is unable to move these funds to another region.

   You assistance is requested as a non-Nigerian citizen to assist the Nigerian National Petroleum Company in moving these funds out of Nigeria. If the funds can be transferred to your name, in your United States account, then you can forward the funds as directed by the Nigerian National Petroleum Company. In exchange for your services, the Nigerian National Petroleum Company would agree to allow you to retain 10%, or US$4 million of this amount.

   However, to be a legitimate transferee of these moneys according to Nigerian law, you must presently be a depositor of at least US$100,000 in a Nigerian bank which is regulated by the Central Bank of Nigeria.

   If it will be possible for you to assist us, we would be most grateful. We suggest that you meet with us in person in Lagos, and that during your visit I introduce you to the representatives of the Nigerian National Petroleum Company, as well as with certain officials of the Central Bank of Nigeria. If this is not possible, could you send me details of your US bank account so an account can be set up for you at the Nigerian National Bank.

   Please call me at your earliest convenience at [Phone Number]. Time is of the essence in this matter; very quickly the Nigerian Government will realize that the Central Bank is maintaining this amount on deposit, and attempt to levy certain depository taxes on it.

Yours truly, etc.

Ben Ahore

Figure 12.23 *A Nigerian scam email*

Security

Security is important in ensuring privacy, data integrity and preventing computer crime. Such crime would not exist if ICT systems were not used and could not be exploited for financial gain. Security precautions are needed to prevent physical access and access via software and networks. In addition, our individual behaviour is important in ensuring our safety and security.

Physical safeguards

Physical safeguards deal with the protection of hardware and software from accidental or malicious damage or destruction. For example:

● **Access control** to ICT rooms using locks that are opened using entry codes, swipe cards, or biometrics such as fingerprints and retinal scans. Security guards can ensure that those entering using entry codes and swipe cards are actually those who are allowed entry.

- **Access monitoring** using CCTV cameras so that those entering and leaving ICT rooms can be recorded.

- **Data security** can be ensured by taking regular backups and storing these in a fireproof safe in another location.

- **Protect hardware from fire, floods, theft and malicious damage** by locating it in buildings and areas where such problems can be reduced; for example, in a concrete underground bunker on top of a hill that is accessible only through a well guarded and narrow passage. Or more usually, not on the ground floor of a building where hardware is accessible to thieves.

- Further precautions to **protect hardware from theft** involve clamping individual computers to desks or securing them to walls; installing burglar alarms attached to individual computers in addition to those already used for the building; and using CCTV cameras in ICT rooms to discourage inappropriate use of computer equipment and to allow any such use to be traced and the culprits identified.

- Make detailed **contingency plans** and **disaster recovery** arrangements so that ICT systems continue operating with a minimum of disruption and recovery is swift. For example, make arrangements with an organisation with similar ICT facilities that is located at a distance so that their ICT facilities can be used should your own be destroyed.

Software safeguards

Software safeguards can protect data from theft or damage by hackers and other unauthorised persons accessing the software to steal or damage it. For example:

- Use of ICT systems and networks is restricted to those who have valid usernames and passwords.

- Access permissions that allow access to the data to the minimum number of people who need it. Others are blocked from accessing the data.

- File-level passwords that restrict access to individual files to those who have appropriate access permissions and passwords.

- Use a virus scanner to prevent viruses entering the system. The intention of some viruses is to damage software recorded on the ICT system or steal it by copying it and emailing it to unauthorised persons.

- Use a firewall. This is a program or hardware device or combination of both that filters the information coming through the Internet connection into a computer or network, to prevent unauthorised users from gaining access. Some firewalls also block cookies, pop-up adverts and spam. Popular firewall software packages are BlackICE Defender, ZoneAlarm and Freedom.

- Data encryption is used so that if data is access by unauthorised persons it cannot be understood. Encrypted data is scrambled during storage and transmission so that it cannot be understood by someone without the encryption key to unscramble it. Wireless networks can be encrypted using WEP (Wired Equivalent Privacy) and WPA (Wi-Fi Protected Access).

- Establish transaction logs to automatically track alterations to ICT systems, including the identity of those who access data and all the changes made.

Figure 12.24 *Logging on to a networked computer*

Individual responsibility

The ways each individual uses the Internet and the Web can have a considerable social impact as this is aggregated and its impact emphasised by the use of networks. It is important to behave sensibly to protect yourself and others because the openness and freedom of the Internet can be abused by criminals.

- Be very cautious who you share personal data with. Don't publish your personal data on web pages that anyone can access. For example, don't give out your name, age, or phone number.

- Don't publish anyone else's personal data anywhere unless you have their permission.

- Make sure you know who stores your personal data and that it is correct. In the UK, the Data Protection Act (1998) gives you this right.

- Don't copy someone else's written work from the Web or books and try to pass it off as your own work. You are permitted to include short quotations in your work if you show that it is a quotation and acknowledge the source. If you copy someone else's work and don't acknowledge it, this is plagiarism.

- Don't download software or music unless it is copyright free. In the UK, copyright material is protected by the Copyright, Design and Patents Act (1988).

- Don't engage in activities such as hacking, etc. Hacking is an illegal activity in the UK under the terms of the Computer Misuse Act (1990).

- Don't believe everything you see or hear online. Make sure you know the source of any information and decide whether it is likely to be true or biased.

- Use virus scanners and other malware detection software. This protects you from others but it also helps keep the Web safe for everyone.

- Be polite and reasonable in all your online interactions. If you feel you are the victim of cyber bullying seek help. Don't bully others.

- Make sure that any wireless networks you use are secure.

Exercise 12.3

1. **a)** Explain what is meant by **teleworking.**

   b) Describe the ICT systems and networks needed at home so that a worker can telecommute.

   c) Discuss the advantages and disadvantages of teleworking to:

      i   A worker

      ii   An employer

      iii The community

2. **a)** Describe what is meant by **privacy.**

   b) List the rights given to individuals by privacy and data protection legislation in the UK.

   c) Give two examples where lack of data privacy can cause embarrassment or undue hardship to an individual.

3. Describe the physical safeguards that can protect hardware from theft or damage.

4. Describe the software safeguards that can protect software from loss, theft or damage.

5. **a)** Describe what is meant by **software piracy.**

   b) Explain why software piracy is illegal.

6. **a)** Define the term **hacking.**

   b) Explain why hacking is illegal.

7. Describe two different types of Internet fraud and say what can be done to avoid having your money stolen.

8. Many hospitals store confidential information about their patients on a central database. Such ICT systems use **wide area networks (WANs)** to make information available to doctors and other medical professionals throughout the community.

   a) Describe two methods that can be used to prevent unauthorised users from gaining access to the ICT system from a remote computer.

   b) Describe two methods that can be used to prevent users who have access to the system from accessing data files that they are not authorised to see.

9. Using a computer for a prolonged period of time can affect your health. State three types of health problem that can arise and say what you can do to avoid each problem.

10. Storing information in databases on a networked ICT system makes it easier to access the information.

    a) Give two reasons why someone may be worried about having information about them stored in a database.

    b) Describe three ways in which a police officer can make use of a database.

1. We are considerably affected in our daily lives by the widespread use of ICT systems.

2. One of the oldest and most common applications of ICT is **payroll processing.** Every company or business has to pay its employees. **Batch processing** can be used because there is usually plenty of time to do the processing and all the data to be processed will be available before processing starts. A **transaction file** that contains details of the hours employees have worked is combined with employees' details saved on the **old master file.** The old master file is updated from the transaction file and a **new master file** is produced. The payroll program prints wage slips and pays employees' wages directly into their bank accounts.

3. An airline booking system keeps details of flight schedules and seat bookings. Passengers can book seats online from a variety of locations. This ICT system must be a fast real-time system as the data input (a seat booking) must be processed before any further input can be accepted.

4. Backups for the airline booking system are produced as the system is running by creating a **fingerprint.** This is a copy of the booking file that is updated at the same time and in the same way as the actual booking file.

5. A supermarket stock control system is an example of an online interactive system. It does not have to be updated instantaneously so the expense of a real-time system is not justified. However, it needs to respond faster than a batch processing system. The stock control system records the sales of goods and prints itemised receipts for customers. Stock sold is deducted from the quantity in stock, and goods arriving at the warehouse are added, so that there is an up-to-date record of stock levels. Goods can be automatically reordered if stocks fall below the reorder level.

6. **Computer-aided design (CAD)** packages are available to make it easier to produce detailed plans and accurate technical drawings. **Computer-aided manufacturing (CAM)** refers to the use of a computer to control manufacturing. CAD and CAM systems are sometimes combined so that engineers can use the system to create the designs for a product and then control the manufacturing process. **Computer-aided engineering (CAE)** systems analyse the engineering designs produced by CAD systems to see if the design will work.

7. **Weather stations** are used to collect information about the weather; for example, the temperature, wind speed, wind direction, whether it is raining, and how much rain has fallen. This information may be collected from a weather station by a computer communicating with it using the telephone network.

8. **Robots** are computer-controlled machines. They are used in manufacturing industries; for example, for making cars.

9. **Process control** refers to the use of digital computers to monitor industrial processes closely and to take corrective action if necessary, in manufacturing environments such as chemical plants, steel mills and oil refineries.

10. **Flight simulators** are very complex constructions involving a wide range of computer control subsystems with highly developed interacting feedback loops. Trainee pilots can learn to fly a variety of aircraft and practise landing and taking off from different airports before they do this in a real plane.

11. Banks make extensive use of ICT systems. For example: cashpoints or automatic teller machines (ATMs); Electronic Funds Transfer (EFT); debit, credit and smart card transactions; and Internet banking.

12. ICT is used extensively to support teaching and learning. With the availability of **virtual learning environments (VLEs)** and **computer-assisted learning (CAL)** software, many teachers are increasingly facilitators of learning rather than dispensers of knowledge.

13. ICT systems can be used to help police officers in their fight against crime. Police officers use computers for preparing reports, case management, circulating photos of wanted criminals and

missing persons on the Internet, and transmitting, exchanging and obtaining information about criminals kept by police officers in other departments or other countries.

14. Law firms have found that the productivity of both the attorney and other staff increases with the use of ICT.

15. ICT systems are increasingly used in healthcare and medicine. Patients' records are stored electronically and can be accessed from a variety of locations. When patients are ill, their progress can be continuously monitored by sensors which measure their blood pressure and heart rate.

16. ICT systems are used in libraries to keep track of books that are borrowed and to provide borrowers with a catalogue of books that can be borrowed.

17. ICT has had a significant impact on society. The use of ICT has affected employment and healthcare.

18. ICT use has to be regulated to protect individual privacy.

19. Software piracy is the illegal use or copying and distribution of software.

20. Copying of some of the material available on the Web is illegal because the owners have **copyright.** The profitability of the music industry has been affected by the illegal downloading of music over the Web.

21. Hackers are unauthorised users who break into ICT systems and steal (copy), alter or damage data.

22. ICT systems and networks have the potential to be used to carry out fraud. Confidence tricks such as identity theft, credit card scams and the Nigerian scam use ICT networks to cheat people out of their money.

23. Data security is ensured by implementing appropriate physical and software safeguards.

✓ **Physical safeguards** include access control, access monitoring, backups, protection from damage and theft, contingency plans and disaster recovery arrangements.

✓ **Software safeguards** include access permissions, usernames and passwords, file-level passwords, data encryption, virus scanners, firewalls and transaction logs. Back up data regularly.

✓ **Individual behaviour** should be defensive and respect others: be cautious who you share personal data with; don't publish others' personal data without their permission; know who stores your personal data and make sure it is accurate; don't use others' work without acknowledgement; respect copyright; don't engage in criminal activity such as hacking; be polite and reasonable; be secure.

Chapter 13: Assessment

Edexcel IGCSE Contacts

The Edexcel IGCSE (International General Certificate of Secondary Education) in ICT is available from Edexcel http://www.edexcel.com

Edexcel provides a specification and sample papers and mark schemes which can be downloaded from the website. These are the definitive source of information about what should be taught and how it will be assessed, and should be used alongside this book. The specification lists the specific ICT skills, knowledge and understanding that should be taught and these are covered in this book. The sample papers are samples of the IGCSE ICT examinations.

> In this chapter you will find an outline of the Edexcel IGCSE assessment procedures and advice on how to prepare for the written and practical examinations.

Assessment requirements

There are two papers, one written and one practical, taken in May/June in the year of entry. The papers are completed in the English language and each contribute 50% of the total marks.

Paper 1

Paper 1 is a written examination that is 1 hour and 30 minutes in length and there is no choice of questions. The paper is in two sections: section A and section B. Questions in section A are multiple choice questions, and in section B questions are structured and require a short written response (a word, phrase or one or two sentences). You will not be asked to write long essays. There will be space below each question for you to write your answer and the marks that can be awarded for each question are printed on the examination paper.

Paper 2

Paper 2 is a practical paper which is 3 hours long, broken down into a number of activities. You are required to carry out practical tasks rather than explain the theory of how the tasks can be completed. The practical tasks, are based on a scenario described at the start of the paper. You can use any hardware, operating system or application software to do the tasks and you will be asked to print out your work so that it can be submitted for assessment.

Preparing for assessment

During your course

Students often find ICT interesting and enjoyable, and it may be a useful preparation for work or further study. Many jobs in ICT are well paid, and knowledge of ICT will help you in your studies in other subjects. Convince yourself it is important to succeed. Always do your best work. If you have a clear idea of why you are studying ICT you may find it easier to put in the effort required to do well. If you are well motivated you are already on the road to success. However, to do well, you also need to pay careful attention to preparing yourself for the examinations.

The purpose of the two papers is to assess.

- Your ICT knowledge and understanding.
- Your ability to apply your ICT knowledge, skills and understanding.
- Your ability to evaluate your own and others' use of ICT.

If you do not know your subject then you cannot expect to do well. Preparation for the examination begins on the first day of the course.

- Try not to miss lessons. If you do, catch up with the work quickly.
- Keep all the notes you write and the work you do.
- Develop your ICT practical skills so that you can work independently and efficiently.
- Make sure that you understand how to use the software tools that you will need for the practical examination.
- Do all your homework to your best standard.
- Learn your work as you progress. If you have any spare time, go back over the course and revise the work. Make sure you understand all the work you do.
- Use the library to look up topics you are unsure of.
- Ask your teacher if you have problems.

You can enrich your skills, knowledge and understanding in a variety of ways:

- Discuss your work with a friend who is doing the same course.
- Read computer magazines.
- Go to local shops that sell computers and ask the sales staff about the computers they sell.
- Go on trips to computer exhibitions.
- Talk to someone who works with ICT systems and ask them about their job.
- Arrange a visit to an office or factory where ICT systems are used.
- Get your own computer and learn to use it.
- Use the Web for research and keep notes about what you discover.
- Practice using the software tools that you will need for the practical examination.
- Always evaluate your work and reflect on whether the products are fit for audience and purpose.

Revision

Start revising in good time and plan your revision carefully. Try to allocate set times each week when you will revise for your examinations. Make sure you allow time to revise all the subjects you are taking, and build in periods for rest and relaxation. Expect to work very hard in the weeks leading up to your IGCSE examinations but leave some time to enjoy yourself. Overwork and worry can be as bad as not doing anything.

When you are revising, this is the time to make sure you have learnt all you need to know. Read the Edexcel IGCSE ICT specification, and be clear about what you have to learn. Make a list of all the topics you should cover.

Revision for the written paper

A useful revision technique is to repeatedly *revise, condense and learn*. Read through your notes and all the work you have done and, as you revise your knowledge, take a brief note of all the topics. These brief notes should cover all the important points in enough detail to refresh your memory of them at a later date. Try to learn these brief notes. Many of the questions in this paper will be set in a context. Make sure that you answer the question in the context. Do not learn set answers and use them without thought.

Preparation for the practical paper

To do well in an ICT practical examination you need to be able to work quickly and accurately using a range of software. The relevant sections of this book provide ideas for you to try out. Try to evaluate any work that you do and improve it until you are satisfied.

For both papers

Practise for the papers by doing questions of the kind you will meet in them. You can download sample papers with a mark scheme from the Edexcel website. Work through them carefully. Your teacher may give you a 'mock' examination and may have papers from previous years that you can practise on. Check your answers to these practice papers and, if you have made a mistake, make sure that you understand why you have made it. It is likely that similar questions will appear on the papers you will take. You can find out what examiners are looking for when they mark your work by checking your answers against the mark scheme.

Revise those topics where you have weaknesses again. You can make extra notes on them if you need to. Do more practice questions in these topic areas until you are confident you understand what is required. Try to complete some of the sample papers under examination conditions in the time allowed for them. This will give you some idea of how quickly you will have to work in the actual papers. If you find you are short of time, plan ahead and use your time effectively.

Before the examinations

However much you know, you will perform better if you are wide awake, healthy and relaxed. Look after yourself! You are likely to do your best work if you are alert. Alertness depends on good health, plenty of sleep and a calm determination to do well.

- Make sure you get plenty of sleep in the days before the examination. Go to bed reasonably early and you will be more alert and will cope with the examination much better.

- You are also likely to perform better if you are fit and healthy. A bad cold, hay fever, headaches, broken bones, sprained ankles and other maladies can distract you from your work in the examination. The best remedy is to avoid accidents and situations that could make you ill. For example, the day before the examination may not be the right time to go horse riding, skiing, sky diving, bungee jumping or motor cycle racing! If you have unavoidable medical problems, your doctor may be able to help.

- Many people find that examinations make them nervous. They get so nervous they make silly mistakes and are unable to do their best. Most people are affected by examination nerves to some extent. Being too nervous will probably have a bad effect on your work. On the other hand, some people are so relaxed they do sloppy, careless work. Being too relaxed is as inappropriate as being too nervous. Make sure you are keen to do well, but keep calm.

The day of the examinations

- Pack your bag the night before the examination, and make sure you have any equipment you will need in the examination. For the written paper you may require a pencil, a pencil sharpener, a rubber, a ruler and at least two pens, in case one runs out. A calculator might be useful. This equipment is essential for accurate, written communication. If you have to borrow a pen, for example, it may not suit you or it may not work properly and consequently you may work at a slower pace. It is possible that equipment may not be available to borrow and you will have to manage without it. For the practical paper take a pencil, a pencil sharpener, a rubber and a ruler. Although you will be working on a computer you may want to do some planning or rough working.

- Make sure you get up in time. You will need plenty of time to have breakfast and get to the examination centre early.

- Make sure you go to the lavatory just before the examination. You could waste five or ten minutes of valuable examination time if you have to go during the examination!

- Always arrive on time for an examination. If you are late it is very unlikely that you will be allowed extra time.

Examination techniques

Examination techniques are common-sense methods to help you communicate what you know more effectively. They are not magic, and using examination techniques will not make up for ignorance or lack of thorough preparation.

- Start work as soon as you are allowed to.

- Read the instructions at the start of the examination very carefully, and do what you are asked.

- There is no choice of questions in either paper.

The written paper

In any examination, you should always make sure that you can do what is required.

- The written paper is divided into two sections. Section A will have 16 multiple choice questions. Section B will have five or six questions divided into sub-questions. The total marks for the paper will be 100 and the time allowed is one hour and 30 minutes. Try to use time wisely. Spend no more than 15 minutes on section A. The marks for each question are on the examination paper. Use these as a guide for the amount of time you should spend on each question.

- Attempt all the questions that you can. This is very important. The first part of each question is often the easiest to answer. You cannot be given marks for questions you haven't answered. Higher marks will almost certainly be given for correct answers to part of all the questions than for complete answers to a very few questions.

- Make sure you read each question carefully. Many students lose marks because they read the question in a hurry and do not fully grasp what it means. They then answer the question they *think* they have read. This means their answer may not relate to the actual question. You will only be awarded marks for a correct answer to the actual question set. Read questions carefully.

- Questions will usually **include** prompts that will help you understand what is needed. **List**, **state** or **identify** require answers that involve a word, a phrase or a short sentence. **Explain** and **describe** require longer answers.

- If you give answers such as 'quicker', 'easier', 'cheaper' or 'more efficient', you are unlikely to be given marks unless you clearly say, for example, what is quicker or why it is quicker.

- You will only be given credit for relevant answers. For example, if the question asks you to give advantages to a customer, then you will only be awarded marks if the advantages are to the customer rather than to some other person or organisation. If you are asked to state what the letters DTP stand for then you will only be awarded marks for the answer 'Desk Top Publishing'.

- If you are asked to describe the difference between two methods (for example, inputting data using a keyboard and an Optical Mark Reader), to be awarded marks you should make a clear statement for each method. For example, 'inputting data by typing it on a keyboard takes much longer than reading an OMR form that has been filled in correctly'.

- If necessary, give examples and draw diagrams to illustrate your answers. It is helpful to label diagrams so the examiner knows what you are illustrating. Communicate clearly and in full.

- If there are two marks for a question, you should make two separate points.

- Handwriting should be neat and easy to read. If answers cannot be read, you will lose marks.

- Pay attention to your spelling, punctuation and grammar. If your answers cannot be understood by the examiner, you will not be awarded marks. Ensure you know how to spell the technical words used in ICT. However, there are no separate marks for spelling, punctuation and grammar.

- Never leave an examination before the end. Spend all the time allowed to you to do the examination answering questions or checking your answers. Make sure that what you can do is correct and make a determined attempt at the more difficult questions. Marks are always given for correct answers. In multiple choice questions you will not be awarded marks if you select more than one option.

The practical paper

- The practical paper is worth 100 marks and you have to answer all questions. The paper will consist of a number of activities, split into tasks. The type of software needed for each activity and the marks available will be clearly stated on the paper.

- You must follow the instructions carefully. The instructions on the labelling and printing of tasks must be followed or your work may not be marked. These instructions will be the same on every paper so make sure that you understand what is needed as you prepare for the examination.

- The paper will start with a brief scenario. It should help you to determine the audience and purpose of any digital product you produce.

- Three hours are allowed for this paper, including printing. You need to manage your time carefully. It is easy to spend too much time on a task.

- You need to work through the tasks in each activity in order but make sure that you allow sufficient time to attempt at least part of every activity.

- All tasks will include a series of detailed instructions that you must follow. There will also be some questions about the products themselves – such as how they work, and whether they are fit for purpose.

- Your centre will have been told what to do if there are hardware problems during the examination session so do not panic if the printer fails or there are other problems. If you have followed the instructions you should have saved your work so it will be easy to redo some printing.

- The most important thing is not to panic. If you have problems with one task, move on to the next. You can do the activities in any order. The simplest thing is to work through the paper in order but if there is one software tool that you feel more confident with you might like to try that one first.

- Make sure that the printouts are labelled correctly and that they are in order of activity and task before you submit them.

Edexcel support for students

Edexcel has support services to help you prepare for the examinations. The Examzone website is for students and gives information on revision, advice from examiners and guidance on results. Links to this site can be found on **www.examzone.co.uk**.

End of Chapter 13 Checklist

1. Edexcel IGCSE ICT is available from Edexcel (website: **www.edexcel.com**).

2. Edexcel provides a specification, sample papers and mark schemes.

3 The examination consists of two papers, 1 and 2, taken in May/June and completed in the English language.

4. Paper 1 is a written examination which is 1 hour and 30 minutes in length and there is no choice of questions. Questions in Section A are multiple choice. In Section B, questions require a short written response.

5. Paper 2 is a practical paper which is 3 hours long. You can use any hardware, operating system or application software to do the tasks. Printouts of your work are submitted for assessment.

6. If you do not know your subject then you cannot expect to do well. Preparation for the examination begins on the first day of the course.

7. Start revising in good time and plan your revision carefully.

8. A useful revision technique for the written paper is to repeatedly **revise**, **condense** and **learn**. For the practical paper you need to practise using the software to do real tasks as quickly and accurately as you can.

9. Practise for the papers by doing questions of the kind you will meet in them. Download sample papers with answers from the Edexcel website. Try to complete some of the sample papers under examination conditions in the time allowed for them.

10. However much you know, you will perform better if you are wide awake, healthy and relaxed. Keep calm.

11. Prepare everything you will need for each exam the night before you sit it. Make sure you get up in time. Go to the lavatory just before the examination. Arrive on time for an examination.

12. Examination techniques are common-sense methods to help you communicate what you know more effectively. Use these to improve your marks.

    • Start work as soon as you are allowed to.

    • For both papers, read the instructions at the start of the examination very carefully, and do what you are asked.

    • Work out how much time you can spend on each question or activity and try to stick to it.

    • Attempt all the questions or activities you are expected to answer.

    • For the written paper, read the question thoroughly and make sure your answers communicate your ideas clearly. Give as much detail as possible in the space provided. Give examples and draw diagrams to illustrate your answers. For the practical paper, read the instructions carefully as you work through a task.

    • If there are two marks for a question, you should make two separate points.

    • Handwriting should be neat and easy to read. Pay attention your spelling, punctuation and grammar.

    • Never leave before the end. Spend all the time allowed to you answering questions or checking your answers.

13. The Examzone website gives information on revision and other advice. You may find this useful: **www.examzone.co.uk**.